GUIDE TO
BACKYARD
BIRDS

GUIDE TO BACKYARD BIRDS

Julie R. Mancini and Pamela L. Higdon

Illustrations by Michele Earle-Bridges

BARRON'S

About the Authors

Pamela Higdon began watching birds as a child on Guam, an island in the Pacific Ocean, before the introduction of the Australian brown snake, which killed so many of the island's birds. She has continued watching them around the world ever since, spotting different species on almost all continents, with special memories of Saudi Arabia, Australia, New Zealand, China, and India. She was an editor of *Bird Talk* magazine and the first managing editor of *Birds USA* magazine. Pamela has nine published books on pet birds as well as numerous educational books and software for children. She has worked as a freelance writer and editor since 1994. She currently lives with four birds and a large dog.

Birds have been an important part of **Julie Mancini**'s life ever since her father built a shelf for the pigeons outside their kitchen window in Culver City, California. He did this to provide her with mealtime entertainment when she was a toddler, and she has been fascinated with both pet and wild birds ever since. Julie has written about birds for *Pet Health News*, *Pet Product News*, and *Birds USA*, and she is also a former editor of *Bird Talk* magazine. Since 1997, Julie has been a freelance writer, with birds (both pet and wild) as her primary focus. She wrote about pet birds for *pets.com* and has written 10 books and numerous articles on both wild and pet birds.

Acknowledgments

Julie would like to thank her husband, Ron Mancini, for sharing her excitement about birds as well as putting up with the demands and deadlines of her writing life.

Pamela would like to thank her friends and family, including Phyllis and Lewis Leis, as well as her daughter Kathie, son-in-law Jon, and grandchildren Nick, Maddie, and Jo Bear for their love and encouragement.

Photo Credits

Cover Photo Credits
Cheryl A. Ertelt: top left, bottom left, bottom right; Norvia Behling: top right.

Interior Photo Credits
Cheryl A. Ertelt: v (top), 1, 10 (bottom), 11, 14, 16, 24, 30, 31, 33, 34, 36, 37, 44, 45, 50, 58, 60, 65, 73, 77, 87, 99, 100, 101, 103, 105, 109, 111, 116, 118, 120, 163, 185. Daniel Johnson: vi, 19, 21, 22, 38, 70, 84, 85, 88, 91, 92, 97, 102, 127, 132, 133, 135, 142, 143, 159, 173. Norvia Behling: v (bottom), 2, 10 (top), 13, 18, 23, 27, 39, 42, 68, 107, 123, 124, 128, 155, 158, 186.

All inquiries should be addressed to:
Barron's Educational Series, Inc.
250 Wireless Boulevard
Hauppauge, New York 11788
www.barronseduc.com

International Standard Book No. 0-7641-2687-3

Library of Congress Catalog Card No. 2004043722

Library of Congress Cataloging-in-Publication Data
Mancini, Julie.
    Guide to backyard birds / by Julie Mancini & Pamela L. Higdon.
        p.   cm
    Includes index.
    ISBN 0-7641-2687-3
    1. Bird-watching. 2. Bird attracting. 3. Birds.
    Higdon, Pam. II. Title
QL677.5.R28   2004
598'.072'34—dc22   2004043722

PRINTED IN CHINA
9 8 7 6 5 4 3 2 1

Contents

5. What to Feed Birds • 78

6. Problems in Paradise • 112

7. Creating a Backyard Habitat • 126

1 Welcome to the World of Bird-watching!

Welcome to the wonderful world of bird-watching! With this book we will help you learn to enjoy one of the world's most popular pastimes. According to the National Survey on Recreation and the Environment, 71 million Americans watched birds in 2001, which is a 250-percent increase from 1982, when the survey was first taken. According to the U.S. Fish and Wildlife Service, Americans spent $6 million on food for wild birds in 2000, and they spent almost $32 billion on wildlife-watching supplies, which was an increase from $30 billion spent in 1996.

A hardy bird, the American goldfinch (also called the thistle bird or the wild canary) breeds and winters across the southern Canadian provinces through much of the American south. It is most beautiful in spring, when the male sports bright yellow plumage. In winter, the male more closely resembles the brownish gray female.

According to a 1996 study by Environment Canada, an estimated 4.4 million Canadians (18.6 percent of the population aged 15 years and over) participated in wildlife viewing. Wildlife watching was the most popular form of residential wildlife-related activity, with 84.2 percent of survey respondents taking part. Purchasing or putting out special feed for wildlife was undertaken by 57.3 percent of participants, and 52.6 percent maintained plants, shrubs, or birdhouses for wildlife. Studying and identifying wildlife (43.3 percent) and photographing wildlife (22.2 percent) were other reported forms of activity. Songbirds, such as warblers and robins, were observed or cared for by 90.7 percent of participants, while 26.7 percent observed or cared for waterfowl, such as ducks and geese.

Why People Watch Birds

People watch birds for reasons as varied as the number of different birds available to observe. Some people find bird-watching a relaxing break from their daily routine, whereas others enjoy the opportunity to connect with nature. Still others use it as a chance to teach their children about ecology and the environment, and others find it a creative way to enhance additional interests, such as drawing, painting, and photography.

You may have begun watching birds from the comfort of your home. As your interest progresses, you will probably move outside, where you can see more birds doing a greater variety of things.

Most people begin to watch birds in their backyards after they first notice an interesting or unusual bird. We believe it's the best place to start because you won't have to transport your equipment. You will find, too, that you will soon begin to compare your sightings with those of your friends and neighbors.

What Is a Bird?

A bird is a warm-blooded animal with a four-chambered heart that has scaly, featherless legs and feet. It has a specialized beak or bill that allows it to crack seeds, extract insects from plants and trees, find nectar, and eat fruit and meat (depending on the species). A bird has air sacs within its body and pneumatized bones that help it fly.

Most species use their wings to fly. Not all birds fly, however; penguins have wings, but they use them to swim. They don't fly. You are unlikely to spot a flightless bird in your backyard, however, unless your neighbor has gone into the ostrich or emu business.

A bird lays hard-shelled eggs that it incubates by sitting on them. The female usually sits on the eggs, but in some species, the males also take turns. Watching birds incubate, hatch, and rear their young can become a part of this delightful hobby.

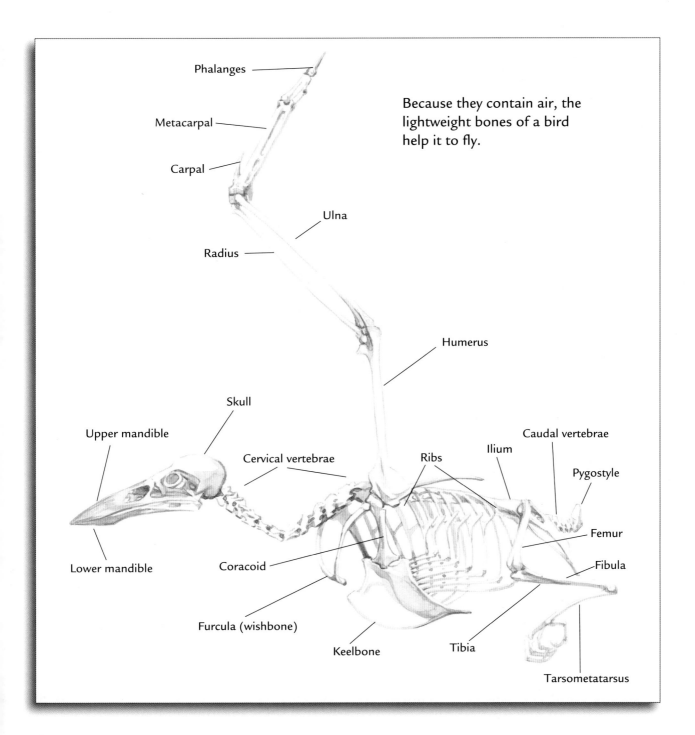

Phalanges

Metacarpal

Carpal

Ulna

Radius

Because they contain air, the lightweight bones of a bird help it to fly.

Humerus

Skull

Upper mandible

Cervical vertebrae

Ribs

Ilium

Caudal vertebrae

Pygostyle

Coracoid

Femur

Lower mandible

Fibula

Furcula (wishbone)

Keelbone

Tibia

Tarsometatarsus

Feathers

Feathers make birds unique from all other animals. The color and patterns formed by feathers help us identify birds.

Feathers are modified parts of a bird's skin made from keratin (the same substance that forms human fingernails). They grow in special rows on the bodies of most birds (except ratites, penguins, and toucans).

Birds have several types of feathers (see diagram at right). Soft, fluffy *down* and *semiplume* feathers lie next to a bird's skin and help trap warmth in winter. *Contour* feathers help define the bird's shape and streamline the bird for effective flight. They also help keep the skin dry. Long *flight* feathers give the bird the lift it needs to take off. *Filoplumes* (bristles) can usually be found around a bird's eyes. They look similar to eyelashes because they are stiff, bare shafts, and they probably serve the same purpose.

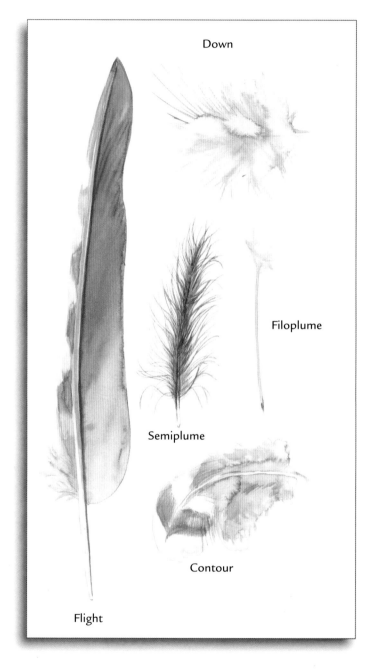

Down

Filoplume

Semiplume

Contour

Flight

Feathers have a central shaft, to which are attached rows of barbs that hook together with tiny barbules. This helps feathers hold tightly together during the arduous conditions of flight, as well as in rain and other circumstances.

Bird feathers derive their color from various sources. Feather colors get their start from the types of pigment found in those feathers. The most common types of pigments are melanins, which produce black, gray, brown, and dull shades of yellow and red, and carotenoids, which produce vibrant red, orange, and yellow shades. Melanins are created by amino acids in a bird's body. A bird ingests carotenoids when it eats certain types of foods. Flamingoes that eat a diet rich in crustaceans and algae containing carotenoid pigments have pinker feathers than those birds whose diets do not contain the special pigments.

In some species, male and female birds are described as dimorphic, which means that they have dramatically different feather colors to differentiate the sexes. Mallard ducks, scarlet tanagers, and rufous towhees are examples of dimorphic birds.

Additionally, some birds, such as tanagers, warblers, and some shore birds, molt (lose old feathers and grow replacements) from their duller winter plumage into bright spring plumages that are called nuptial, or breeding, plumage. These help them attract mates. Other birds molt their old feathers for new, but the feather colors never change. Still other birds molt in the late summer after the chicks have fledged, getting ready for a harsh, wet winter.

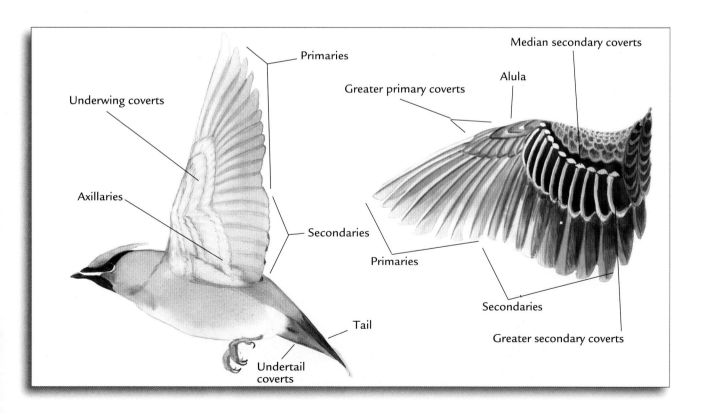

How to Use the Regional Information Features in this Book

We divided the United States and Canada into areas. Each area is represented by a specific color. In each chapter when we have information on birds specific to the part of the country you live in, the information will be presented in a sidebar with a specific color. So, in each chapter, look for your color and then check out the local birds or other information that is specific to where you live.

 **Canada**

Canada is a vast country with many ecozones. These areas are defined by the kind of weather that occurs there, which in turn determines what plants and animals can thrive in that area. Harsh weather cuts a wide swath across the northern part of the country, while relatively temperate regions can be found near water in the east and areas along the Pacific Coast, for example. By dividing the country by province and territory, we hope to make it easier for you to learn more about the birds you can see in your backyard.

British Columbia

Manitoba

Québec

Newfoundland and Labrador

Alberta

Ontario

New Brunswick

Yukon

Saskatchewan

Nova Scotia

Northwest Territories

Prince Edward Island

Nunavut

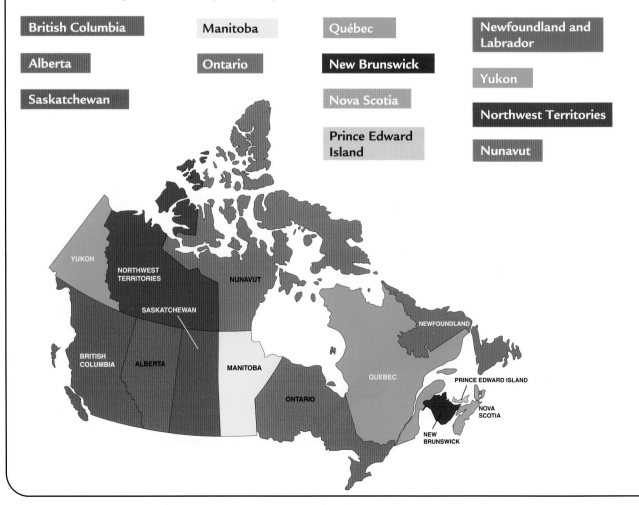

United States

Where birds choose to live is determined by weather patterns, which have a direct impact on food sources. The United States is divided into areas that likely attract particular bird species at various times of the year. In general, the Pacific Coast and southern United States have milder weather than the north central or eastern part of the country, for example. This type of information determined how we divided the country to make it easier to spot birds in your backyard and the general area where you live, as you begin to broaden the regions where you search for birds.

Pacific
Alaska, Washington, Oregon, California, Nevada, and Hawaii

Mountain
Idaho, Montana, Wyoming, Colorado, Utah, Arizona, and New Mexico

West North Central
North Dakota, South Dakota, Minnesota, Iowa, Missouri, Nebraska, and Kansas

West South Central
Oklahoma, Texas, Arkansas, and Louisiana

East North Central
Wisconsin, Illinois, Indiana, Ohio, and Michigan

East South Central
Mississippi, Alabama, Tennessee, and Kentucky

Middle Atlantic
New York, New Jersey, and Pennsylvania

South Atlantic
Delaware, District of Columbia, Maryland, Virginia, West Virginia, North Carolina, South Carolina, Georgia, and Florida

New England
Maine, New Hampshire, Vermont, Massachusetts, Rhode Island, and Connecticut

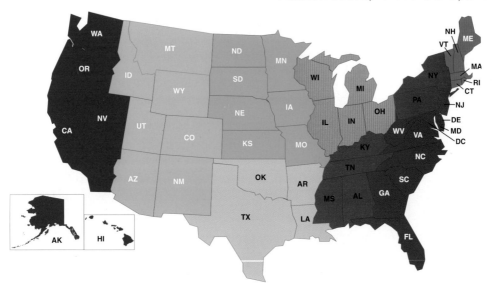

How to Identify Birds

How do you tell one bird from another? At first, they may all look somewhat similar, but over time and with careful observation, you'll learn to sort out the different species based on certain characteristics, including:

Size: Is the bird larger, smaller, or the same size as other birds you've seen?

Color: What color predominates the bird's feathers? In addition to the color, are the feathers marked in any way—that is, are they striped, spotted, barred, or a solid color?

Shape: What shape is the bird's body? Is it short and stout or long and slender?

Movement: How does the bird walk? Does it strut confidently; make short, quick runs; or hop from place to place?

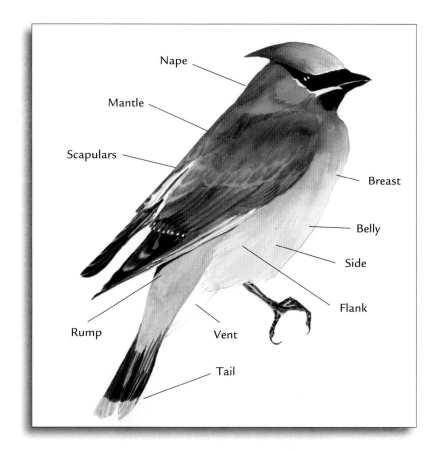

Head: Does the bird have a tuft or crest on its head, or is the head rounded?

Beak: What shape is the bird's beak? Is it curved or cone shaped, for example? What color?

Wings: What shape are the bird's wings? Are they long and wide like a vulture's, for instance, or are they more like a gull's wing that is slender and narrow? Are they marked or colored in an unusual way?

Wings in flight: How does the bird hold its wings in flight? Are they level with the bird's body, or are they slightly above the bird's back? What is their in-flight shape?

Flight characteristics: How does the bird fly? Does it fly in a straight line, or does it seem to move up and down with noticeable changes in direction as it goes from place to place?

Feet: Do the bird's feet appear distinctive in any way? Are they webbed? Do the feet have noticeable talons? What color are the feet?

Tail: Is it long and slender or short and square? Does the bird hold the tail up, level with its body, or down?

Note these characteristics. Doing so will make it easier to find the bird in various bird guides.

Other important considerations when identifying birds are the habitat and the time of year in which you see them. Forest birds aren't often seen in fields and, vice versa, and migrating birds tend to turn up in fall and in spring.

Before you start flipping through your identification books to determine which bird you've just seen, take the time to really study the bird. Notice its colors, watch its flight pattern and listen to its song. Describe the bird to yourself as you watch it eat or bathe or do whatever it was doing when you noticed it.

Here, a pileated woodpecker visits a feeder. The number of species you attract to your feeders will depend on which birds spend the summer, winter, or all year in your area and the varieties of food you offer.

Make a sketch; even if you think you can't draw, you can make a crude drawing, with colors noted. After you have a good, clear mental picture of this bird, pick up your identification guide and start looking for it.

Practice your identification skills on some common birds in your area. Really study the sparrows, robins, or chickadees that pop up regularly in the trees outside your kitchen window or at your neighbor's feeder.

Watch these birds through binoculars to become comfortable with handling the binoculars and focusing them on birds. Concentrate on the birds' colors and field marks (marks on the bird's chest or wings that set it apart from other similar-looking birds).

The American robin is found across the United States—through Alaska—in summer and across the southern states in winter. It breeds across the northern part of the continent from Labrador to Alaska and as far south as Arkansas, Texas, and California. It flies south to winter mainly in the northern part of the United States and from British Columbia to Newfoundland. It feeds on fruit and insects, including caterpillars. It's easily recognized by its orange-red breast and the grayish brown plumage on the rest of the body. Look for a white ring around its eyes.

The black-capped chickadee is a common feeder visitor. It breeds in northern areas of the continent from Alaska east to Newfoundland and south to Northern California and New Mexico and to northern New Jersey. It winters farther south from Maryland to Texas. It has a distinguishing black cap and bib with white cheeks and breast. White edges on its wing feathers will help you differentiate it from a Carolina chickadee. In summer it eats insects and their eggs, as well as snails; in winter it eats berries.

By learning how to use the tools of your newfound hobby, such as binoculars, and by studying the coloration and markings of common birds and comparing them with the descriptions found in your field guide, you'll soon learn what to look for in birds to help you identify them quickly.

Your bird identification tactics will improve with time and practice, so don't give up if all the birds seem like colorful blurs at first. With a little practice, you'll soon be able to sort the birds by color, size, or another identifying trait. Before long, you'll identify those yellow, orange, red, blue, purple-black, brown, and black birds at your feeder as goldfinches, orioles, cardinals, jays, martins, sparrows, and starlings.

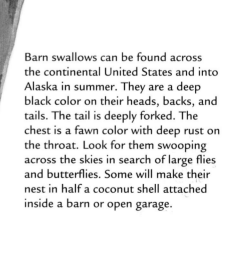

Barn swallows can be found across the continental United States and into Alaska in summer. They are a deep black color on their heads, backs, and tails. The tail is deeply forked. The chest is a fawn color with deep rust on the throat. Look for them swooping across the skies in search of large flies and butterflies. Some will make their nest in half a coconut shell attached inside a barn or open garage.

Learning the Lingo

As with any hobby, bird-watching has a vocabulary that newcomers need to learn in order to enjoy the hobby more fully. Here are some bird-watching terms to help get you started:

Aerie: The nest of a bird of prey, such as an eagle.

Allopreening: Mutual preening of feathers, usually done by mated pairs.

Altricial: Descriptive of baby birds that hatch naked and blind. They require parental care to survive.

Anisodactyl: Descriptive of a bird's foot that has three toes facing forward and one toe facing backward.

Anting: Some birds sit on anthills and allow the ants to run through their feathers, whereas other species place ants on their feathers. Both behaviors may help control external parasites on the birds, but experts are unsure of the cause.

Axilla: The area under the wing of a bird.

Beveled: Descriptive of a chisel-tipped beak.

Birding: The art of watching wild birds. Used interchangeably with bird-watching.

Blocking: Technique for counting a large flock of birds that involves counting a block of birds at the end of the flock and then visually estimating how many times the block you counted would fit over the entire flock.

Cere: The bare skin covering the top of some birds' upper beaks. Ceres are especially easy to see on raptors and most species of parrots.

Checklist: A list of birds found in a particular area, with a place for bird-watchers to check off the birds as they see them.

Checklists Galore!

As you explore a wider range of locations in which to watch birds, you'll soon encounter a wide variety of checklists by which you can track the birds you see. Some lists are simply that—the common and scientific names of the birds and a place for you to mark them off as you see them. Other checklists provide additional information for bird-watchers, including a detailed map of the location in which you're looking for birds; information about the avian seasonal visitors to the location; the abundance or rarity of different species found in the area; and habitat preferences of different bird species.

Consider keeping your checklists in a binder so you can refer to them more easily. Over time, you may find you've created your own specialized field guide based on your checklists that you can refer to as you develop your bird-watching skills.

Clock technique: Method used by bird-watchers to help others locate the position of a bird. For example, birds directly in front of a bird-watcher are at 12 o'clock, those directly behind are at 6 o'clock, those to the immediate left are at 9 o'clock, and those to the immediate right are at 3 o'clock. By the same token, birds at the top of a tree are at 12 o'clock and those at the bottom are at 6 o'clock.

Crown: The top of a bird's head.

Decurved: A downward-turning beak.

Disruptive coloration: Patterns in a bird's feathers that help camouflage it in the wild.

Dusting: Some species of birds take dust baths instead of or in addition to water baths.

Mourning doves live in a wide variety of habitats, including fields, parks, and residential areas.

Those birds are described as dusting themselves to clean their feathers or, possibly, to rid themselves of parasites, such as mites.

Family: A group of closely related species of birds that look, sound, and act similarly, but do not interbreed successfully. Examples include European starlings and red-winged blackbirds, which are part of the starling family but do not interbreed.

Field guide: Informative book about the birds you'll watch, many of which are organized by scientific name and full of colorful paintings or photos.

Field marks: Marks on a bird's body seen in the field that help a bird-watcher identify that bird. These include eye rings, wing bars, and breast spots or stripes.

Field notes: Comments made by a bird-watcher in the field about a particular species' color, song, nesting habits, location, and other identifying characteristics.

Frontal shield: A flat portion of a bird's bill that extends onto the bird's forehead.

Gape: A bird's mouth.

Habitat: A combination of landscape and plants that is home to certain species of birds or animals.

Life List: Record of birds seen by an individual bird-watcher in the course of his or her lifetime of watching birds.

Lobed: Descriptive of a bird's foot with flat, paddle-like toes.

Mobbing: Behavior in which several smaller birds gang up on or mob a larger bird or predator (such as a cat or predatory bird) to drive it away from a feeder or nest site.

Niche: An animal's particular place in its environment, which includes how it lives, where and what it eats, and where it lives.

The blue jay's range includes large areas of the United States and Canada.

Palmated: Descriptive of a bird's foot that has webbing between the front three toes; also semipalmated (partial webbing between the front toes) and totipalmated (webbing between all four toes).

Passerine: Adjective meaning "perching" that's used to describe many types of song-birds.

Pelagic: Adjective meaning "of the open sea" that's used to describe many seabirds.

Pileated: Having a crest.

Pishing: Noise made by bird-watchers who say the word "pish" with an extended exhale to attract songbirds that scold larger predatory birds. The "pish" sound mimics the sound of a bird scolding another bird. Ethical birders take care not to overuse this technique.

Precocial: Descriptive of chicks that hatch with downy feathers and open eyes. They require little parental care.

Preening: Behavior in which birds routinely clean and rearrange their feathers in order to maintain them in top condition.

Range: Region or area of the country in which a particular species is found.

Recurved: Descriptive of an upward-turning beak.

Rufous: Reddish brown, as in the rufous-crested towhee.

Serrate: Descriptive of a bill that appears to have small teeth on its edge.

Species: A group of birds that look, sound, and act similarly and interbreed success-fully.

Squeaking: Noise made by bird-watchers who kiss the backs of their hands to attract birds. The squeak imitates the sound of a bird in distress. Ethical bird-watchers take care not to overuse this technique.

Suet: Fat from around the kidneys of cattle. It is used as a bird food in suet feeders and attracts woodpeckers, chickadees, titmice, and jays, among others.

Taxonomy: Method of organizing birds that is based on their evolution.

Tit: A small, active bird, such as a titmouse.

Zygodactyl: Descriptive of a bird's foot that has two toes that face forward and two toes that face backward.

Getting Started

The North American continent is home to some 700 species of wild birds. With a little practice and luck, many bird-watchers can see about 100 of those species in a simple backyard setting.

Begin your bird-watching by getting to know your field guide. Review it carefully before you watch birds in your yard or neighborhood. Don't worry about birds found primarily in Alaska if you're bird-watching in Nebraska, or in British Columbia if you primarily watch birds in Newfoundland. Mark your guide (if you haven't done so already) to make species location easier for those birds found in and around the area in which you'll be watching. Also, take the time to familiarize yourself with the guide as it relates to the area in which you'll watch birds. Because you'll probably start to bird-watch by looking at the birds you'll see in your backyard or at the feeders you'll set up, get to know the sections of your guide that deal with passerine (perching) and nonpasserine (nonperching) birds.

When you're out in your yard, take the time to really look for and listen to the birds. Scan the trees and bushes carefully while you're looking. Move quietly so you don't disturb the birds and scare them away. Relax and enjoy the bird-watching experience, and you'll get more out of it.

Have a pair of binoculars handy as you look out at your yard and feeders. Binoculars will make watching the birds easier and more enjoyable. (We offer some tips on how to select the right pair of binoculars for you in Chapter 2.) Learn how to use them to get the most from your birding adventure.

You'll notice as your bird-watching skills improve that you learn to see things in a new way. You'll train your eyes to discern the differences between the patterns of light and shadow made by leaves in the trees, and you'll learn to detect the slightest movement in the reeds or underbrush. At first, you may scare more birds than you see, but you'll learn from these experiences how to move about confidently in wildlife areas without frightening away the animals you've come to see.

The male red-winged blackbird is easy to identify with his red shoulders.

If you learn to recognize just eight birds that you might see in your yard, such as the robin, the eastern or western kingbird, the barn swallow, the red-eyed vireo, the red-winged blackbird, the American goldfinch, and the chipping sparrow, you'll be ready to identify almost any North American songbird based on its similarity to or differences from these common bird families. For a complete list of birds you can find in your area, check the "Real birds" section of *www.virtualbirder.com*, where you can double click on your state.

When identifying birds, you start working from the known to the unknown. You can either begin by comparing the unknown species to a known species (this bird is the same size as a sparrow) or by recognizing differences between a known and the unknown species (this bird is smaller and lighter in color than a crow). Before long, you'll sort those birds quickly and come up with some solid identifications.

Another way to approach the process of identifying a bird is to think of it as a process of elimination. You can immediately discount species that aren't found in your current habitat or elevation, and you can further eliminate species that are considered winter visitors if you're bird-watching in July. The elimination process continues further as you discount all the characteristics the bird you're observing isn't or doesn't have. If it doesn't have a crest, for instance, it isn't a northern cardinal. Finally, focus on the characteristics your bird does have, and you'll soon have a good idea of what you're looking at.

U.S. Bird-watching Statistics

According to the U.S. Fish and Wildlife Service, more than 40 million Americans watch birds around their homes, and 18 million take special bird-watching trips. More than 14 million people watch waterfowl on their vacations, and 12.9 million people seek out songbirds. Also, 12.5 million people look for birds of prey; 10.5 million people watch water birds, such as herons or pelicans; and 7.9 million people seek out game birds, such as turkeys and pheasants—all while away from home. Approximately 34 million Americans said they could identify between 1 and 20 different species of wild birds. Another 6 million could identify between 21 and 40, and almost 4 million said they could identify more than 41 species of wild birds.

2 What You'll Need to See Birds

Now that you have a brief introduction to the world of bird-watching, it's time to get equipped so you can start identifying some of the birds in your world.

Your Shopping List

Your equipment list for bird-watching in your backyard is fairly simple:

- A good pair of binoculars
- A camera
- A field guide
- Insect repellent

You're probably wondering where you should shop for a good pair of binoculars and a field guide. If you're fortunate enough to live in an area where bird-watching or bird feeding specialty stores exist, look in your Yellow Pages under "Feed Dealers" or search online using a search engine such as *www.google.com* for "wild bird store." Otherwise, go to a sporting goods or camera store for your binoculars and a bookstore for your field guide.

Selecting Binoculars and Spotting Scopes

At first, it may seem a bit intimidating and bewildering as you scan the choices in the case. What do all the numbers mean? What size binoculars do you want? How much do you want to spend?

Buy the best binoculars you can afford. Good-quality binoculars will last a lifetime of bird-watching, so although you may spend a little more initially, you will receive many years of bird-watching enjoyment from your investment. Besides, if you purchase lower-quality binoculars, eventually you'll have to replace that pair, spending time and money to select the pair you should have purchased in the first place.

Let's look at some key terms you'll need to know when shopping for binoculars:

First check the magnification, or *power*, which is expressed in figures that look like a multiplication problem, such as 7 × 35 or 7 × 50, on the flat surface of the binoculars' housing near the eyepieces.

The first number expresses the power of that pair of binoculars. Seven-power binoculars make an item appear seven times larger than it appears with the naked eye. For bird-watching, 7× to 10× binoculars are good choices. Keep in mind, however, that the higher the power number, the more difficult it will be for you to see a steady image through the binoculars because the higher magnification will exaggerate any movements you make. Most bird-watchers use 7× to 8× binoculars successfully.

A good pair of binoculars will last many years and will enhance your enjoyment of your new hobby by allowing you to see details of birds that you might otherwise miss.

Next, let's consider the lens diameter, or *objective*, which is the second number in the figure described above. The lens diameter in question is that of the objective lenses, which are located at the lower end of the binoculars. When selecting binoculars for bird-watching, try to select as large a lens diameter as possible. Lens diameters between 35 and 50 are good choices for bird-watching.

Now let's look at the *field of view* of the binoculars. This term describes the width of the image you see when using the binoculars, and it usually measures the area that's visible to you from 1,000 yards away. The field of view measurement is usually found near the power measurement on the flat surface of the binoculars' housing. On some, it is expressed as a measurement of degrees, while on others it is a measurement of the number of feet visible at 1,000 yards. Beginning bird-watchers will want to invest in binoculars with a wide field of view (about 6 degrees or

300 feet at 1,000 yards) because these binoculars make it much easier to follow birds in flight or scan an area rapidly for birds.

Another important concept to consider when selecting binoculars is the *exit pupil*. This is the image that you see through the eyepiece when you hold a pair of binoculars away from you at arm's length. With a good-quality pair of binoculars, the image should appear as a full circle with clear, well-defined edges. On the other hand, a lower-quality pair of binoculars will produce an exit pupil with grayed-out edges.

Prisms are an essential part of every pair of binoculars because they alter the path that light takes through the binoculars. The prisms reflect the light that enters the binoculars through the large objective lenses at the bottom of the binoculars and direct it toward the ocular lenses, or eyepieces. In high-quality binoculars, the prisms are held in place with metal brackets, whereas in lower-quality binoculars they are held in place with glue. In case of hard knocks, the metal brackets are better able to hold the prisms in place than glue, so high-quality binoculars are better able to take a few bumps and jostles than lower-quality models.

Another difference between high- and low-quality binoculars is the amount of *coated optics* that you find in the binoculars. High-quality binoculars have fully coated optics, whereas lower-quality ones have coated optics only on the outer surfaces of the objective lenses and the eyepieces. To determine whether or not a pair of binoculars has fully coated optics, hold them under a fluorescent light and look at the objective lenses. Those with fully coated optics will reflect a bluish or amber cast from inside, whereas those with uncoated optics will reflect a whitish light.

A recent development in binoculars is the use of image-stabilizing technology. Binoculars with this feature have a built-in microcomputer, a tilt mechanism, and a special series of prisms that compensate for shaking hands and other vibrations.

Cleaning your binoculars with special tissues and other manufacturer-recommended supplies will extend the life of your binoculars—a good investment for a costly piece of equipment.

Another new trend brings binoculars together with digital photography. Several manufacturers offer binoculars with a built-in camera that records either still photos or short snippets of video. This allows bird-watchers to photograph what they see as they bird-watch. Visit your local camera store and ask to see several models of this combination device to determine which one is best for you.

When you purchase your binoculars, you may receive some accessories, such as a neck strap, a carrying case, and lens covers. As soon as possible, trade in the neck strap for a wider one that's made of soft cloth or neoprene rubber, because these will feel better on your neck than the original strap. Check the strap often, and replace it immediately when you see signs of wear, especially near the loops that fasten the strap to the binoculars.

> ### Binocular Care
>
> Clean your binoculars often to keep them at their optical best. Use lens-cleaning tissues suitable for eyeglasses or a camera-cleaning kit to remove dust and dirt.
>
> Protect your binoculars when climbing, jumping, or otherwise moving in ways that might cause you to drop them. Make sure the strap is securely around your neck whenever you use your binoculars, and don't swing them by the neck strap.
>
> Keep them dry! If your binoculars are dropped into fresh water, you will need to have them professionally cleaned to prevent rust from forming in the inner workings. If they fall into salt water, rinse them off with fresh water and seal them in a plastic bag, then take them for professional cleaning as soon as possible.

Choosing a Camera

Photographing birds at your backyard feeder is often a natural progression of your bird-watching hobby. Over time, you will have not only a great record of the different birds that have visited your feeder but also a new interest and new skills that you can use in other photography situations.

To truly enjoy your photography hobby, you'll first need a good camera. As with binoculars, it's essential to buy the best camera you can afford to get the most out of your hobby. This doesn't mean that you have to buy the most expensive camera or the one with the most features. You'll need to determine which is the best camera for you and make your purchase accordingly.

A good camera should be relatively easy for you to operate. For some photographers, this means purchasing a good-quality auto-focus camera, sometimes called a "point-and-shoot camera." These auto-focus cameras are ideal for beginners because they let you enjoy taking photos without having to worry about a lot of different settings on the camera before the shutter is snapped. Some come with zoom-telephoto lenses, which may help bring the birds at your feeder into better focus than a standard 50-mm lens.

Other photographers may find that a 35-mm camera with interchangeable lenses is the best solution. Advantages of the 35-mm camera with interchangeable lenses are that you can expand your skills as you become more comfortable with the equipment. If you want to shoot extreme close-ups, for instance, you can select from several different types of telephoto lenses (a lens with a minimum of 70–210 mm is a good starting point for close-up photography). If you want to shoot photos at sunrise or sunset, you can change the shutter speeds or aperture openings to make the final photo look even more dramatic than it does naturally. If you become really serious about the hobby, you can even have the glass in your camera's eyepiece ground to match your prescription if you wear corrective lenses.

Still other photographers go for the latest digital camera. If the world of digital photography appeals to you, purchase a camera with enough megapixels to allow you to be a successful photographer. If you want to save your photos and send them electronically to bird-watching friends in other parts of the country, a camera with 2 or 3 megapixels should be adequate, but if you plan to enlarge your bird photos to 11-by-17 posters, then you'll need a camera with 4 or more megapixels. Make sure you have enough digital media cards (they replace film in the digital world) to save your photos, and also be sure the camera is compatible with other electronic gear in your home, whether it's your computer, your printer, or your scanner. Then start snapping away!

The camera you choose for your backyard bird photos will depend on your needs and your comfort level with the different cameras. Go to a camera store and

Choose a camera with care. Although a high-quality camera can be expensive, it might give you better photos. Research carefully before buying, and then purchase the best you can afford.

handle as many different types of cameras as you wish. Ask for recommendations from the staff as to which types of cameras they recommend for photographing backyard birds. Also, check on the availability of used equipment, which is often a more affordable way to get into photography.

The Importance of a Field Guide

Field guides are very important to a bird-watcher. Without one, you won't be able to easily tell sparrows from warblers or gulls from terns. Take some time at the bookstore to peruse the different guides available. Make sure the one you select is the correct one for your area, and go through it to make sure that you are comfortable with the layout and that the text and illustrations make sense to you.

Once you get home from the bookstore, sit down with your field guide and begin to go through it carefully. Note which species are common to your area, and consider highlighting or flagging these entries to make finding them easier when you're in the field.

Go ahead and write in your field guide. Mark or flag birds that you will likely see in your yard. You can use removable, colored plastic strips to mark the birds you hope to see and those you've seen.

U.S. Wildlife-Watching Participants by Region

According to the most recent Hunting, Fishing, and Wildlife-Associated Recreation survey by the U.S. Fish and Wildlife Service, which measures various outdoor activities Americans take part in, 42.1 million U.S. residents watch wildlife and 96 percent of them, or 40.3 million people, watch birds. Here is how the country's participation breaks down by region:

Pacific

25 percent of region's residents watch wildlife

Mountain

32 percent of region's residents watch wildlife

West North Central

41 percent of region's residents watch wildlife

West South Central

24 percent of region's residents watch wildlife

East North Central

33 percent of region's residents watch wildlife

East South Central

34 percent of region's residents watch wildlife

Middle Atlantic

28 percent of region's residents watch wildlife

South Atlantic

28 percent of region's residents watch wildlife

New England

36 percent of region's residents watch wildlife

Beginning bird-watchers owe a debt of gratitude to naturalist, artist, and author Roger Tory Peterson (1908–1996), who revolutionized bird-watching beginning in 1934. That year, Peterson's *Field Guide to the Birds* introduced "the Peterson System" of classifying birds, which emphasized a visual identification system based on patternistic drawings with arrows pinpointing the key field marks bird-watchers needed to pay attention to. Peterson differed greatly from the previous system, which based itself on a top-to-bottom description of the bird being observed.

These white ibises and snowy egrets were spotted in Myakka River State Park in Florida.

Interest in Wildlife Watching in Canada

In a 1996 survey by Environment Canada, Canadians were asked to express their interest in wildlife watching activities. Following are the percentages of residents who expressed some interest to a great deal of interest in watching wildlife: (Note: Results for Northwest Territories and Nunavut were unreported in the survey.)

British Columbia
60.7 percent

Manitoba
57.3 percent

New Brunswick
57.2 percent

Newfoundland
52.2 percent

Alberta
57.1 percent

Ontario
55.0 percent

Nova Scotia
60.8 percent

Yukon Territory
78.0 percent

Saskatchewan
53.7 percent

Québec
57.8 percent

Prince Edward Island
61.0 percent

Canadian Bird-watching Statistics

About 1.2 million Canadians consider themselves serious bird-watchers able to name more than 100 different species. An additional 3.6 million Canadians consider themselves casual backyard bird-watchers.

The average Canadian bird-watcher spends $859 for bird-watching supplies, including a telescope ($350), a tripod ($220), binoculars ($100), a bug hat and vest ($85), a rain guard ($79), and a field guide ($25).

These evening grosbeaks are enjoying a snack.

3 Where You'll See Birds

Obviously, this book is about backyard bird-watching, so you're likely to see a number of birds in your yard. However, you can also find them in other places. You'll soon find that you can see birds almost anywhere, especially when you know the best times of day to watch and some of the places birds are most likely to be seen.

Time of Day to Watch

In most areas, the best times to bird-watch are early in the morning or late in the afternoon, when birds are most active. They are either waking up or settling down for the night and need something to eat to start or end their day. As you watch the birds in your yard or neighborhood, you'll soon learn the activity periods for the birds in your area.

Each season of the year has special bird-watching rewards. Fall and winter bring unexpected migratory guests to your feeder, whereas spring and summer allow you to watch the next generation of wild birds hatch, grow, and fledge.

In Your Backyard

Your backyard is probably the best and most accessible place for you to see birds. By the time you finish this book, you'll have all the necessary items in place that will bring birds to you. You'll have set up a bird-friendly habitat with the right mix of hiding places for wild birds, along with sheltering shrubs and trees. You'll have feeders to stock, birdbaths to fill, and birdhouses and nest boxes to maintain—each of which will bring certain types of birds to your yard for you to watch and enjoy.

In the City

If you reside in a major city, you can still see birds nearby. Birds can be found in city parks and public squares; apartment dwellers who put out feeders on their balconies or patios are often rewarded with a variety of visitors. (Make sure a bird feeder doesn't violate complex rules before you set it up.)

How to Behave While Watching Birds

Birds have a keen sense of danger, and although you may not view yourself as a predator, a bird will. You have all the qualifications: large size, unpredictable behavior and movements, and a loud voice. When you watch birds, you should sit, because doing so allows you to be immobile for a longer period than if you were standing. Don't move or talk if you're outside. Wear neutral clothing in greens and browns to blend in with the shrubs and trees. You're not trying to hide, but you are trying to calm the wildlife. A bright red shirt and pants might not help you achieve your goal.

When birds have gotten used to your presence, they will tolerate slow movement, so you can raise your binoculars or camera if you do so slowly.

After a few days, the birds in your area will get used to your presence, but will never totally accept you. Don't try to tame wild birds or get them to sit on you. Consider it a privilege to observe wildlife in a natural setting.

By watching birds this way, you can truly observe their natural behavior, a much more rewarding goal than to try to tame a wild animal, which could leave it open to harm from someone not as kind as you are.

Crossing the Border

Someday, you may want to bird-watch beyond your backyard. Wildlife viewing is big business on both sides of the U.S.-Canadian border. About 1.1 million Americans visited Canada to see wildlife, and about 438,000 Canadians visited the United States for the same reason, based on a 1996 survey conducted by Environment Canada. Here are some highlights:

- Wildlife viewing was the reason 331,000 Canadians took trips to the U.S. and the reason 526,000 Americans went to Canada.
- The American states to which Canadians went the most were Florida, Washington, and New York. U.S. visitors tended to concentrate their visits in two provinces: Ontario (50.0 percent of U.S. visitors) and British Columbia (20.9 percent of U.S. visitors).
- Most Canadians who traveled to the United States for wildlife viewing came from three provinces—Ontario (42.7 percent of travelers), Québec (25.5 percent), or British Columbia (21.1 percent).

If a chick falls out of its nest in your yard, put it back if you can. If you cannot find the nest and the chick is fully feathered, leave the chick and watch from a distance. It's likely that the parents will find and feed the chick.

If the chick is not fully feathered or is in imminent danger from other animals, such as cats or dogs, pick it up and keep it warm. Ideally, put it in a box or clean aquarium that sits on top of a heating pad, turned to a low setting. Wrap the chick in a clean cloth. Call your local veterinarian for the name and phone number of a licensed wildlife rehabilitator or wildlife rehabilitation center quickly, because the chick's life may depend on it. They will either arrange for a pickup or ask you to drive the chick to a central point where they can pick it up, usually at the office of an avian veterinarian. For laws on keeping wild birds native to your country, see Chapter 9. Most importantly, the bird is a wild creature and belongs in the wild. A rehabilitator will know how to care for it and train it to live again in the wild as an adult bird.

Once you learn the proper behavior for watching birds, you might be able to get this close (to a sandhill crane)!

Who's Who in the North American Bird World?

The North American continent is home to 92 families of birds. We've listed them below by the regions in which they are found. Keep in mind that these birds may be in your area at different times of the year. They are listed in taxonomic order, as you will find them in other ornithological publications. Some pass through during migration, while others are summer, winter, or year-round residents:

United States

Pacific

Accipiters
Albatrosses
Auks, murres and
   puffins
Babblers
Barn Owls
Blackbirds
Orioles
Bushtits
Buteos
Cardinals
Grosbeaks
Dickcissels
Buntings
Chickadees
Titmice
Cormorants
Creepers
Dippers
Diving Ducks
Eagles
Falcons

Finches
Siskins
Redpolls
Crossbills
Flycatchers
Geese
Goatsuckers
Grebes
Grouse
Gulls
Harriers
Herons
Hummingbirds
Jaegers
Skuas
Jays
Crows
Kingfishers
Kinglets
Kites
Larks
Loons

Mergansers
Mockingbirds
Thrashers
New World Quail
Nuthatches
Old World Sparrows
Old World Warblers
Ospreys
Oystercatchers
Parrots
Pelicans
Pigeons and Doves
Pipits
Wagtails
Plovers
Rails
Granules
Coots
Sandpipers
Phalaropes
Shearwaters
Petrels

Shrikes
Sparrows
Towhees
Starlings
Stiff-tailed Ducks
Stilts
Avocets
Storm Petrels
Swallows
Swans
Swifts
Tanagers
Terns
Thrushes
Tropicbirds
Typical Owls
Vireos
Vultures
Waxwings
Wood Warblers
Woodpeckers
Wrens

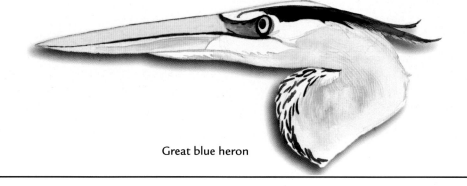

Great blue heron

Mountain

Accipiters
Blackbirds
Orioles
Bushtits
Buteos
Cardinals
Grosbeaks
Dickcissels
Buntings
Chickadees
Titmice
Cormorants
Cranes
Creepers
Dippers
Diving Ducks
Eagles
Falcons
Finches
Siskins

Redpolls
Crossbills
Flycatchers
Geese
Gnatcatchers
Goatsuckers
Grebes
Gulls
Harriers
Herons
Hummingbirds
Jays
Crows
Kingfishers
Kinglets
Kites
Larks
Mergansers
Mockingbirds
Thrashers
New World Quail

Nuthatches
Old World Sparrows
Parrots
Partridges
Pheasants
Pelicans
Pigeons
Doves
Pipits
Wagtails
Plovers
Rails
Granules
Coots
Sandpipers
Phalaropes
Shrikes
Silky-flycatchers
Sparrows
Towhees
Starlings

Stiff-tailed Ducks
Stilts
Avocets
Swallows
Swans
Swifts
Tanagers
Terns
Thrushes
Trogons
Turkeys
Typical Owls
Verdins
Vireos
Vultures
Waxwings
Whistling-ducks
Wood Warblers
Woodpeckers
Wrens

West North Central

Accipiters
Blackbirds
Orioles
Buteos
Cardinals
Grosbeaks
Dickcissels
Buntings
Chickadees
Titmice
Cormorants
Creepers
Diving Ducks
Falcons
Finches

Siskins
Redpolls
Crossbills
Flycatchers
Geese
Gnatcatchers
Goatsuckers
Grebes
Grouse
Harriers
Herons
Hummingbirds
Jays
Crows
Kingfishers
Kinglets

Larks
Mergansers
Mockingbirds
Thrashers
Nuthatches
Old World Sparrows
Parrots
Pigeons
Doves
Plovers
Rails
Granules
Coots
Sandpipers
Phalaropes
Shrikes

Sparrows
Towhees
Starlings
Stilts and Avocets
Swallows
Swifts
Tanagers
Terns
Thrushes
Typical Owls
Vireos
Vultures
Waxwings
Wood Warblers
Woodpeckers
Wrens

Scarlet ibis

West South Central

Accipiters
Anhingas
Blackbirds
Orioles
Boobies
Gannets
Buteos
Caracaras
Cardinals
Grosbeaks
Dickcissels
Buntings
Chachalacas
Chickadees and
    Titmice
Cormorants
Creepers
Dabbling (surface-
    feeding) Ducks
Diving Ducks
Falcons
Finches
Siskins
Redpolls
Crossbills
Flycatchers
Frigatebirds
Geese
Goatsuckers
Grebes
Gulls
Harriers
Herons
Hummingbirds
Ibis
Spoonbills
Jays
Crows
Kingfishers
Kinglets
Kites
Mergansers
Mockingbirds
Thrashers
Nuthatches
Old World Sparrows
Ospreys
Oystercatchers
Parrots
Pelicans
Pigeons and Doves
Plovers
Rails
Granules
Coots
Sandpipers
Phalaropes
Shrikes
Skimmers
Sparrows and
    Towhees
Starlings
Stiff-tailed Ducks
Storks
Swallows
Swifts
Tanagers
Thrushes
Typical Owls
Vireos
Vultures
Waxwings
Whistling-ducks
Wood Warblers
Woodpeckers
Wrens

East North Central

Accipiters
Blackbirds
Orioles
Buteos
Cardinals
Grosbeaks
Dickcissels
Buntings
Chickadees
Titmice
Creepers
Diving Ducks
Eagles
Falcons
Finches
Siskins
Redpolls
Crossbills
Flycatchers
Geese
Goatsuckers
Grebes
Harriers
Herons
Hummingbirds
Jays
Crows
Kingfishers
Kinglets
Larks
Loons
Mergansers
Mockingbirds
Thrashers
Nuthatches
Old World Sparrows
Ospreys
Parrots
Pigeons
Doves
Plovers
Rails
Granules
Coots
Sandpipers
Phalaropes
Shrikes
Sparrows
Towhees
Starlings
Stilts
Avocets
Swallows
Swifts
Tanagers
Thrushes
Typical Owls
Vireos
Vultures
Waxwings
Wood Warblers
Woodpeckers
Wrens

Hairy woodpecker

East South Central

Accipiters
Anhingas
Blackbirds
Orioles
Boobies
Gannets
Buteos
Cardinals
Grosbeaks
Dickcissels
Buntings
Chickadees
Titmice
Creepers
Diving Ducks
Eagles
Falcons
Finches
Siskins
Redpolls
Crossbills
Flycatchers
Frigatebirds
Geese
Goatsuckers
Grebes
Harriers
Herons
Hummingbirds
Ibis
Spoonbills
Jays and Crows
Kingfishers
Kinglets
Kites
Loons
Mergansers
Mockingbirds
Thrashers
Nuthatches
Old World Sparrows
Ospreys
Oystercatchers
Parrots
Pelicans
Pigeons
Doves
Plovers
Rails
Granules
Coots
Sandpipers
Phalaropes
Shrikes
Skimmers
Sparrows
Towhees
Starlings
Stiff-tailed Ducks
Stilts
Avocets
Storks
Swallows
Swifts
Tanagers
Terns
Thrushes
Typical Owls
Vireos
Vultures
Waxwings
Wood Warblers
Woodpeckers
Wrens

Red-eyed vireo

Middle Atlantic

Accipiters
Barn Owls
Blackbirds
Orioles
Boobies
Gannets
Buteos
Cardinals
Grosbeaks
Dickcissels
Buntings
Chickadees
Titmice
Cormorants
Creepers
Cuckoos
Diving Ducks
Falcons
Finches
Siskins
Redpolls
Crossbills
Flycatchers
Geese
Gnatcatchers
Goatsuckers
Grebes
Gulls
Harriers
Herons
Hummingbirds
Jaegers
Skuas
Jays
Crows
Kingfishers
Kinglets
Larks
Loons
Mergansers
Mockingbirds
Thrashers
Nuthatches
Old World Sparrows
Ospreys
Oystercatchers
Parrots
Partridges
Pheasants
Pigeons
Doves
Plovers
Rails
Granules
Coots
Sandpipers
Phalaropes
Shearwaters and
    Petrels
Shrikes
Sparrows and Towhees
Starlings
Storm Petrels
Swallows
Swans
Swifts
Tanagers
Terns
Thrushes
Typical Owls
Vireos
Vultures
Waxwings
Wood Warblers
Woodpeckers
Wrens

South Atlantic

Accipiters
Anhingas
Blackbirds and Orioles
Boobies and Gannets
Buteos
Caracaras
Cardinals
Grosbeaks
Dickcissels
Buntings
Chickadees
Titmice
Cormorants
Cranes
Creepers
Cuckoos
Diving Ducks
Falcons
Finches
Siskins
Redpolls

Crossbills
Flycatchers
Geese
Gnatcatchers
Goatsuckers
Grebes
Gulls
Harriers
Herons
Hummingbirds
Ibis
Spoonbills
Jaegers
Skuas
Jays
Crows
Kingfishers
Kinglets
Kites
Limpkins
Loons
Mergansers

Mockingbirds
Thrashers
New World Quail
Nuthatches
Old World Sparrows
Ospreys
Oystercatchers
Parrots
Pigeons
Doves
Pipits
Wagtails
Plovers
Rails
Granules
Coots
Sandpipers
Phalaropes
Shearwaters
Petrels
Shrikes
Sparrows

Towhees
Starlings
Stilts
Avocets
Storm Petrels
Swallows
Swans
Swifts
Tanagers
Terns
Thrushes
Tropicbirds
Turkeys
Typical Owls
Vireos
Vultures
Waxwings
Whistling-ducks
Wood Warblers
Woodpeckers
Wrens

New England

Accipiters
Barn Owls
Blackbirds
Orioles
Buteos
Cardinals
Grosbeaks
Dickcissels
Buntings
Chickadees
Titmice
Cormorants
Creepers
Cuckoos
Diving Ducks
Falcons
Finches

Siskins
Redpolls
Crossbills
Flycatchers
Geese
Goatsuckers
Grebes
Grouse
Gulls
Harriers
Herons
Hummingbirds
Jays and Crows
Kingfishers
Kinglets
Larks
Mergansers
Mockingbirds

Thrashers
Nuthatches
Old World Sparrows
Parrots
Partridges
Pheasants
Pigeons
Doves
Plovers
Rails
Granules
Coots
Shrikes
Sparrows
Towhees
Starlings
Swallows
Swifts

Tanagers
Terns
Thrushes
Typical Owls
Vireos
Vultures
Waxwings
Wood Warblers
Woodpeckers
Wrens

Black-capped chickadee

Canada

British Columbia

Loons/Huards
Grebes/Grèbes
Albatrosses/Albatros
Shearwaters and fulmars/Puffins et fulmars
Storm-petrels/Océanites
Pelicans/Pélicans
Cormorants/Cormorans
Frigatebirds/Frégates
Herons and bitterns/Hérons et botaurs
Ibises/Ibis
Storks/Cigognes
Geese/Oies
Swans/Cygnes
Ducks/Canards
American vultures/Urubus
Ospreys/Balbuzard
Hawks and eagles/Buses et aigles
Falcons/Faucons
Pheasants/Faisans
Turkeys/Dindons sauvages
Grouse/Tétras
Rails, gallinules, and coots/Râles, gallinules, et foulques
New World quail/Colin
Cranes/Grues
Plovers/Pluviers
Oystercatchers/Huîtriers
Avocets and stilts/Avocettes et échasses
Sandpipers and phalaropes/Bécasses et phalaropes
Skuas and Jaegers/Labbes
Gulls/Goélands
Terns/Sternes
Auks, murres, and puffins/Alques, guillemots, et macareux
Pigeons and doves/Pigeons et tourterelles

Cuckoos/Coulicous
Barn owls/Effraies
Owls/Hiboux
Vireos/Viréos
Goatsuckers/Engoulevents
Swifts/Martinets
Hummingbirds/Colibris
Kingfishers/Martins-pêcheurs
Woodpeckers/Pics
Tyrant flycatchers/Moucherolles et tyrans
Flycatchers/Moucherolles
Shrikes/Pies-grièches
Jays and crows/Geais et corneilles
Larks/Alouettes
Swallows/Hirondelles
Titmice/Mésanges
Nuthatches/Sittelles
Creepers/Grimpereaux
Wrens/Troglodytes
Dippers/Cincle plongeurs
Kinglets/Roitelets
Gnatcatchers/Gobemoucherons
Thrushes/Grives
Mockers/Moqueurs
Accentors/Accenteurs
Starlings/Étourneaux
Pipits/Pipits
Waxwings/Jaseurs
Warblers/Parulines
Tanagers/Tangaras
Blackbirds and allies/Ictérides
Cardinals/Cardinals
Buntings and sparrows/Bruants
Finches/Fringillidés
Old World sparrows/Moineaux

Northern tufted titmouse

Alberta

Loons/Huards
Grebes/Grèbes
Tropicbirds/Phaétons
Pelicans/Pélicans
Cormorants/Cormorans
Herons and bitterns/Hérons et botaurs
Ibises/Ibis
Geese/Oies
Swans/Cygnes
Ducks/Canards
American vultures/Urubus
Ospreys/Balbuzard
Hawks and eagles/Buses et aigles
Falcons/Faucons

Pheasants/Faisans
Turkeys/Dindons sauvages
Grouse/Tétras
Rails, gallinules, and coots/Râles, gallinules, et foulques
Cranes/Grues
Plovers/Pluviers
Avocets and stilts/Avocettes et échasses
Sandpipers and phalaropes/Bécasses et phalaropes
Skuas and Jaegers/Labbes
Gulls/Goélands
Terns/Sternes
Auks, murres, and puffins/Alques, guillemots, et macareux
Pigeons and doves/Pigeons et tourterelles
Cuckoos/Coulicous

Eagles have eyesight up to eight times sharper than humans.

Barn owls/Effraies
Owls/Hiboux
Vireos/Viréos
Goatsuckers/Engoulevents
Swifts/Martinets
Hummingbirds/Colibris
Kingfishers/Martins-pêcheurs
Woodpeckers/Pics
Tyrant flycatchers/Moucherolles et tyrans
Flycatchers/Moucherolles
Shrikes/Pies-grièches
Jays and crows/Geais et corneilles
Larks/Alouettes
Swallows/Hirondelles
Titmice/Mésanges
Nuthatches/Sittelles
Creepers/Grimpereaux
Wrens/Troglodytes
Dippers/Cincle plongeurs
Kinglets/Roitelets
Gnatcatchers/Gobemoucherons
Thrushes/Grives
Mockers/Moqueurs
Starlings/Étourneaux
Pipits/Pipits
Waxwings/Jaseurs
Warblers/Parulines
Tanagers/Tangaras
Cardinals/Cardinals
Blackbirds and allies/Ictéridés
Buntings and sparrows/Bruants
Finches/Fringillidés
Old World sparrows/Moineaux

Brown pelican

Saskatchewan

Loons/Huards
Grebes/Grèbes
Pelicans/Pélicans
Cormorants/Cormorans
Herons and bitterns/Hérons et botaurs
Ibises/Ibis
Geese/Oies
Swans/Cygnes
Ducks/Canards
American vultures/Urubus
Ospreys/Balbuzard
Hawks and eagles/Buses et aigles
Falcons/Faucons
Pheasants/Faisans
Turkeys/Dindons sauvages
Grouse/Tétras
Rails, gallinules, and coots/Râles, gallinules,
    et foulques
Cranes/Grues
Plovers/Pluviers
Avocets and stilts/Avocettes et échasses
Sandpipers and phalaropes/Bécasses et
    phalaropes
Skuas and Jaegers/Labbes
Gulls/Goélands
Terns/Sternes
Auks, murres, and puffins/Alques, guillemots,
    et macareux
Pigeons and doves/Pigeons et tourterelles
Cuckoos/Coulicous
Barn owls/Effraies
Owls/Hiboux
Vireos/Viréos
Goatsuckers/Engoulevents
Swifts/Martinets
Hummingbirds/Colibris
Kingfishers/Martins-pêcheurs
Woodpeckers/Pics
Tyrant flycatchers/Moucherolles et tyrans

Raptors use their sharp,
down-turned beaks to
tear apart prey.

Flycatchers/Moucherolles
Shrikes/Pies-grièches
Jays and crows/Geais et corneilles
Larks/Alouettes
Swallows/Hirondelles
Titmice/Mésanges
Nuthatches/Sittelles
Creepers/Grimpereaux
Wrens/Troglodytes
Dippers/Cincle plongeurs
Kinglets/Roitelets
Thrushes/Grives
Mockers/Moqueurs
Starlings/Étourneaux
Pipits/Pipits
Waxwings/Jaseurs
Warblers/Parulines
Tanagers/Tangaras
Cardinals/Cardinals
Buntings and sparrows/Bruants
Blackbirds and allies/Ictéridés
Finches/Fringillidés
Old World sparrows/Moineaux

Manitoba

Loons/Huards
Grebes/Grèbes
Boobies and gannets/Fous
Pelicans/Pélicans
Cormorants/Cormorans
Herons and bitterns/Hérons et botaurs
Ibises/Ibis
Geese/Oies
Swans/Cygnes
Ducks/Canards
American vultures/Urubus
Ospreys/Balbuzard
Hawks and eagles/Buses et aigles
Falcons/Faucons
Pheasants/Faisans
Turkeys/Dindons sauvages
Grouse/Tétras
Rails, gallinules, and coots/Râles, gallinules,
  et foulques
Cranes/Grues
Plovers/Pluviers
Avocets and stilts/Avocettes et échasses
Sandpipers and phalaropes/Bécasses et
  phalaropes
Skuas and Jaegers/Labbes
Gulls/Goélands
Terns/Sternes
Auks, murres, and puffins/Alques, guillemots,
  et macareux
Pigeons and doves/Pigeons et tourterelles
Cuckoos/Coulicous
Barn owls/Effraies
Owls/Hiboux
Vireos/Viréos
Goatsuckers/Engoulevents
Swifts/Martinets
Hummingbirds/Colibris
Kingfishers/Martins-pêcheurs
Woodpeckers/Pics
Tyrant flycatchers/Moucherolles et tyrans
Flycatchers/Moucherolles

Tricolored heron

Shrikes/Pies-grièches
Jays and crows/Geais et corneilles
Larks/Alouettes
Swallows/Hirondelles
Titmice/Mésanges
Nuthatches/Sittelles
Creepers/Grimpereaux
Wrens/Troglodytes
Gnatcatchers/Gobemoucherons
Thrushes/Grives
Mockers/Moqueurs
Starlings/Étourneaux
Pipits/Pipits
Waxwings/Jaseurs
Warblers/Parulines
Tanagers/Tangaras
Buntings and sparrows/Bruants
Cardinals/Cardinals
Blackbirds and allies/Ictéridés
Finches/Fringillidés
Old World sparrows/Moineaux

Ontario

Loons/Huards
Grebes/Grèbes
Shearwaters and fulmars/Puffins et fulmars
Storm-petrels/Océanites
Boobies and gannets/Fous
Pelicans/Pélicans
Cormorants/Cormorans
Anhingas/Anhinga d'Amerique
Frigatebirds/Frégates
Herons and bitterns/Hérons et botaurs
Ibises/Ibis
Storks/Cigognes
Geese/Oies
Swans/Cygnes
Ducks/Canards
American vultures/Urubus
Ospreys/Balbuzard
Hawks and eagles/Buses et aigles
Falcons/Faucons
Pheasants/Faisans
Turkeys/Dindons sauvages
Grouse/Tétras
Rails, gallinules, and coots/Râles, gallinules,
    et foulques
Cranes/Grues
Plovers/Pluviers
Oystercatchers/Huîtriers
Avocets and stilts/Avocettes et échasses
Sandpipers and phalaropes/Bécasses
    et phalaropes
Skuas and Jaegers/Labbes
Gulls/Goélands
Terns/Sternes
Skimmers/Becs-en-ciseaux
Auks, murres, and puffins/Alques, guillemots,
    et macareux
Pigeons and doves/Pigeons et tourterelles
Cuckoos/Coulicous
Barn owls/Effraies
Owls/Hiboux
Vireos/Viréos

Goatsuckers/Engoulevents
Swifts/Martinets
Hummingbirds/Colibris
Kingfishers/Martins-pêcheurs
Woodpeckers/Pics
Tyrant flycatchers/Moucherolles et tyrans
Flycatchers/Moucherolles
Shrikes/Pies-grièches
Jays and crows/Geais et corneilles
Larks/Alouettes
Swallows/Hirondelles
Titmice/Mésanges
Nuthatches/Sittelles
Creepers/Grimpereaux
Wrens/Troglodytes
Kinglets/Roitelets
Gnatcatchers/Gobemoucherons
Thrushes/Grives
Mockers/Moqueurs
Starlings/Étourneaux
Pipits/Pipits
Waxwings/Jaseurs
Warblers/Parulines
Silky-flycatchers/Ptilogons
Tanagers/Tangaras
Cardinals/Cardinals
Buntings and sparrows/Bruants
Blackbirds and allies/Ictéridés
Finches/Fringillidés
Old World sparrows/Moineaux

Female northern shoveler

Robin eggs in a nest.

Québec

Loons/Huards
Grebes/Grèbes
Albatrosses/Albatros
Shearwaters and fulmars/Puffins et fulmars
Storm-petrels/Océanites
Boobies and gannets/Fous
Pelicans/Pélicans
Cormorants/Cormorans
Frigatebirds/Frégates
Herons and bitterns/Hérons et botaurs
Ibises/Ibis
Storks/Cigognes
Geese/Oies
Swans/Cygnes
Ducks/Canards
American vultures/Urubus
Ospreys/Balbuzard
Hawks and eagles/Buses et aigles
Falcons/Faucons
Pheasants/Faisans
Turkeys/Dindons sauvages
Grouse/Tétras
Rails, gallinules, and coots/Râles, gallinules,
    et foulques
New World quail/Colin
Cranes/Grues
Plovers/Pluviers
Oystercatchers/Huîtriers
Avocets and stilts/Avocettes et échasses
Sandpipers and phalaropes/Bécasses
    et phalaropes
Skuas and Jaegers/Labbes
Gulls/Goélands
Terns/Sternes
Skimmers/Becs-en-ciseaux
Auks, murres, and puffins/Alques, guillemots,
    et macareux
Pigeons and doves/Pigeons et tourterelles
Cuckoos/Coulicous
Barn owls/Effraies
Owls/Hiboux

Vireos/Viréos
Goatsuckers/Engoulevents
Swifts/Martinets
Hummingbirds/Colibris
Kingfishers/Martins-pêcheurs
Woodpeckers/Pics
Tyrant flycatchers/Moucherolles et tyrans
Flycatchers/Moucherolles
Shrikes/Pies-grièches
Jays and crows/Geais et corneilles
Larks/Alouettes
Swallows/Hirondelles
Titmice/Mésanges
Nuthatches/Sittelles
Creepers/Grimpereaux
Wrens/Troglodytes
Kinglets/Roitelets
Gnatcatchers/Gobemoucherons
Thrushes/Grives
Mockers/Moqueurs
Starlings/Étourneaux
Pipits/Pipits
Waxwings/Jaseurs
Warblers/Parulines
Tanagers/Tangaras
Cardinals/Cardinals
Buntings and sparrows/Bruants
Blackbirds and allies/Ictéridés
Finches/Fringillidés
Old World sparrows/Moineaux

New Brunswick

Loons/Huards
Grebes/Grèbes
Albatrosses/Albatros
Shearwaters and fulmars/Puffins et fulmars
Storm-petrels/Océanites
Boobies and gannets/Fous
Pelicans/Pélicans
Cormorants/Cormorans
Herons and bitterns/Hérons et botaurs
Ibises/Ibis
Storks/Cigognes
Geese/Oies
Swans/Cygnes
Ducks/Canards
American vultures/Urubus
Ospreys/Balbuzard
Hawks and eagles/Buses et aigles
Falcons/Faucons
Pheasants/Faisans
Grouse/Tétras
Rails, gallinules, and coots/Râles, gallinules, et foulques
Cranes/Grues
Plovers/Pluviers
Oystercatchers/Huîtriers
Avocets and stilts/Avocettes et échasses
Sandpipers and phalaropes/Bécasses et phalaropes
Skuas and Jaegers/Labbes
Gulls/Goélands
Terns/Sternes
Skimmers/Becs-en-ciseaux
Auks, murres, and puffins/Alques, guillemots, et macareux
Pigeons and doves/Pigeons et tourterelles
Cuckoos/Coulicous
Barn owls/Effraies
Owls/Hiboux
Vireos/Viréos

Goatsuckers/Engoulevents
Swifts/Martinets
Hummingbirds/Colibris
Kingfishers/Martins-pêcheurs
Woodpeckers/Pics
Tyrant flycatchers/Moucherolles et tyrans
Flycatchers/Moucherolles
Shrikes/Pies-grièches
Jays and crows/Geais et corneilles
Larks/Alouettes
Swallows/Hirondelles
Titmice/Mésanges
Nuthatches/Sittelles
Creepers/Grimpereaux
Wrens/Troglodytes
Kinglets/Roitelets
Gnatcatchers/Gobemoucherons
Thrushes/Grives
Mockers/Moqueurs
Starlings/Étourneaux
Pipits/Pipits
Waxwings/Jaseurs
Warblers/Parulines
Tanagers/Tangaras
Cardinals/Cardinals
Buntings and sparrows/Bruants
Blackbirds and allies/Ictéridés
Finches/Fringillidés
Old World sparrows/Moineaux

A blue jay chick.

Nova Scotia

Loons/Huards
Grebes/Grèbes
Albatrosses/Albatros
Shearwaters and fulmars/Puffins et fulmars
Storm-petrels/Océanites
Tropicbirds/Phaétons
Boobies and gannets/Fous
Pelicans/Pélicans
Cormorants/Cormorans
Frigatebirds/Frégates
Herons and bitterns/Hérons et botaurs
Ibises/Ibis
Geese/Oies
Swans/Cygnes
Ducks/Canards
American vultures/Urubus
Ospreys/Balbuzard
Hawks and eagles/Buses et aigles
Falcons/Faucons
Pheasants/Faisans
Grouse/Tétras
Rails, gallinules, and coots/Râles, gallinules, et foulques
Limpkins/Courlan brun
Cranes/Grues
Plovers/Pluviers
Oystercatchers/Huîtriers
Avocets and stilts/Avocettes et échasses
Sandpipers and phalaropes/Bécasses et phalaropes
Skuas and Jaegers/Labbes
Gulls/Goélands
Terns/Sternes
Skimmers/Becs-en-ciseaux
Auks, murres, and puffins/Alques, guillemots, et macareux
Pigeons and doves/Pigeons et tourterelles
Cuckoos/Coulicous
Barn owls/Effraies
Owls/Hiboux

Vireos/Viréos
Goatsuckers/Engoulevents
Swifts/Martinets
Hummingbirds/Colibris
Kingfishers/Martins-pêcheurs
Woodpeckers/Pics
Tyrant flycatchers/Moucherolles et tyrans
Flycatchers/Moucherolles
Shrikes/Pies-grièches
Jays and crows/Geais et corneilles
Larks/Alouettes
Swallows/Hirondelles
Titmice/Mésanges
Nuthatches/Sittelles
Creepers/Grimpereaux
Wrens/Troglodytes
Kinglets/Roitelets
Gnatcatchers/Gobemoucherons
Thrushes/Grives
Mockers/Moqueurs
Starlings/Étourneaux
Pipits/Pipits
Waxwings/Jaseurs
Warblers/Parulines
Tanagers/Tangaras
Cardinals/Cardinals
Buntings and sparrows/Bruants
Blackbirds and allies/Ictéridés
Finches/Fringillidés
Old World sparrows/Moineaux

Wood duck

Prince Edward Island

Loons/Huards
Grebes/Grèbes
Shearwaters and fulmars/Puffins et fulmars
Storm-petrels/Océanites
Boobies and gannets/Fous
Pelicans/Pélicans
Cormorants/Cormorans
Herons and bitterns/Hérons et botaurs
Ibises/Ibis
Geese/Oies
Swans/Cygnes
Ducks/Canards
American vultures/Urubus
Ospreys/Balbuzard
Hawks and eagles/Buses et aigles
Falcons/Faucons
Pheasants/Faisans
Grouse/Tétras
Rails, gallinules, and coots/Râles, gallinules,
    et foulques
Cranes/Grues
Plovers/Pluviers
Avocets and stilts/Avocettes et échasses
Sandpipers and phalaropes/Bécasses
    et phalaropes
Skuas and Jaegers/Labbes
Gulls/Goélands
Terns/Sternes
Skimmers/Becs-en-ciseaux
Auks, murres, and puffins/Alques, guillemots,
    et macareux
Pigeons and doves/Pigeons et tourterelles
Cuckoos/Coulicous
Barn owls/Effraies
Owls/Hiboux
Vireos/Viréos
Goatsuckers/Engoulevents
Swifts/Martinets
Hummingbirds/Colibris

Blue jay

Kingfishers/Martins-pêcheurs
Woodpeckers/Pics
Tyrant flycatchers/Moucherolles et tyrans
Shrikes/Pies-grièches
Jays and crows/Geais et corneilles
Larks/Alouettes
Swallows/Hirondelles
Titmice/Mésanges
Nuthatches/Sittelles
Creepers/Grimpereaux
Wrens/Troglodytes
Kinglets/Roitelets
Gnatcatchers/Gobemoucherons
Thrushes/Grives
Mockers/Moqueurs
Starlings/Étourneaux
Pipits/Pipits
Waxwings/Jaseurs
Warblers/Parulines
Tanagers/Tangaras
Cardinals/Cardinals
Buntings and sparrows/Bruants
Blackbirds and allies/Ictéridés
Finches/Fringillidés
Old World sparrows/Moineaux

Look for raptors, including hawks and eagles, high up in trees or on telephone poles, where they look for prey.

Newfoundland

Loons/Huards
Grebes/Grèbes
Albatrosses/Albatros
Shearwaters and fulmars/Puffins et fulmars
Storm-petrels/Océanites
Tropicbirds/Phaétons
Boobies and gannets/Fous
Pelicans/Pélicans
Cormorants/Cormorans
Frigatebirds/Frégates
Herons and bitterns/Hérons et botaurs
Ibises/Ibis
Geese/Oies
Swans/Cygnes
Ducks/Canards
American vultures/Urubus
Ospreys/Balbuzard
Hawks and eagles/Buses et aigles
Falcons/Faucons
Pheasants/Faisans
Grouse/Tétras
Rails, gallinules, and coots/Râles, gallinules, et foulques
Cranes/Grues
Plovers/Pluviers
Oystercatchers/Huîtriers
Avocets and stilts/Avocettes et échasses
Sandpipers and phalaropes/Bécasses et phalaropes
Skuas and Jaegers/Labbes
Gulls/Goélands
Terns/Sternes
Skimmers/Becs-en-ciseaux
Auks, murres, and puffins/Alques, guillemots, et macareux
Pigeons and doves/Pigeons et tourterelles
Cuckoos/Coulicous
Barn owls/Effraies
Owls/Hiboux
Vireos/Viréos
Goatsuckers/Engoulevents
Swifts/Martinets
Hummingbirds/Colibris
Kingfishers/Martins-pêcheurs
Woodpeckers/Pics
Tyrant flycatchers/Moucherolles et tyrans
Flycatchers/Moucherolles
Shrikes/Pies-grièches
Jays and crows/Geais et corneilles
Larks/Alouettes
Swallows/Hirondelles
Titmice/Mésanges
Nuthatches/Sittelles
Creepers/Grimpereaux
Wrens/Troglodytes
Kinglets/Roitelets
Gnatcatchers/Gobemoucherons
Thrushes/Grives
Mockers/Moqueurs
Starlings/Étourneaux
Pipits/Pipits
Waxwings/Jaseurs
Warblers/Parulines
Tanagers/Tangaras
Cardinals/Cardinals
Buntings and sparrows/Bruants
Blackbirds and allies/Ictéridés
Finches/Fringillidés
Old World sparrows/Moineaux

Yukon Territory

Loons/Huards
Grebes/Grèbes
Shearwaters and fulmars/Puffins et fulmars
Cormorants/Cormorans
Herons and bitterns/Hérons et botaurs
Geese/Oies
Swans/Cygnes
Ducks/Canards
American vultures/Urubus
Ospreys/Balbuzard
Hawks and eagles/Buses et aigles
Falcons/Faucons
Pheasants/Faisans
Grouse/Tétras
Rails, gallinules, and coots/Râles, gallinules, et foulques
Cranes/Grues
Plovers/Pluviers
Avocets and stilts/Avocettes et échasses
Sandpipers and phalaropes/Bécasses et phalaropes
Skuas and Jaegers/Labbes
Gulls/Goélands
Terns/Sternes
Auks, murres, and puffins/Alques, guillemots, et macareux
Pigeons and doves/Pigeons et tourterelles
Owls/Hiboux
Vireos/Viréos
Hummingbirds/Colibris
Kingfishers/Martins-pêcheurs
Woodpeckers/Pics
Tyrant flycatchers/Moucherolles et tyrans
Flycatchers/Moucherolles
Shrikes/Pies-grièches
Jays and crows/Geais et corneilles
Larks/Alouettes
Swallows/Hirondelles
Titmice/Mésanges
Nuthatches/Sittelles
Creepers/Grimpereaux
Wrens/Troglodytes
Dippers/Cincle plongeurs
Kinglets/Roitelets
Thrushes/Grives
Mockers/Moqueurs
Starlings/Étourneaux
Pipits/Pipits
Waxwings/Jaseurs
Warblers/Parulines
Tanagers/Tangaras
Cardinals/Cardinals
Buntings and sparrows/Bruants
Blackbirds and allies/Ictéridés
Finches/Fringillidés
Old World sparrows/Moineaux

Northwest Territories

Loons/Huards
Grebes/Grèbes
Shearwaters and fulmars/Puffins et fulmars
Storm-petrels/Océanites
Boobies and gannets/Fous
Pelicans/Pélicans
Cormorants/Cormorans
Herons and bitterns/Hérons et botaurs
American vultures/Urubus
Geese/Oies
Swans/Cygnes
Ducks/Canards
Ospreys/Balbuzard
Hawks and eagles/Buses et aigles
Falcons/Faucons
Grouse/Tétras
Rails, gallinules, and coots/Râles, gallinules, et foulques
Cranes/Grues

Plovers/Pluviers
Avocets and stilts/Avocettes et échasses
Sandpipers and phalaropes/Bécasses et
    phalaropes
Skuas and Jaegers/Labbes
Gulls/Goélands
Terns/Sternes
Auks, murres, and puffins/Alques, guillemots,
    et macareux
Pigeons and doves/Pigeons et tourterelles
Owls/Hiboux
Vireos/Viréos
Goatsuckers/Engoulevents
Swifts/Martinets
Hummingbirds/Colibris
Kingfishers/Martins-pêcheurs
Woodpeckers/Pics
Tyrant flycatchers/Moucherolles et tyrans
Flycatchers/Moucherolles
Shrikes/Pies-grièches
Jays and crows/Geais et corneilles
Larks/Alouettes
Swallows/Hirondelles
Titmice/Mésanges
Nuthatches/Sittelles
Wrens/Troglodytes
Dippers/Cincle plongeurs
Kinglets/Roitelets
Old World Warblers and Gnatcatchers/Sylviidés
Thrushes/Grives
Mockers/Moqueurs
Accentors/Accenteurs
Starlings/Étourneaux
Pipits/Pipits
Waxwings/Jaseurs
Warblers/Parulines
Tanagers/Tangaras
Cardinals/Cardinals
Buntings and sparrows/Bruants
Blackbirds and allies/Ictéridés
Finches/Fringillidés
Old World sparrows/Moineaux

Baltimore orioles usually eat insects, but will sometimes drink from hummingbird feeders.

Red-headed woodpecker

Nunavut

Loons/Huards
Grebes/Grèbes
Shearwaters and fulmars/Puffins et fulmars
Storm-petrels/Océanites
Boobies and gannets/Fous
Pelicans/Pélicans
Cormorants/Cormorans
Herons and bitterns/Hérons et botaurs
Geese/Oies
Swans/Cygnes
Ducks/Canards
American vultures/Urubus
Ospreys/Balbuzard
Hawks and eagles/Buses et aigles
Falcons/Faucons
Grouse/Tétras
Rails, gallinules, and coots/Râles, gallinules,
    et foulques
Cranes/Grues
Plovers/Pluviers
Avocets and stilts/Avocettes et échasses
Sandpipers and phalaropes/Bécasses
    et phalaropes
Skuas and Jaegers/Labbes
Gulls/Goélands
Terns/Sternes
Auks, murres, and puffins/Alques, guillemots,
    et macareux
Pigeons and doves/Pigeons et tourterelles
Owls/Hiboux
Vireos/Viréos
Goatsuckers/Engoulevents
Swifts/Martinets
Hummingbirds/Colibris
Kingfishers/Martins-pêcheurs
Woodpeckers/Pics
Tyrant flycatchers/Moucherolles et tyrans
Flycatchers/Moucherolles
Shrikes/Pies-grièches

Broad-billed hummingbird

Jays and crows/Geais et corneilles
Larks/Alouettes
Swallows/Hirondelles
Titmice/Mésanges
Nuthatches/Sittelles
Wrens/Troglodytes
Dippers/Cincle plongeurs
Kinglets/Roitelets
Old World Warblers and Gnatcatchers/Sylviidés
Thrushes/Grives
Mockers/Moqueurs
Accentors/Accenteurs
Starlings/Étourneaux
Pipits/Pipits
Waxwings/Jaseurs
Warblers/Parulines
Tanagers/Tangaras
Cardinals/Cardinals
Buntings and sparrows/Bruants
Blackbirds and allies/Ictéridés
Finches/Fringillidés
Old World sparrows/Moineaux

Outdoor Health Hazards

While we like to concentrate on the positive aspects of this enjoyable hobby, it's always a good idea to learn about the risks and to take precautions. Here we will discuss those associated with watching birds and ways to help you remain healthy.

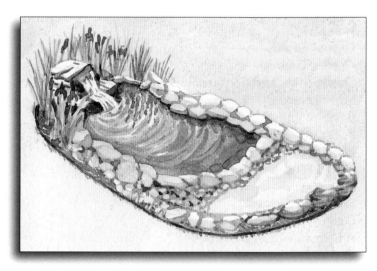

Standing water in your yard can be a major attraction for mosquitoes.

Keep in mind as you read this that the chance that you will become ill with a mosquito-borne illness is extremely slim, particularly if you heed the appropriate precautions.

We've long known that mosquitoes carry a host of diseases. This is because the female periodically needs a blood meal to support the reproduction of her species. She bites one animal, and then another, spreading any virus one may carry in its system on to another. Among the diseases mosquitoes carry are yellow fever, Japanese encephalitis, dengue fever, St. Louis encephalitis, and West Nile virus. Common sense and a few simple precautions can help you, whether you look at birds from the comfort of your backyard or you venture out into the field.

Keep in mind that mosquitoes are most active at dawn and dusk, but are also plentiful in shady areas, like under trees.

A Few Tips for Bird-watchers

Insect repellents: *Always* read and follow the directions. Some contain chemicals that can be harmful. Apply it to exposed skin, but never under clothing. Carefully spray the repellent on top of your clothing.

Clothing: Wear a hat and long-sleeved shirt with a high neck. Long pants and socks will help protect your legs and feet.

Backyard cleanup: To prevent an infestation of mosquitoes in your yard, make sure you have no standing water in discarded tires, potholes, or buckets. If you have a birdbath, change the water every other day (at a minimum) in warm weather, when mosquitoes can hatch in just two days. If you have a deep bath or pond, add fish.

"Feeder" goldfish are sold in pet stores and are inexpensive and hardy in outdoor ponds. These will eat the larvae and provide a nice bath and drinking spot for birds.

In addition, many gardening supply companies now sell machines that emit warm carbon dioxide, which attracts mosquitoes. Some machines also have vacuums that suck in the mosquitoes when they approach. An advantage to this over spraying an area or using a kill-all bug zapper is that you have *selective* control, an ecologically preferable method. (You kill only mosquitoes, not other insects that birds eat.) Position one nearby as you watch for birds in your yard.

West Nile Virus

This mosquito-borne illness was first identified in Uganda, Africa in 1937. It was then isolated to areas of Africa, West Asia, Europe, and the Middle East.

According to the National Institute of Health Web site, it appeared in North America in 1999 for the first time with a case in New York City. It has since spread across the North American continent with cases being found in Canada as well as the United States. This is not a cause for alarm, however. Emi Sato, West Nile Surveillance Coordinator for the U.S. Geological Survey National Wildlife Health Center, told the National Wildlife Federation, "West Nile Virus is much more a wildlife disease than it is a human disease."

To protect yourself from contracting the disease, take all precautions against mosquito bites whenever you go outside to watch birds.

In this disease, birds carry the infecting virus; after a mosquito bites a sick bird it can carry the virus to the next animal it bites, including humans. Crows and jays are particularly susceptible, but watch groups have noted that hummingbirds, owls, eagles, hawks, and other native North American species are dying as well. House sparrows, an introduced, old-world species, are also a possible carrier of the disease. This supposition arose because the disease spread relatively slowly once it arrived on this continent. If migratory birds had been likely carriers, the virus would have spread across the continent very quickly.

If you see dead crows or other native birds, contact local health officials. Do not attempt to dispose of a dead bird carcass yourself; health authorities will want to test the bird for the virus.

At present, West Nile virus has no vaccine and no cure; however, the chance that you will become ill with the disease is slight.

Symptoms of West Nile virus mimic those of the flu. For further, in-depth information on the disease please check the following Web sites:

- Canada: *www.hc-sc.gc.ca/english/westnile/* (Health Canada)
- United States: *www.cdc.gov/ncidod/dvbid/westnile/* (Centers for Disease Control)

Bird Droppings

In general, avoid bird droppings wherever possible. Two potentially dangerous diseases are carried in bird fecal matter: avian (or bird) flu and histoplasmosis. Of the two, avian flu has gotten the most publicity, but histoplasmosis has the potential for a tremendous health impact on an individual. If you track through wet bird droppings, use a hose to wash it off your shoes. Never scrape or stir up dried bird droppings because fungal spores, or a virus or bacteria that carries a disease could become airborne and then be easily absorbed by your body when you inhale. Not all bird droppings are infectious, but assuming that they are will help you handle them in a manner that will best protect your health. Try not to sit in dried bird droppings, or if you have gotten them on your clothing or hands, wash them in hot water with soap. Don't allow pieces of clothing to dry before you handle them again.

Avian (or bird) flu

Although a lot of information hit the press in late 2003 and early 2004, avian flu has been around in various forms for many years, including in the Western hemisphere. It has not been noteworthy except to poultry farmers and those who track the health of wild birds affected by it because it is usually, like many diseases, species specific. The worry occurs when a disease jumps from one species to another. When that happens, the newly affected species has no defense and affected members tend to die quickly. In the cases seen in 2003–2004, for a reason not yet entirely understood, bird flu has begun to jump from chickens to humans, as we have seen in Asia with a strain called H5N1, which can easily attach to cells in the nose and throat. "What scares scientists most about H5N1 [Asian bird flu] is that someone eventually will be stricken by the bird flu and a human flu at the same time, allowing the viruses to swap genetic material. The resulting hybrid could be both deadly and virulent. Even if it weren't immediately contagious, it could quickly evolve." (Anthony Spaeth, *Time*, Feb. 9, 2004.)

Although the disease has also been identified in the United States, it is a different strain, called H7. (Human flu strains are labeled H1, H2, H3, etc.) While deadly to waterfowl and chickens, as of press time, avian flu had not yet mutated to humans.

The evolution of the disease in humans would make it particularly deadly, because humans would have no antibodies for this new disease.

What can bird-watchers do to protect themselves and others? Common sense will serve us well. Migratory birds, such as shorebirds and ducks, may carry the disease, but develop only a mild form of the illness. Bob Dietz, spokesman for the World Health Organization was quoted on the *New York Times* Web site on January 27, 2004: "Migratory birds are what carry the disease. If they're dying, it's an awfully strong disease."

For more information, go to the following Web sites:

- *www.webmd.com* (Online medical information: WebMD)
- *www.cdc.gov* (Centers for Disease Control)
- *www.who.int* (World Health Organization)
- *www.cnn.com* (Cable News Network)
- *www.nytimes.com* (*New York Times* online)
- Canada: *www.ccohs.ca* (Canadian Centre for Occupational Health and Safety)

Use the search function to look for "avian flu."

Histoplasmosis

This disease primarily affects the lungs, but can also involve other organs; then it's called *disseminated* histoplasmosis. According to the CDC, it can cause death if left untreated.

Histoplasmosis is caused by a fungus called *Histoplasma capsulatum* found in soil worldwide, but especially in moderate temperatures in river valleys and other places likely to collect bird or bat droppings. When contaminated soil is disturbed, microscopic spores of this fungus are released into the air. Breathing this air pulls the spores into the lungs, where they can cause infection and scarring.

According to the CDC, most infected people will show no symptoms or ill effects, but those with an acute form of the disease could have "respiratory symptoms, a general ill feeling, fever, chest pains, and a dry, or nonproductive, cough. ... The disseminated form is fatal unless treated."

For more information on histoplasmosis, check the following Web sites:

- *www.cdc.gov* (Centers for Disease Control)
- *www.who.int* (World Health Organization)
- *www.nei.nih.gov* (National Institutes of Health)

4 What You'll See and Hear While You Watch Birds

A great deal of bird-watching is spent refining your observational skills. At first, watching birds may seem a constant blur of color, noise, and movement. But if you sit still and remain quiet for prolonged periods looking at one area of your yard, you will begin to make mental notes about what's normal for most birds, or some specific birds.

As you become more comfortable with the birds, you'll note behavior specific to certain times of the year and to particular birds. You may learn that there are names for much of this behavior. For instance, when some small birds have chicks in the nest, they become bold enough to chase aggressive birds such as hawks, owls,

The chipping sparrow is a common backyard visitor throughout North America.

and grackles away from the nest area. Sometimes one small bird, such as a mockingbird, will fly at a larger bird, such as a red-tailed hawk, with such fury the larger bird will flee. Sometimes several birds will join together to rid a nesting area of a predator, whether real or perceived, and that behavior is called *mobbing*. Some birds will also fly at humans in a group or as a single attacker. (The best advice: Leave the area to enable the parent bird to get back to feeding or protecting its chicks.)

You'll also see some behavior that will be hard to watch, such as a raptor killing a smaller bird, or some larger chicks pushing smaller ones out of the nest, but your role in this is to observe. You can use snake and squirrel baffles and prevent ants from invading nests, but you cannot save all the birds from the natural cycle that will play out in your view. If you save the life of a bird that couldn't make it on its own, it may still die later when released.

Listening to birds sing is relaxing, and you may even have purchased a feeder with a built-in microphone or an inexpensive baby-monitoring device so the sounds of your backyard birds can come into your home. Once you've learned more about the meaning of these sounds, you may be less relaxed, but more intrigued.

Birdcalls and songs will become an important tool in your bird "watching" kit. As you begin to take a serious interest and keep records, note which birds sing one song and which sing many. Sparrows generally sing about 10 songs; marsh wrens, as many as 200 different songs; and brown thrashers, as many as 2,000 songs. A study of warblers done at the University of Massachusetts, Amherst, found that each male had a primary song that he used to attract a mate, and the rest of his songs were to define and defend his territory.

Listening: A Valuable Part of Bird-watching

Often, before you see birds, you will hear them. When you learn their songs and calls, then you'll know they're in the area and you can concentrate your search. The best time to listen for birds is in the early morning, about dawn, before the wind picks up and other environmental noises make it more difficult to differentiate the songs and calls.

Bird songs and birdcalls can mean many things. A *call* is a short, inborn vocalization, such as the "chip, chip" of a northern cardinal. A *song* is a longer, more complex pattern the bird learns or knows intrinsically. Some male birds use their song to define and defend their territory, essentially saying to other males, "This is mine. It holds enough food for me to support my family. Find your own."

At specific times of the year, usually spring, males use their song to attract females. A strong song may indicate to females that a male is healthy. Innately, a female knows that a healthy male is a good candidate for producing robust young and has the strength to help her find food for their family. Older males who have survived several seasons usually have more complex song, and the females respond to the potential such a male offers for helping her chicks stay alive.

Some birds have an inborn song pattern. Others learn the songs. Mockingbirds are an example of the latter; they learn the songs of other birds and mimic them well. Other mockingbird males in the area seem to recognize the voice of the singer, no matter what song he sings.

Two species are special favorites of new American bird-watchers because they sing loudly and distinctively. The whip-poor-will and the common poorwill live both summer and winter in the United States. In woodlands of the East, listen for the whip-poor-will, whose name comes from the loud sound of its call. These birds make this call many times consecutively at dusk in early summer. Whip-poor-wills winter in the southern United States. In the West, listen for common poorwills all year.

In most of northern Canada, from west to east, listen and look for Swainson's thrush in summer, but not in winter. Across Canada in all but the most northern parts of each province, listen for the song of the red-winged blackbird in summer, but in winter this bird migrates south, except for warmer areas of British Columbia.

Mockingbirds and starlings include the songs of other birds in their repertoire, so check the bird visually to know for sure which bird you've heard.

Generally, only male birds sing, and females and males call, but the female red-winged blackbird (year-round across Canada—except in the coldest part of the north—and the United States) sings during the breeding season to communicate with her mate and to scare off other females.

A hanging flowerpot can be a good makeshift nest for your local birds.

Common ravens (found in the western United States into Alaska all year and across Canada, except in the far north) have distinct calls and will use the partner's call as a location tool. This call seems to be a way to tell the mate to return.

When you begin, listen for the wrens, known for their strong, intricate songs. Wrens can be found across Canada and the U.S. (see "Wrens Near You" starting on page 54). The Internet makes it easy to learn the song of the wren that either lives in your area year-round, migrates through at specific times of the year, or winters in your vicinity—maybe in your own backyard. Listed in the sidebar are Web sites relevant to each wren. At those sites, you will see either a photo or a drawing so you can more easily spot the bird. At *www.mbr-pwrc.usgs.gov* you will find lists of birds and can listen to the songs of many of the birds you could hear in your own backyard.

Useful Web Sites

We are frequently asked how to find useful and accurate information on the Internet. We use it as a search tool because it's powerful and fast, and it adds many sites each day; however, if you type in a subject, you may find that your search engine, such as Google, has listed thousands of pages of good, bad, and mediocre information.

Remember, however, that people enter the information into a computer, so the degree of correctness depends on a human, and humans make mistakes. We believe in checking information (note, we didn't say facts just yet) gleaned from one site with at least one other well-respected site. Some sites offer CDs with birdsongs specific to areas of North America or elsewhere.

We've found an easy way to limit the number of selections to exactly what we want: We encase our subject in quotation marks. For instance, if you want to search for a species by name, put quotation marks around the name: "northern mockingbird." The search engine will then look in all of its possible files for the whole term. If you don't encase your title, the search engine will give you all sites it finds on the Web with "northern" and then it will give you all it finds for "mockingbird," and it may also give you sites with the whole term. In any case, unless you encase the whole phrase, you may get thousands of sites to check, instead of the few with useable information.

Once the search engine gives you the site addresses, sort through them for likelihood of accuracy. Some general advice: Look for the place the site originates—".*gov*" in the site name indicates that it's generated by a government agency; ".*edu*," on the other hand, indicates that it's generated by a university or other educational institution. Avoid those many chatty, self-generated sites put on the Web by individuals until you are surer of yourself and can separate fact from fiction.

You'll soon see sites developed by the U.S. Geological Survey (*www.usgs.gov* and *www.mbr-pwrc.usgs.gov*), the Audubon Society (*www.audubon.org*) and Cornell University (*birds.cornell.edu*). For Canadian information, check out the Canadian Wildlife Service (*www.cws-scf.ec.gc.ca*), the Canadian Wildlife Federation (*www.cwf-fcf.org*), and World Wildlife Fund Canada (*www.wwf.ca/default.asp*). The National Wildlife Federation now sponsors a site: *eNature.com*. To listen to bird songs, go to *www.enature.com/audio/audio_home.asp*. Those are a good place to begin because they are all excellent, well-researched sites you can count on for accuracy.

Wrens Near You

A wren is a small, appealing bird whose color ranges from dark brown to tan to white. It has a long, tapered, downward-curving beak, a design that allows it to easily pry insects from tight spaces. Its short, wide tail is most often held up for balance, and the wren has a well-rounded chest. You could easily miss it, however, if you didn't listen first for its beautiful song. Following is a list of types of wrens you can find across the continental United States, Alaska, and Canada. Use the following Web site to listen to wren songs: *www.junglewalk.com/sound/Wren-sounds.asp*. Then, go outside and listen.

   Wrens eat insects, so a tray of mealworms and the proper place to build a nest could bring them to your yard.

Bewick's wren: **(United States)**

This 4 $^1/_2$-inch (11.4-cm) bird looks similar to the house wren, but it has a white, curved line of feathers above each eye. *Summers:* It usually breeds from Washington state south along the West Coast and through Arizona and New Mexico through central Texas. More rarely, it can be found as far north as Nevada, Colorado, Kansas, and Missouri. *Winters:* Although it may migrate south a short distance, you can generally see it in the same area as in summer. Nests are in scrub grass. It feeds on insects. Listen for its song at dawn. More information on this species is available on the Patuxent Wildlife Research Center's Web site (*www.mbr-pwrc.usgs.gov*). (This URL is case sensitive; lowercase letters must be typed exactly as they appear here.)

Cactus wren: **(United States)**

This bird is larger than other wrens, at about 6 $^1/_2$ inches (16.5 cm) long. Its bill is not as curved as that of other wrens. It has a white stripe above each eye and spots on its body. Its range is limited to Arizona, southern California, southern New Mexico, Utah, and west Texas. It doesn't migrate in winter. It nests in spiny plants, especially the cholla cactus. Cactus wrens eat insects and some fruit. See a photo of this bird and specific maps for its range, and listen to its call online at *animaldiversity.ummz.umich.edu*.

Cactus wren

Canyon wren: (United States)

It's about 4 $\frac{1}{2}$ inches (11.4 cm) long with white feathers under its beak and on its upper chest. The lower chest is a distinctive rust color. The beak is especially long, thin, and curved, which makes it ideal for the bird to grab insects hiding in tiny crevices and under rocks. During mating season, the male fans his tail like a turkey or a peacock. The canyon wren's habitat is mainly along the Rio Grande River in Texas, southern Arizona, the Central Valley in California, southeastern Nevada, and eastern Utah. It doesn't migrate. Both male and female use song to define their territory, nest in low rock crevices, and are monogamous. Check out this Web site for its spiraling song: *www.junglewalk.com/sound/Wren-sounds.asp*; or *www.mbr-pwrc.usgs.gov/id/framlst/i7170id.html* for a photo.

Carolina wren: (United States)

This hardy little bird ranges as far east as Virginia, west to central Texas, and north to Kansas, Missouri, Illinois, Indiana, Ohio, Michigan, and West Virginia. In warm winters it can be seen in New York, Rhode Island, Pennsylvania, and New Jersey. It is about 5 $\frac{1}{2}$ inches (14 cm) long, with the characteristic shape of body, tail, and long, curved bill. The head (crown) is a rusty brown with a white (superciliary) line above each eye, with a black stripe on either side of the white line. White feathers cover its lower cheeks, throat, and chin. The rest of the bird has gradations of the rust color. To read John James Audubon's account of this bird and see his drawing of one of them, go to *www.50states.com/bird/carwren.htm*. This bird generally does not migrate unless winter is unusually harsh. It makes its nest low to the ground and eats insects and spiders.

Rock wren: (United States)

This medium-sized wren is a grayish brown overall with a pale buff colored throat and chest. The line above its eyes is gray. Its tail is barred, as are the flight feathers. Dots of black and white appear on the back and crown of the head. The profile of this bird is similar to most wrens, with the tail held up as a balancing tool. The bill is not as long or curved as that of most wrens. It is about 5 to 6 $\frac{1}{2}$ inches (12.7 to 16.5 cm) long. It's a western American bird, ranging north from New Mexico, through Colorado, Wyoming, and Montana. In winter it migrates short distances throughout the Southwest and as far east as central Texas. For a not yet understood reason, the rock wren lays down a path of small rocks, shell, bone, and small pieces of metal leading to its nest in crevices of rock walls or in dry washes. It eats insects.

You can see a John James Audubon painting of a rock wren by searching for it in the "plates" section, located in the Audubon Birds of America section of *www.abirdshome.com*, or view photos by searching for "rock wren" at *www.enature.com*.

Rock wrens sing all year, but the song varies slightly in spring. The song is distinct and easily remembered. To hear both songs on a University of Michigan Web site, go to *animaldiversity. ummz.umich.edu* and search the "birds sounds" section.

House wren: **(United States and Canada)**

This feisty little bird is 4 $\frac{1}{4}$ to $\frac{3}{4}$ inches long (11.4 to 12 cm). It has the characteristic well-rounded chest and upright tail. The white line above its eyes is more of a light beige than white. The body is brown in the East, but more grayed brown in the West. The tail and back have distinct black bars. It sings all spring and summer, almost continuously during the day. For a photo and to listen to the song, go to *www.mbr-pwrc. usgs.gov*. In winter it migrates to tropical climates south of the United States. Both males and females sing a complicated song to defend their territory.

House wren

They will nest in barns, cavities in trees, flowerpots, or hats, and take readily to nest boxes, which they clean out and redo when they arrive to nest each year.

During breeding season, the house wren can be found all across the United States except central and west Texas, though some can be found in the Piney Woods of east Texas. It lives in only the central part of Georgia and the Carolinas. It lives across Canada, in the warmer parts of the south, but does not winter there!

Marsh wren: **(United States and Canada)**

This relatively tiny wren is about 4 inches (10.16 cm) long. Compared with other wrens, its beak is short, but still thin enough to get into narrow places to look for insects. It also eats some snails.

Its throat and chest are white, and it has a distinctive white line above each eye. Its back is black, speckled with white. The wings and tail have black bars. The crown is black. Its breeding areas are mainly in the American wetlands of California, Oregon, Washington, Nevada, Idaho, Nebraska, North and South Dakota, Minnesota, and the swamps of southeast Texas. In Canada, it breeds in British Columbia, Alberta, Saskatchewan, Manitoba, and southern Ontario.

In winter, it migrates relatively short distances to British Columbia in Canada, and in the United States to the marshes of California, along the Rio Grande River, and the swamps of the Gulf Coast, including Texas, Louisiana, Mississippi, Alabama, Georgia, and Florida. To listen to a recording of this shy bird, and many others, use the following: *www.mbr-pwrc.usgs.gov*. Male marsh wrens will duel for territory, and females are more willing to mate with males that have the most complex song.

Sedge wren: **(Canada and the United States)**

This small bird is only 3 $^1/_2$ to 4 $^3/_4$ inches (8.9 to 12.1 cm) long. It has a typical wren profile, with its tail commonly held upright, but it has a relatively short, slender beak. It's a soft fawn color with dark brown or black bars on its back, wings, and tail.

Because the sedge wren lives in wet grasslands with clumps of sedges, grasses, rushes, and scattered shrubs, its habitat is disappearing as such areas are drained for development. In Canada, it breeds in some parts of Alberta, more heavily in Saskatchewan, and most often in Manitoba. It does not winter in Canada. In the United States, it breeds mainly in North Dakota, Minnesota, and Michigan. It migrates to winter along the Gulf and Atlantic coasts, going inland in some cases as far as central Texas.

Look for a photo of the sedge wren and listen to its song on *www.enature.com*. This is a reclusive bird, so you may hear its song well before you spot the bird.

Winter wren: **(Canada and the United States)**

This tiny—about 3-inch-long (7.6 cm)—bird has a huge territory; it's the only wren that can be found outside the New World. Most types of winter wren live in dense coniferous forests near creeks or small streams, where it nests in tangled tree roots and abandoned woodpecker nest holes. In the United States, it can be found mainly along the West Coast of California, Oregon, and Washington, but also in the Appalachian and Rocky mountains. Look for it as well during breeding season in heavily forested areas in Wisconsin, Minnesota, Michigan, and New York. In Canada, it breeds heavily in British Columbia and across central Alberta, Saskatchewan, Manitoba, central and southern Ontario and Québec, New Brunswick, Nova Scotia, and Prince Edward Island. It winters along the western coast of and in the interior of British Columbia, spreading somewhat into western Alberta.

Its feathers are reddish brown, and its tail, that of a typical wren, held upright. This adaptable species is darker in the western part of the North American continent than in the eastern part. In the Aleutian Islands, its paler coloring helps camouflage it against the rocky cliffs where it lives and breeds. Look for a painting of the winter wren in the "Birds of the Week" section of the Cornell Web site (*birds.cornell.edu*) or by searching for the winter wren on *www.mbr-pwrc.usgs.gov*.

The song of the winter wren differs from coast to coast, with the song more complex on the West Coast. Listen to a song and call of the winter wren by searching the "Birds of the Week" section of the Cornell Web site (*birds.cornell.edu*). The winter wren eats insects, reportedly (according to a Stanford Web site) dunking its head completely into a stream to catch a water insect.

Getting Physical

Some things birds do every day will surprise a new birder—yawning and stretching, for instance. Birds do this for the same reasons other animals, including humans, do it: to relax, to keep muscles limber, to take in more oxygen. They also blink their eyes, and close their eyes when they sleep.

Birds have a remarkable ability to turn their heads 180 degrees, which most other animals cannot do. This helps them look out for predators—and for prey.

Eating

Birds spend most of the daylight hours searching for food and eating. In summer they have lots of food available, but they must also feed chicks, so the job is still an all-consuming one. Putting out feeders with many types of food, including various seeds, mealworms, fruit, and nectar, will help ease the burden. In winter, birds must eat enough food to keep warm, so your feeders will make their lives easier then, too. In winter, include suet, which you can purchase by the block in most pet and feed stores. You will soon know which types of birds eat seeds and which seeds they prefer.

You will learn which birds eat insects and where they hunt for them. It will also become apparent whether you've provided the trees and shrubs that help make your yard the perfect habitat.

Some birds, such as robins and blackbirds, eat worms and insects on the ground, walking as they look for them. Others, such as purple martins and swifts, catch insects as they fly.

Who Eats What?

Birds eat a wide variety of food. One way to tell what type they eat is by looking at the bird's bill. The bill shape determines what the bird can eat. A woodpecker has a sharp, hard bill that allows it to dig into

It won't take you too long to learn the favorite snacks of your local birds.

wood for the insects that form its diet. Various species live and breed across the United States; the pileated woodpecker lives in all southern Canadian provinces, from west to east.

Raptors (including kestrels, kites, falcons, eagles, owls, goshawks, harriers, ospreys, and vultures) have sharp, hooked beaks that permit them to tear open animals, such as rodents, foxes, and birds, to eat. Raptors live throughout the United States and Canada.

The northern flicker has a long tongue with which it grabs ants to eat. This bird summers as far north as Alaska, the Yukon, the Northwest Territories, Nunavut, and the Maritime Provinces in Canada. They live year-round as far south as Florida and south Texas. They migrate only short distances.

Finches vary widely and have diverse bills: Crossbills (Rocky Mountains and west to the Pacific Coast to northern British Columbia) use their odd-looking bills to dig out seeds from cones, and to eat insects buried in bark and fruit seeds. Many small finches roll seeds in their cone-shape bills until the shell breaks away.

Wrens and creepers have long, curving, slender bills that enable them to dig deep into crevices to catch spiders and insects.

Begin to make note of the types of bills on the birds in your yard and the foods they prefer—fruit, insects, small seeds, or sunflower seeds. Offer more of these foods to help ease their burden in spring and summer when they feed young and in winter when food is short. Continue to offer it in spring, too, when some will have just completed a long migration.

Some birds will amuse you by storing food in your yard. Jays (including blue, green, stellar, gray, and western) are found across the United States and Canada (except the Northwest Territories and Nunavut), and always want more than enough to suffice for a meal, burying nuts or peanuts and retrieving them during winter. Other birds that behave similarly include nuthatches and chickadees, woodpeckers and crows (various species across North America). According to the PBS show *Bird Brains*, the Clark's nutcracker crow (western United States and British Columbia) buries as many as 30,000 pine nuts in November and remembers where to retrieve them during the following winter.

To attract the widest variety of birds to your yard, offer fruit, insects (mealworms), and small and large seeds. (See Chapter 5.) Placing your bird feeders in sheltered areas will help prevent the birds you attract from becoming prey to birds that prefer to eat animals, such as raptors.

Hunting

Some birds in your backyard hunt for and eat live prey, including rodents, snakes, and other birds. Owls hunt at night. If you are lucky enough to have an owl to observe, sit quietly near its usual roosting place, such as in a barn or in a large tree. If you can see it well, you'll notice it cocking its head to listen for the rustle of a mouse or other nocturnal animal. Soon, it will dive silently and snatch the prey in its talons, and then return to its roost to eat. Relatively affordable night-vision spotting scopes are available in catalogs, online, and in retail stores. These can help you get an up-close view of owls at work.

Bald eagles steal food from one another.

Other raptors, such as hawks and eagles, circle high above or sit on cliffs, posts, trees, or wires to hunt for live prey during daylight hours, which means you may see one concentrate on the birds in your feeding area. If so, it may dive and grab the slowest among them. Usually, though, smaller birds are well aware of raptors in the air, and they will dive quickly for cover and your yard will fall silent. The small birds will remain hidden in the brush and trees until the raptor has moved on.

Animal behaviorists, ornithologists, and ecologists have combined talents in recent years to study the hunting behavior of raptors, especially Harris's hawks (the southwestern United States). Harris's hawks hunt in teams. Some birds flush the prey, whereas other hawks wait in the direction the prey will run, where they attack and kill the prey. The group of hawks then shares the kill, taking food back to nestlings when they have them. This allows the group to have more food than one hawk could kill by itself, but it indicates to us the high degree of intelligence of these birds. An online account posted by Texas A&M University, College Station, gives an account of this bird's behavior at the following Web site: *http://ccwild.cbi.tamucc.edu/naturalhistory/harris'_hawk/hrshacc.htm*. This behavior is also seen in golden eagles, which can be found across the United States where there is open country. Watching hunting parties formed of such birds will amaze you.

Bald eagles spend summers from the Aleutian Islands (Alaska), through the Yukon, the Northwest Territories, northern British Columbia and Alberta, as well as Ontario, Québec, and Newfoundland, and year-round in the western provinces and states, south to Mexico. They winter as far south as Florida. To protect its own kill, a bald eagle will hold out its wings over the dead animal, perhaps making itself look as large as possible; this lets other birds know it will fight for the food. These large birds steal food from each other and other birds.

The gyrfalcon lives year-round in the arctic tundra across the North American continent and is also cunning in finding prey. Some were reported following a trapper because his presence in the area flushed other birds the gyrfalcon would eat. This raptor is also seen in the northern parts of the United States and across Canada, especially in summer. Take notes as you watch birds to see which food they prefer and if you note any interesting or unusual feeding behavior.

Preening/Caring for Feathers

A bird must spend a great deal of time taking care of its feathers. If the feathers get into disrepair, the bird cannot fly and then it will die.

Birds molt at least once a year, usually after the chicks are raised and before migration or winter, when birds need all their feathers to be in top condition. During molt, birds gradually replace old feathers with new. This is hard on the bird's body, and during this time songbirds will not sing.

You may see birds wallowing in dust, appearing to thoroughly enjoy themselves. Experts believe this may be a way birds rid themselves of pests, such as mites, and keep their feathers in top shape. If you provide a dust-bath area in your yard, make sure it's far away from plants where a cat could hide.

To maintain feather health, birds must bathe. At all times of the day, you can see birds bathing, both in fine dirt and in water. Provide an area of your yard with a bare patch where birds can get a dust bath. (Refer to Chapter 7 for guidance and precautions.) Also, offer clean water in a safe place where they can bathe. Watch birds in a rainstorm and you may see some, such as doves, spread their wings to get wet before preening. In summer, many birds will seek out lawn sprinklers. If yours are set to go off at a certain time, you may see the birds hanging out every day, waiting for a shower, especially in late afternoon.

You will sometimes also see birds spread their wings and bask in the sun, some on the ground and some on the barest branches of trees.

Fighting

Occasionally, you will see two male birds that square off for territory, whether for a breeding area or just for the rights to food at your patio feeder. They'll puff out their feathers and perhaps flap their wings. They may strike at each other in a menacing fashion. The idea is to look as big as possible to frighten away the other bird. If things go far enough between two birds of equal stature (mature birds, for instance) they may actually get into a physical fight, but birds rarely fight to the death or even to the point of serious injury, although feathers may fly. Too much is at stake. An injured bird would soon be food for a predator.

You may sometimes see a bird attack a mirror or a reflective window. The bird apparently believes it's attacking an equal bird that has entered his territory. If you can, put some sort of covering over the "offending" area so the bird doesn't get hurt.

Timing

As you watch the birds in your yard begin to mate and build nests and then hatch and raise chicks, you will soon note that not all species do so at the same time of the year—or even at the specific time of year you would guess. Timing for each species is based on the availability of the food it needs. Raptors that feed young rodents to their chicks may go to nest the soonest, in early spring, when those animals are the most abundant. Raptors that feed on young songbirds hatch their young later in the year when those chicks are fledging and vulnerable. Plant-eating birds feed their chicks on insects and will go to nest in warm weather when insects thrive.

Courting

No matter what the species, many courting behaviors look ridiculous—and fascinating. During mating season, male birds work hard to impress females with complicated song or impressive dances and other displays. This seems to serve mainly as a way to demonstrate the vigor and hardiness of the male, which the female needs for the health of her young, ensuring their survival as much as she can. Some behaviors may appear odd to you, but to the female, they have great significance.

When you begin keeping your notebook on bird facts, mating behaviors may be among the first you want to record, simply because they are so interesting. As you watch, think about how each behavior might have evolved for that particular species. Watch for any variation, however slight. There may be some surprises for you, as a new bird-watcher, in avian mating and relationship behavior. A wild male turkey fluffs his head and neck feathers and fans his tail, shaking his feather pinions to get a rattling sound. Some male eagles fly in dizzying circles in updrafts to impress females, who may join them before mating. Watch their dizzying display of locking talons in midflight, cartwheeling from high in the air. Some actually mate up there!

Delineating territory is important behavior for survival of many animal species.

When eagles fly the perimeters of their territory, other birds know that the area is taken.

Eagles fly the perimeters of their territory on a regular basis to let other raptors (potential competitors for food) know the territory is taken. Songbirds use their impressive vocalizations to define and to defend territory, as well as to attract mates.

Although some birds seem to be monogamous, many are not. And those who do seem to mate for life may also mate with other birds. This behavior may strengthen the particular bird's line, whether male or female, by introducing new genes. Ornithologists now differentiate between *genetically monogamous* and *socially monogamous*. Genetic monogamy means that the two birds mate with only each other, ensuring that their offspring all have the same gene pool. A bird that mates on occasion with other birds, but helps his or her mate raise the chicks in their nest, is socially monogamous. These definitions have been determined by banding and close observation.

Divorce is also a factor among birds, and apparently the female initiates the split, probably because the eggs were infertile or the male was otherwise not good at his job. His duties are specific to the species. After the breakup, the two will go on to look for other mates and try again. The survival of the species is a strong instinct in all animals, including birds.

The factors for determining a territory depend on the species, but generally, birds need food, safety, water, and materials for building the nest. If you offer all of those necessities in your backyard, more birds will choose it as theirs and succeed at raising chicks.

Some species will want others of their species to live far away because they won't want the food source threatened. Other species—only about 13 percent—will breed and nest in large colonies of birds, perhaps finding safety in numbers. The great blue heron covers all bases (breeding and nesting across the United States, Saskatchewan, Manitoba, and Ontario in wetlands). It has large, strong wings that allow long flights to find food, but it normally lives near food sources, so it doesn't matter that other birds live nearby. A large, ungainly bird, the great blue heron nests in the tops of tall trees that stand in water, which helps prevent predators from killing chicks. As its habitat shrinks, it may have no choice but to live close to others.

Other birds nest in colonies, too, including cedar waxwings (found across North America from the west to east coasts in summer, the south of Alaska, and the northern provinces and territories of Canada). Terns, including the Caspian, common, Arctic, Forster's, and black tern, can be found across the North American continent, from north to south. These birds nest in colonies and fight off predators in groups, which maximizes the survival chance of their offspring.

In only about 100 species worldwide, birds work closely together to feed and care for the young of one pair with the aid of helper birds. Sometimes these helpers are relatives, such as older offspring, and sometimes the helpers are unrelated birds that hope to eventually claim a part of a large territory belonging to the parent birds. In North America, look for this behavior in the scrub jay (California coast and Florida), the Mexican jay (southwestern United States), the acorn

Mexican jays use helper birds to raise their young. They are one of only 100 bird species worldwide that do this.

woodpecker (central California coast), the red-cockaded woodpecker (American southwest and south), and the Harris's Hawk (Texas's Rio Grande Valley, southernmost Arizona and California).

Among the most unusual mating behaviors are *polygyny* and *polyandry*. In polygyny, a male mates and forms pair bonds with several females. This occurs mainly in areas rich in food. The female, who cannot necessarily rely on the male for help in finding food, must be able to feed her chicks easily. In the United States, such birds live in grasslands and marshes and include some members of the grouse family (across North America) and shorebirds.

It also happens among red-winged blackbirds (across the United States and Canada), yellow-headed blackbirds (breeds in the Midwest and western United States and into the prairies of British Columbia, Alberta, and Saskatchewan), and indigo buntings (from the East through the Midwest of the United States and southern regions of Manitoba, Ontario, and Québec). In polyandry, the female mates and forms pair bonds with several males, who incubate and rear the chicks. Look for this behavior among some shorebirds, such as phalaropes, along eastern, western, and northeastern shores of the continent.

One of the most unusual mating and nesting behaviors occurs among chimney swifts, which live across the United States and into the southern parts of Saskatchewan, Manitoba, Ontario, Québec, New Brunswick, Nova Scotia, and Prince Edward Island. These birds, which winter in South America, do everything but sleep in the air. That includes finding food (insects) and even mating! They make their nests mostly in brick chimneys and occasionally in hollow trees. They use matchstick-size twigs, which they've broken from trees while still flying, and glue with their saliva to the rough texture of the bricks on the inside of chimneys. Once their chicks are old enough to leave the nest and get close to fledging, these young birds have already learned to cling to the bricks with their sharp nails. Adult birds fly together in a twisting circle, somewhat like a tornado, to get into chimneys at dusk and to leave them in the morning, and remain in the air all day searching for food. A large chimney, such as old factories had, could hold thousands of birds. As these buildings are torn down and house chimneys are capped, swifts are losing their habitat. If you are lucky enough to have them living in your chimney, they will return each year. In the early spring, have the creosote cleaned from your chimney so the swifts can cling to the rough surface and close your damper so young chicks don't fall into your house. Another interesting behavior: Swifts are not able to perch; they cling to rough surfaces with their nails.

Some animals, including a few bird species, mate in *leks*. In this relatively unusual mating behavior, males gather in an area to carry out elaborate displays. Females come to that area to choose a male to mate with based on his performance on the lekking ground—also called an arena, a booming ground, or a strutting ground. The male's display and the mating are the only part the male will take in ensuring his line. He will not help incubate the eggs, he will not protect or feed the female while she does so, nor will he help feed the chicks. In North America, birds that mate in leks include the grouse, the snipe, the buff-breasted sandpiper, and some hummingbirds. To see a photo of a sage grouse in full display on the lekking ground, check the following website: *www2.mcgill.ca/biology/undergra/c465a/ biodiver/2000/sage-grouse/sage-grouse.htm.*

Hummingbird

Building Nests

The types of nests are many and varied. Species develop certain nest types for many reasons, including the types of predators the species must protect against, the materials at hand, and the amount of food available.

Once you determine the species in your backyard, you can look for nest types online or in guidebooks to help you locate likely spots to look for them. Do so from a distance with binoculars to avoid frightening the parents, who may leave your yard for a place they view as more secure.

Laying and Hatching Eggs

Eggs are the perfect way for young birds to develop. Most birds are built for flight with hollow bones and air sacs throughout their bodies. (Penguins, emus, ostriches, and a few other flightless birds are the exceptions.) A female bird couldn't fly if she had to develop her young in her body for live birth. Instead, she forms an egg and lays it. During formation, the yolk passes through her body until the last stage, when calcium begins to form around the yolk. The shell hardens when air hits the surface. The oval shape makes it particularly strong. And its porosity allows the chick just the right amount of oxygen as the young bird develops.

Go House Hunting

Following are a few interesting nests.

- The western meadowlark (West Coast through the Midwest and Great Lakes regions, British Columbia, Alberta, Saskatchewan, and Manitoba) female builds a dome of grass over a space she has smoothed in the ground.
- House sparrows (common across the continental United States and Canada) build their nests in the crevices or holes of houses or in nest boxes and in crevices of business signs. The parents line the space with their own feathers.
- Bullock's orioles and Baltimore orioles (ranges overlap in the Midwest; combined, they cover all of the continental United States in summer months; in Canada, Bullock's orioles can be seen in southern British Columbia and Alberta. Look for Baltimore orioles in Alberta, Manitoba, Ontario, Québec, New Brunswick, Nova Scotia, and Prince Edward Island) build complicated pouch nests that hang from the tips of branches of large trees. These pouches are woven from animal hair, spiderwebs, and plant fibers. They will use fibers and hair that you leave out for them.
- Some birds, such as the yellow-breasted chat (in summer, in most of the United States and in Canada, southern British Columbia, Alberta, and Saskatchewan), build nests of twigs shaped into a cup.
- Barn swallows and cliff swallows use mud to make nests stuck in sheltered parts of buildings, bridges, freeway overpasses, and rocky areas, such as cliffs. (Look for cliff swallows in Alaska, across Canada, and into the continental United States except for the southeast.)

Instinctively, birds know that this protein-rich egg is highly prized as food among predators, so parent birds choose nesting sites carefully. They then incubate the eggs by sitting on them, warming the eggs with their own body heat. Parents may take turns incubating the eggs or the male will feed the female as she sits tight. Take note of which style of parenting the birds in your yard use.

As they near time to hatch, chicks begin making sounds, which the parents seem able to interpret. According to a PBS program, *The Life of Birds*, American white pelican chicks, found all year along the western coast of North America, through British Columbia and Alaska and the American Gulf Coast, communicate their temperature needs before they hatch, leading the parents to turn eggs, or sit back on eggs to warm them. Their cries are those of a distressed pelican.

Although laying and hatching eggs may seem pretty straightforward, it sometimes takes unusual turns. Cowbirds never build their own nests; they lay eggs in the nests of other birds. The host bird might then incubate the cowbird's eggs along with its own. The cowbird chick is usually larger and demands more food than the young of the parents, eventually leading to the starvation of the smaller chicks. Sometimes, however, parent birds notice the cowbird eggs and destroy them

Always try to be extra careful when observing any nest on your property.

by pushing them out of the nest or by abandoning the invaded nest to make a new one where they rear only their own offspring.

The yellow warbler breeds mainly across North America, through Alaska, and across Canada to the Maritime provinces. Its nests are often invaded by cowbirds, so they tend to form a false floor over a cowbird egg, which prevents the cowbird egg from hatching and allows the warblers to raise their own chicks without abandoning their nest. According to Audubon research, cowbirds invade nests near feeding sites such as woodlands and home feeders. If you think a cowbird has laid eggs in the nest of another bird, you can remove the egg. Be sure, however, that you can identify a cowbird egg or, more specifically, that you can identify the eggs of the host parents.

Occasionally, a female bird, such as a duck or a pheasant, whose nest is destroyed will lay her eggs in the nest of another bird of the same species.

Make a list of the birds in your yard. Without disturbing or touching eggs, determine the types of nests in your yard and their location. Describe the eggs in a journal.

Protecting the Nest

Once the eggs are laid, birds must protect the nest from predators, and many have elaborate strategies. Some aggressive birds, such as the northern mockingbird (found across the U.S. in the south, southeast, and southwest) and the red-winged blackbird (found year-round across the U.S. and summers across Canada, except Newfoundland), will fly directly at the predator and attack it. Several birds may join in, chasing the predator away. When several birds of the same species join in the attack, it's called *mobbing*, and it could happen to you if you get too close to a nest. Or, you may observe birds that chase larger birds away, even raptors.

Another common tactic is leading the predator away from the nest. The parent bird may pretend to be injured and then take off when it has led the predator in another direction. Or the parent may rustle through grasses making a lot of noise so the predator will follow. When the parent determines it has misled the predator, it will return to the nest.

The white-breasted nuthatch (found across the United States in summer except the Great Plains from Canada to South Texas, and across southern Canada from British Columbia to Nova Scotia and Prince Edward Island) will hang on the bark of the tree near its nest and flap its wings to scare away predators. And it may work! An aggressive small bird can frighten a larger animal.

Caring for Chicks

The amount of energy parent birds must give to care for their chicks varies based on the types of chicks they have: *altricial* or *precocial*.

Shorebirds, ducks, and quail have precocial chicks, which hatch with downy feathers and eyes open, and soon can run and swim. The parents help them find food and protect them from predators.

Altricial chicks are born naked, blind, and helpless. They need constant warmth and cannot feed or care for themselves. These chicks require constant care from the parents. Various species of songbirds, woodpeckers, hawks, kingfishers, and owls have altricial chicks. (Look for all of these across the North American continent at various times of the year.)

Parents of altricial chicks invest a great deal of time and energy into finding food for their hungry family. You can help by keeping your feeders full and by offering a variety of foods. Some species, such as woodpeckers, may eat bread, mealworms or fruit from your feeders to supplement the food they hunt for their young.

Parents rush back and forth from food sources to their nest, where they thrust food into the wide-open mouths of their young. Any chick that doesn't open its mouth wide will not get fed. In the nest, only the fit and healthy survive. Some chicks have bright colors inside their mouths to help the quickly moving parents see where to push the food.

Shortly, the chicks will develop down feathers to help keep them warm, but until they do, one parent must sit on the nest to keep the chicks warm enough to stay alive, while the other seeks food. The chicks will grow rapidly, gaining weight and growing feathers until they are soon heavier than their parents. At that point, you may see them on telephone wires, tree limbs, or brush piles, still begging from their parents.

They will hold their wings out slightly, hold their mouths open, and quiver to indicate their hunger. In a few days or a week, you'll notice the parents trying to lead the chicks away to fledge—or fly—for the first time. This can be difficult to watch because you'll fear for the chick's life, but leave them

Until chicks, like these baby sparrows, develop feathers, a parent bird must keep them warm by sitting on them.

alone. The parents know what they're doing. When chicks fall to the ground, even before they fly, the parents find them and feed them. Soon you'll see the chicks flying.

Sibling Rivalry

If you watch the nest closely after the chicks have hatched, you will notice in some that the siblings fight. They may even fight to the death. When eggs are laid with a significant time period between, such as a day or two, they will hatch in consecutive order. The older chick has a major advantage in the amount of strength it has gained in that time period. The parents will not intervene in this fight for life. They can support only so many chicks, and perhaps to support the survival of the species, they pay most attention to the strongest of their offspring. In a year with abundant food, all chicks may survive. In a lean year, only the strongest will grow to adulthood. Don't attempt to interfere. Our role in bird-watching is to observe. We can protect birds by offering enough food and water, by not using pesticides, and by reducing the number of outdoor cats—but we shouldn't interfere in normal behaviors, such as sibling rivalry.

Adapting to Temperature

Birds in North America live in various climates, from the rocky frozen lands of northern Canada, to the rain forests of the Pacific Coast and Hawaii, to the prairies and deciduous forests across the continent. Some migrate to accommodate to the changes in temperature across our huge continent, whereas others stay put year-round, which can make it especially interesting for you as you watch them adapt.

Birds have down feathers next to the skin. So effective are they that these light, fluffy feathers are used to fill some coats to keep humans warm. In cold weather, a bird fluffs its outer, or contour, feathers, which creates air pockets between the down and contour feathers. These pockets trap air that becomes warmed by the bird's body heat. The bird may pull its head closer to its body and pull up one foot into its feathers. This will make the bird look much larger and rounder than normal.

Other birds can tolerate a lower core body temperature and go into a state of torpor, in which they move little—if at all—in very cold weather, especially during nighttime. Nighthawks (found across the continent except the far northern Canadian provinces and Alaska, and the deserts of California, Arizona, and Nevada) and hummingbirds use this method of survival.

According to *Grzimek's Animal Life Encyclopedia*, the white-throated poorwill may sleep for long periods, perhaps months, during the coldest weather in Arizona, where many of them spend the winter. Ornithologist examinations have shown that these birds go into a "cold rigor" in rocky niches during especially cold days or longer. In that state, a white-throated poorwill will have "body temperature, heartbeat, respiration and all other bodily functions... reduce[d] to absolute minimum... [with] fat reserves stored during the fall." The Native Americans in the southwestern U.S. call these birds "holhke," or "sleeper." When warmed, the birds spring back to life, ready to fly away.

Another unusual sight also involves survival in cold weather: Inca doves (Texas and Arizona in the United States) may roost in a triangular-shaped group to maintain the heat of all of them. Other birds seek shelter in brambles, bushes, tree holes, under the leaves of evergreen trees, or even in holes in the ground made by other animals, as is the case of burrowing owls (western prairies from Mexico to Alberta, Saskatchewan, Manitoba, and southern Florida).

Heat also requires adaptation. In hot weather, a bird will pull in its feathers to avoid trapping hot air next to its body. This gives the bird an especially streamlined profile. It will also hold its wings away from its body and may, in very hot weather, hold its beak open and pant. Both legs will probably be down, even in rest during summer months. Birds instinctively know to bathe and drink more often during hot weather. Keeping water available in your yard will help to attract them.

Behaving Curiously: Oddities and Incomparables

If you are a careful observer, you'll see birds do some amazing, interesting, and seemingly odd things. Once, not so long ago, many people believed only humans could reason. Now, we know better. Crows, while they might not look spectacular, are right near the top of avian intelligence. Some have been photographed dropping walnuts on roads and waiting for cars to run over the nuts to break open the shell, which crows can't do because of the shape of their beaks. If cars don't drive over the nuts, the crows get back on the highway and move the nuts to another place until they succeed. People have recorded crows in Japan and California doing this. See if you can spot any unusual or especially intelligent behavior among the birds in your yard.

It has been proven that some birds, most notably crows, make tools, by shaping twigs with their beaks to just the right shape to scrape insects out of tight spaces. North American ravens notify others of a carcass and share it with other ravens.

This behavior helps to ensure more food for each than it could find on its own. Crows and ravens range over all of North America.

Renee and James Ha, both affiliated with the University of Washington's psychology department, observed complex behavior among crows, which they reported in March 2003. These birds steal food from each other, but they treat relatives with greater care than those crows they are not related to. When stealing food from a non-relative, they use more aggressive techniques; when stealing from a relative, a passive technique.

Peregrine falcons now occupy both city and country, making use of the updrafts of natural canyons and those created by buildings in big cities. It is pos-

The peregrine falcon is, perhaps, the fastest bird.

sibly the fastest bird—its dive has been timed at 180 miles per hour. This bird is seen year-round along the west coast of the continent through Alaska, along all continental American coasts in winter, and in the Rocky Mountains in summer.

Hummingbirds, which summer in the continental United States, have a fast heartbeat—clocked at 16 beats per second, according to PBS. Also, they are the only bird that can hover for more than a few seconds. The hummingbird does this with specially constructed wings that move in a figure-eight pattern. This is the only bird that can fly backward.

The green-backed heron (found in the wetlands across the United States and into southern Québec) has been seen using bread scraps it floats on water. It waits for a fish to come for the bread and then grabs the fish. If a duck comes near to get the bread, the heron will chase it away.

If you live in the southern part of the United States, you may notice an odd invasion by birds that normally winter north. This is triggered by a reduction in the food supply in their normal wintering area, causing the birds to flee to an area that has a food supply abundant enough to sustain them for the winter. The behavior is called an *irruption*.

You may notice birds near ant mounds picking up ants one at a time and putting the ants in their feathers or holding the ants on their feathers before, sometimes, eating the ant. This is called *active anting*. Some birds will sit on ant mounds, allowing the ants to get on their feathers. This is called *passive anting*. Some scientists have speculated that the formic acid sprayed by the ants will rid the bird of pests, such as mites, but that hasn't been proven. Starlings (an introduced species that lives across the North American continent, but lives in Canada and Alaska only in summer) and tanagers (four species, across the United States and southern Canada) perform this odd procedure.

Sleeping

At dusk, especially in summer when there are many birds in the backyard, you'll hear a lot of noise as flocks of birds flutter to their favorite roosts. Some may remain all summer, and others will move on in a week or so. They'll settle into trees, on power lines, or near small ponds or lakes.

Those that sit on hard, stable surfaces may soon draw up one leg into their feathers to control their temperature. Although it looks awkward, birds rest easily on one leg. Some may turn their heads 180 degrees to tuck their beaks in the soft down feathers of their backs. As the sun sets, the birds will hush and sleep until dawn, when they start the whole process again.

Migrating

Not all birds migrate. In your backyard, you will see birds that live in your area that will stay year-round, such as house sparrows. You will also see birds that live in or around your yard just for the summer, but then leave in the fall, when they fly to warmer climates. Purple martins and chimney swifts fall into that category. A third group comprises the birds that only winter in your area, such as those that summer in the Arctic Refuge, including the green-winged teal, the northern shrike, or the golden eagle. (For a complete list see the sidebar, "Wintering in Your Yard" on page 75.) A fourth group is considered transient to your area—that is, it summers farther north than you live and winters farther south.

Migration is one of the most wonderful and mysterious of bird behaviors. Hummingbirds, although tiny and seemingly fragile, fly great distances from South America to North America in spring and back again in fall to feed on the nectar from flowers in each area. Some fly 500 miles across the Gulf of Mexico.

About 180 species of birds spend their summers in the Arctic Refuge of Alaska, raising their families. They then fly south to various parts of the continent for winter.

The Arctic tern seems to hold the record for long-distance flying during migration. It summers in the Arctic Circle, where it breeds. Then it flies to the Antarctic ice packs to spend the other half of the year (summer in the southern hemisphere). The round-trip journey is estimated to be 22,000 miles.

But how do they do it? Scientists believe songbirds and shorebirds have a sort

Wintering in Your Yard

Of the 180 species that spend a short time in summer rearing chicks in the Arctic Refuge of Alaska, some may come to your backyard for the relatively mild winter. The following list was obtained from a chart in the August/September 2003 *National Wildlife* magazine (Page 37), with information gleaned from the U.S. Fish and Wildlife Service. If drilling is allowed in the Arctic Refuge, many of these birds may die because of loss or pollution of their breeding grounds.

Pacific

Snow goose
Varied thrush
Brant
Green-winged teal
Redpoll
Wandering tattler (Hawaii)

Mountain

Golden eagle
Fox sparrow
Bohemian waxwing
Short-eared owl
Sandhill crane
White-crowned sparrow
Townsend's solitaire

West North Central

Red-legged hawk
Northern shrike
Sharp-shinned hawk
Red-throated loon
American pipit

Wilson's warbler
Smith's longspur
American pipit

West South Central

Savannah sparrow
Long-billed Dowitcher
Greater white-fronted goose

East North Central

Northern flicker
Wilson's snipe
Dark-eyed junco
American tree sparrow
Oldsquaw

East South Central

Long-tailed duck
Northern waterthrush
Yellow-rumped warbler
Ruby-crowned kinglet

Middle Atlantic

Canvasback
Semi-palmated sandpiper
Lapland longspur

South Atlantic

Grey-cheeked thrush
Peregrine falcon
Lesser scaup
Ruddy turnstone
Semi-palmated plover
Tundra swan
Rusty blackbird

New England

Horned grebe
Golden plover
Dunlin
Snow bunting
Greater scaup
Least sandpiper
Long-tailed duck

of internal compass sensitive to the earth's magnetic field. Studies at Lund University, Sweden, have shown that birds use the geomagnetic field, sun, sunset, skylight polarization pattern, and stars for their orientation during flight. Successful migration also depends on an adequate amount of food in their summer nesting grounds, as well as stopping sites along the way.

Your role could be to supply food for migrating birds, whether you live in their summering area or in their migrating path. For example, hummingbirds migrate from the United States to South America. If your local newspapers don't publish the dates migrating birds come through on their way north in spring or south in the fall, gather the information from a local university, zoological park, agricultural agent, or the Internet. Write an article and take it to the newspaper office. Newspapers are often glad to have the information at hand.

Sometimes, for reasons not easily understood, migrating birds get lost. If you notice birds migrating through that you don't normally see, investigate their needs in books and online, and offer food and water. There are laws that protect migrating birds in both Canada and the United States. (See Chapters 9 and 10 for more information.)

Waterfowl migrate, but they are taught the migration route by older birds of the same species or by their parents. Ducks join large groups of older birds of their species. Geese, swans, and cranes fly with both parents. On this initial flight, the young birds apparently learn to orient themselves by the position of the sun and the stars, and by using landmarks and the earth's magnetic field.

Some birds, including ducks, migrate as families—old and young, males and females. Others, including purple martins, travel by gender, with the males leaving wintering sites first to arrive at yearly summering sites to choose nests, perhaps to eject

Summering in Alaska

Those of you who live in Alaska know you can see an amazing and diverse number of animals year-round, but especially in spring and summer, although breeding areas are being compromised by habitat destruction by growing communities and oil and gas drilling. Following is a list of birds to look for.

Golden eagles	Baird's sandpiper
Buff-breasted sandpipers	Long-billed dowitcher
Bald eagles	Pacific loon
King eiders	Lapland longspur
Red-necked phalaropes	Gyrfalcon
Snowy owls	Rock ptarmigan
Spectacled eider	American golden plover
Steller's eider	Red-breasted merganser

sparrows that have taken over old nests. Some older birds leave the young and migrate as a group, leaving the young to follow. All in all, migration is an amazing aspect of birds and bird-watching.

Check the feature starting on page 98 for your area to find which migrating birds you might see in your area.

For more in-depth studies on migration, use the following Web sites:

orn-lab.ekol.lu.se/birdmigration/orient.html (Lund University, Sweden)

www.birdnature.com/timetable.html (Spring and fall migration patterns of specific birds for the United States from *Birds and Nature Magazine*.)

Gyrfalcons change coloring as they mature. This is a juvenile; as it ages, it will have a darker head and back feathers.

www.birdnature.com/flyways.html (Migratory flight paths for the United States, from *Birds and Nature Magazine*.)

www.npwrc.usgs.gov/resource/othrdata/migratio/migratio.htm (U.S. Fish and Wildlife information on migration. A complete site on migration information.)

www.ebird.org/content/news/RadarTracking.html (A joint Web site of Cornell University, New York and the Audubon Society, offers migratory and other information, including tracking migration by radar.)

www.mbr-pwrc.usgs.gov/ (Patuxent Wildlife Research Center, has information on specific birds with a search function.)

fathergoose.durham.net/ (A Canadian/American program to teach the young to conserve and help whooping cranes.)

www.nebulasearch.com/directory/search/Migratory.html (Use this as a general search site for migratory birds and conservation programs in the United States and Canada.)

For a visual treat, see the film *Winged Migration* (2001). The filmmakers used planes, gliders, helicopters, and balloons to fly alongside, above, below, and in front of various species of birds across 40 different countries to chart the migration of birds.

5 What to Feed Birds

To attract birds to your yard, provide three basic things: food, water, and shelter. In this chapter, we'll look at bird foods and bird feeders, and we'll provide information on water and shelter in later chapters.

Bird Food Basics

What does bird food provide? Like any animal, a bird needs to eat to maintain its life and health, and to grow. At certain times of the year, wild birds also need food to breed, lay eggs, and raise young. Depending on the species, a wild bird receives its nutrition in the wild from a variety of sources, including insects, plants, mollusks, fish, and invertebrates.

A backyard bird feeder can't provide as diverse a food source as Mother Nature, but it provides some key nutrients birds need, especially during cold weather when natural sources of fats and oils are difficult to find. Birds require fats and oils for additional energy during cold weather. It also helps them to stay warm and to produce healthy feathers.

Offer birds food, shelter, safety, and water, and they will come to your backyard feeders. Hummingbirds migrate through many areas of the United States in spring and fall.

The primary foods served at a backyard bird feeder are seeds and grains. These generally provide fats, carbohydrates, vitamins, minerals, and oils birds need to maintain good health. Listed below are the key ingredients in common birdseeds:

Black Oil Sunflower:
  high fat content
Striped Sunflower:
  high oil content
Niger: rich in protein and oil
Safflower: high oil content
Millet: high in starch,
  vitamins, and minerals
Peanuts: high in fat and
  protein
Cracked corn: high in oil
  and starch

A platform feeder is ideal for offering cracked corn, whole peanuts, and nuts. Jays tend to grab one nut and leave to eat it elsewhere, so the mess can be minimal if you plan to feed select birds.

FOOD	WHO EATS IT	HOW TO SERVE IT	CAUTIONS
Black oil sunflower *Note: Black oil sunflower seed has an easier-to-crack shell and a larger seed than striped sunflower.	cardinals finches jays chickadees pine siskins sparrows titmice woodpeckers redpolls goldfinches sparrows	hopper feeder, tube feeder with tray	Discarded seed hulls could harm the lawn if allowed to build up.
Striped sunflower	cardinals, titmice, jays, cardinals, grosbeaks, woodpeckers	hopper feeder, tube feeder with tray, platform feeder	

FOOD	WHO EATS IT	HOW TO SERVE IT	CAUTIONS
Fruit	orioles, tanagers, mockingbirds, woodpeckers, cedar waxwings, jays, chats, bluebirds	fruit feeder, platform feeder with fruit	Fruit can attract ants and other insect pests if feeder isn't kept clean.
Cracked corn	pheasants, quail, doves, sparrows, starlings, blackbirds, brown-headed cowbirds, jays, grackles	platform feeder	Cracked corn can bring aggressive birds to your feeder.
Millet	doves, sparrows, juncos, blackbirds, brown-headed cowbirds, starlings	platform feeder	
Milo/sorghum	doves, quail, towhees, sparrows, blackbirds	platform feeder, ground feeder	Milo is considered a "last-resort food" by many birds at feeders. It is also a filler ingredient for seed mixes. Buy milo only if you plan to feed the birds it attracts.
Nectar	orioles, tanagers, hummingbirds	nectar feeder	Nectar feeders can attract ants and other pests if not kept clean.

*Note: Cracked corn is especially attractive to blackbirds, grackles and sparrows, which some backyard bird feeders find too aggressive. You may want to limit offerings of cracked corn to prevent these birds from monopolizing your feeders.

FOOD	WHO EATS IT	HOW TO SERVE IT	CAUTIONS
Suet	mockingbirds, flickers, woodpeckers, goldfinches, jays, wrens, juncos, chickadees, titmice, bluebirds	suet feeder	Suet is ideal to feed in the winter, but it can become rancid in warm weather. Suet feeders can be messy because the birds scatter suet bits around the feeder as they eat.
Suet cakes	nuthatches, kinglets, starlings, thrashers, chickadees, flickers, woodpeckers, wrens	suet feeder	See above. Also, suet can attract squirrels.
Niger seed	finches, pine siskins, chickadees, sparrows	tube feeder with tray, platform feeder with fine mesh, thistle sock	Niger seed can become moldy in warm weather.
Peanuts	cardinals, sparrows, starlings, chickadees, juncos, finches, titmice, grackles, doves, jays	tube feeder, platform feeder	Peanuts can become moldy or rancid in warm weather.
Day-old baked goods	sparrows, starlings, grackles, robins, mockingbirds	crumbled on ground, platform feeder	Don't offer moldy bread to birds. Never feed chocolate to birds.

FOOD	WHO EATS IT	HOW TO SERVE IT	CAUTIONS
Fat and meat Scraps	roadrunners, woodpeckers, crows, magpies	platform feeder, scattered on ground	Meat scraps can attract vermin if left out too long.
Insects	hummingbirds, woodpeckers, robins, thrushes, bluebirds, purple martins, phoebes, flycatchers	found naturally in yard, mealworms served in small bowls on platform feeder	Except for mealworms, it's difficult to provide insects for wild birds.

Freshness Matters!

When purchasing birdseed for your feeders, buy the freshest seed. Shop at stores that seem to have good sell-through of their stock, and avoid stores with products that seem to sit on the shelf and collect dust. Shake the bag slightly and examine the contents. Are the seeds clean and fresh looking? Do any appear moldy? If you see signs of mold or other problems with the seeds, shop elsewhere.

If you purchase your seed in bulk from bins at a feed store or bird specialty store, sift through the seed with the scoop and look for clumped or webby seed. (These signs can indicate moth infestation.) Also, look for other signs of insect damage, such as holes in the seed hulls or light or empty hulls. If you plan to store the seed in your home, freeze it for a few days to kill any weevils or moths and their eggs.

Check the Labels

When selecting birdseed for your feeder, check the bag's label before you buy. The ingredients are listed from the most-used item to the least-used items. Look for mixes that have high concentrations of sunflower, millet, and finely cracked corn.

Steer clear of mixes with lots of milo or sorghum in them, unless you feed a lot of quail, doves, and towhees. Other wild birds routinely turn their beaks up at milo, but some bird food manufacturers include it in their mixes because milo is less expensive than other seeds, and its size allows it to take up more space, which fills up the bags more quickly. Other ingredients that aren't attractive to most wild birds include wheat, oats, rye, and rice.

What Does My Bird Feeder Provide?

Although bird feeders cannot completely duplicate a wild bird's natural diet, they do provide some important nutrients at key times during the year, especially during winter and summer.

During winter, birds need the extra food that feeders provide to help them cope with winter's cold, frosty weather, offering them more calories with little effort. During summer, bird feeders also provide supplemental food for parent birds that are busy raising nests full of hungry young. These birds can stop at a feeder for a snack as they obtain food for their nestlings.

Who Eats What and When?

In the course of a normal day, you may not see many birds at your feeder during daylight hours. A number of species feed early in the morning or at sunset, so be sure to watch your feeders during these peak feeding times. Other birds may drop by for a midday snack as they fly by, and these visitors are welcome surprises for bird-watchers. As you learn the habits of the birds that visit your feeder, you'll soon know the best times to watch for them!

During the year, you will likely see waves of birds that visit your feeder. The first wave will start in late fall, as migratory birds visit your feeder before flying south. It will last through winter with some resident visitors, then another wave will begin in spring as the migrants return and begin building nests. This wave will crest in early summer as the nests full of baby birds fledge and become adults. Late summer and early fall are likely to be the least busy time at your bird feeders, but you'll likely see a few birds drop by from time to time.

Contrary to popular opinion, you can allow your bird feeders to go empty for a few days from late spring through early fall. From late fall through early spring, though, it's best to keep the feeders full so that visiting birds and migrants can take advantage of the additional food during times when their natural food supplies may be low, but they need the calories to nourish them during migration or simply to sustain life in your area.

The Needs of Specialty Eaters

Birds with specialty diets can be broken into three main categories—insect eaters, fruit eaters, and nectar eaters.

Short of offering mealworms from time to time, there isn't much a backyard bird feeder can do to provide additional insects for the birds that come to visit, but Mother Nature has a way of providing ample bugs and arachnids for your visitors. You have to do your part, however, and not overuse pesticides and other chemicals that will not only kill insects but also may harm wild birds.

To please the palate of the fruit-eating birds at your feeder, offer a variety of fresh fruits in season in bird-size servings. Slice or chop fruit to make it easier for the birds to eat. Don't worry about the fruit being picture-perfect—wild birds don't mind slightly bruised fruit. Make sure the fruit is fresh, and remove uneaten portions promptly to reduce the number of pests, such as ants, you may attract. Save some of the fruits the birds at your feeder like best by freezing or drying because dried or frozen fruit can be served in winter for some much-needed variety at the feeder.

Hummingbirds will not drink from feeders that have any ants in them. Keep the feeders clean. If you find ants in the nectar, remove the feeder and wash it with hot water and soap. Take recommended actions to prevent ants and replace the feeder with fresh nectar.

Nectar-eating birds are best served with the use of special nectar feeders and nectar diets. You can purchase nectar powder at discount or bird specialty stores, or you can make your own mixture by using 1/2 cup of sugar in two cups of boiling water. Allow the mixture to cool before pouring it into the feeder, and refrigerate unused nectar to ensure its freshness.

Types of Feeders

Backyard bird-watchers have several feeder styles to choose from. The one you select will depend on the type of birds you want to attract. Many backyard bird feeders provide more than one feeder style to attract the widest variety of birds possible. Let's look at the most common feeder styles:

Platform Feeders

These come in two styles—open and covered. The open platform is nothing more than a wooden frame lined with fine mesh (such as window screen) that sits on a pole and is filled with seeds. Make sure the pole is tall enough to protect visiting birds from cats, and install the open platform feeder far enough away from ground cover so that your diners aren't surprised by a predatory ambush from the bushes.

Open platform feeders are useful in initially attracting birds to your yard because almost all wild birds, including chickadees, finches, jays, cardinals, nuthatches, and siskins, are attracted to them. They provide an easily accessible food source for the birds and a clear viewing area for you.

The open platform feeder needs to be emptied, scraped, and washed regularly with soap and water and a 10-percent dilute bleach solution in order to maintain the health of visiting birds. Rinse thoroughly and allow the feeder to dry completely before refilling it.

Because of their open design, open platform feeders can also attract squirrels, deer, and raccoons. Seeds in an open platform feeder are also constantly exposed to the elements, which can cause the seeds in them to become soggy or moldy. Clean the feeder at least once a day.

You can purchase open platform feeders at discount or bird specialty stores, or you can easily build one from plywood. Whether you buy one or build it yourself, make sure the open platform feeder has a drainage system in place to keep the seeds as dry as possible when it rains.

As the name suggests, a *covered platform feeder* has a cover over it to protect the seeds inside from becoming wet. The cleaning and maintenance requirements for a covered platform feeder are the same as for an open platform feeder.

Suet Feeders

Suet is a popular wild-bird food because it provides fat that birds need for energy. It is derived from the hard fat found near the loin and kidneys of cattle, and you can find it in your local market's meat department. If your store has a butcher on the premises or if you visit a special butcher shop, you can ask for suet at the counter.

A suet feeder and package of suet.

Suet feeders attract a wide variety of birds, including woodpeckers, chickadees, nuthatches, and mockingbirds, and suet can be offered in a number of ways. Suet feeders can be as simple as a block of suet from the meat counter at your local market hung in an empty mesh bag used to market onions, or you can use a commercially made suet log from your bird specialty store.

Premade suet cakes are also available at your bird specialty store and discount stores, and these may provide the easiest method by which to offer suet. Some of these cakes come with hangers attached, whereas others are designed to be served in a cage-style suet feeder. Suet feeder cages are also available in many stores including discount stores as well as those that sell feed, pet supplies, and bird provisions.

In addition to attracting a number of desirable birds to your feeder, suet can bring in some of the less-desirable species, such as crows or starlings. It is also attractive to raccoons and squirrels, but using pest-proof feeders will deter them. Suet is easier to serve in winter than in summer because the colder winter temperatures make it less likely to melt. However, you can serve suet year-round as long as the summer servings are rendered to make them less likely to melt. You can purchase commercially made suet blocks in summer, or you can render your own suet by heating it on the stove over a low heat and using only the material that rises to the top to fill your feeders.

Hopper Feeders

These feeders look like covered platform feeders, and they attract the same birds that platform feeders do. Besides attracting many different types of birds, hopper feeders offer the additional benefit of seed storage in the feeder unit, which means that you don't have to refill them as often as platform feeders. Unused seed is stored in a covered container, and the feeder refills itself through a small opening in the bottom of the container.

Hopper feeders can be purchased at discount or bird specialty stores, or you can make them at home, using a wood-and-mesh platform and an inverted glass jar as the hopper.

The main drawback to the hopper feeder is that the storage container takes up what would otherwise be feeding space for visiting birds. However, the automatic refilling capability of a hopper feeder makes it a good choice during your vacations or during inclement weather.

Bowl Feeders

These types of feeders are sometimes marketed as squirrel-proof or baffle feeders, and they offer a covered source of seeds for a variety of birds. Among the birds attracted to bowl feeders are nuthatches, chickadees, finches, cardinals, and grosbeaks.

The squirrel-proof portion of the bowl feeder comes into play if the bowl has a large plastic dome, or baffle, over it. The dome keeps not only the seeds dry in rainy weather but also helps deter squirrels from eating the seeds. The dome can also be adjusted, if you wish, to limit the size of birds that access the food inside. Watch the baffle, though; determined squirrels will chew plastic and can break it. If this happens, offer squirrels food in another part of your yard. Squirrel feeders are available. (See Chapter 6 for ways to deal with squirrels and other pests.)

Bowl feeders are easy to maintain. They can be filled quickly, and they can be cleaned easily with soap and water. Rinse the feeder thoroughly, and allow it to dry completely before refilling it.

When purchasing a bowl feeder, look for one that is made of sturdy, unbreakable plastic. Feeders that are made of flimsy or brittle plastic are more likely to break or crack, which means they will need to be replaced sooner than a sturdy model. Consider those made of metal. Talk with personnel in a wild-bird specialty store if squirrels are a big problem in your area.

Tube Feeders

These offer an economical opportunity to feed several birds at the same time. The feeder openings are designed to dispense a single seed at a time, which reduces the amount of wasted seeds.

Depending on what type of seed is served, tube feeders can attract goldfinches, siskins, redpolls, and other small birds. Larger birds and squirrels aren't as likely to visit tube feeders because they aren't able to access the seeds well, thanks to the tubular design and short perches found on these feeders.

Tube feeders are suitable for small birds like this house finch. Buy one with metal reinforced seed holes because squirrels may chew the openings to make them larger to dispense more seed. If you have many squirrels in your yard, they may try to take over a feeder.

Tube feeders are an excellent way to serve niger and other specialty seeds. To vary the choices for visiting birds, you can fill the tube feeder with layers of seed so birds eating at the bottom level have a different seed choice than birds eating at a middle or upper perch.

When selecting a tube feeder, try to find one that has metal to reinforce seed openings and metal perches. The reinforced openings also help deter squirrels, preventing them from chewing at the openings of the plastic tubes to try to get the seeds inside. All-metal tube feeders are also available if the squirrels in your area are particularly persistent.

Nectar Feeders

Although primarily used to attract hummingbirds, nectar feeders can also attract orioles, tanagers, woodpeckers, warblers, grosbeaks, and jays. You can provide a prepackaged nectar mix in your feeder, or you can offer a homemade mixture of four cups of water to one cup of sugar. (Red dye isn't required to attract hummingbirds or other nectar drinkers; the red base or nectar bottle tips found on most feeders should do the trick.) Boiling water dissolves the sugar more quickly than room-temperature water, and any leftovers should be refrigerated after the feeder is filled. Don't substitute honey in place of the sugar because honey spoils more quickly, which can create potential disease problems in your feeder. Honey may also carry botulinum, a naturally occurring bacteria.

Make sure to choose a nectar feeder with a clear bottle so you can see when the nectar level is getting low. Nectar feeders need to be cleaned about every 2 days in warm weather to ensure the health of birds. To prevent mold growth, select a feeder style that's easy to clean. You may also want to purchase specially designed bottlebrushes to clean out the nectar bottle tips, and a regular bottlebrush make cleaning the main bottle assembly quicker and easier.

Ants repel hummingbirds in some way, and these birds will not feed when ants are in the nectar. Once ants find a feeder, they will need to be deterred. You may have to apply petroleum jelly to the feeder's hanger. Ants can't get

You don't need to add color to the nectar. Most feeders have a red plastic tip that will attract birds.

a solid footing on the petroleum jelly, so they won't be able to get into the feeder. If the petroleum jelly gets dusty, however, the ants can walk on the surface with no trouble. Look for ant trails on the ground at the base of the feeder, and put small ant traps there. The traps contain liquid sealed inside that attracts ants. Once the ants are inside the trap, they die in the sticky fluid. Bees and wasps can be kept at bay by attaching bee guards to the nectar bottle tips. Hummingbirds can still consume the nectar, but the bees and wasps will have to go elsewhere.

Other Feeder Types

Preformed feeders

These types of feeders, sometimes referred to as "feederless feeders," are often the introduction to backyard bird feeding. How many of us started by hanging a seed bell near our family room window, or by placing a seed block in our yard for ground-feeding birds? Preformed feeders do double duty because they are both food and feeder in one. Birdseed is molded into shapes and held together with a binding agent, like gelatin. Popular shapes include bells, blocks, and cakes.

Scrap basket

If you have an abundance of bread crusts or other food scraps at your house, you can feed them to wild birds in your area by using a scrap basket. A scrap basket for the birds can be as simple as a plastic berry container or an empty tuna can with the top removed and edges blunted, or it can be a cage-type suet holder. Fill the container with your food scraps, and set it out for the birds.

Wild birds may also enjoy the discarded seeds from fruits and vegetables, such as tomatoes, melons, bell pepper, or squash. Offer these seeds and their pulp on a platform feeder or as part of the scrap basket.

Stick-on window feeders

These feeders are also popular introductions to backyard bird feeding. They are plastic devices with suction cups attached that allow you to fasten the feeder directly to a window for easier viewing of the visiting birds.

Stick-on window feeders are best used to supply specialty seeds for smaller quantities of birds, rather than as the main food source in your yard. Another drawback of these feeders is that the suction cups attached to some feeders may not adequately support the weight of feeder, seeds, and visiting birds, so the feeder may fall off the window, spilling the seeds and scaring away the birds (at least temporarily).

Specialty feeders

If you wish to provide corn, nuts, or fruits to the birds in your yard, you may find that a specialty feeder is just the right serving device for these foods. You can serve dried corn on the cob, which will attract cardinals, jays, woodpeckers, pheasants, quail, and even wild turkeys, in two main ways. Either distribute it on spike feeders around your yard or suspend the dried ears from hangers in trees. Avoid placing it near other bird feeders, though, because it will attract legions of squirrels.

Nuts can bring jays, nuthatches, chickadees, and woodpeckers to your yard, especially during winter. You can serve nuts on a platform feeder. Before serving, place the nuts in a sock and give the sock a few taps with a hammer to crack some of the tougher shells.

Fruit, such as oranges, apples, or berries, can bring bluebirds, cardinals, orioles, robins, catbirds, thrushes, and thrashers to your yard. Specially designed fruit feeders can be purchased that allow you to serve halved fresh apples or oranges, or you can provide the same service by setting out an old muffin tin full of fruit halves. Remove apple seeds, which are not good for birds because they contain a toxin that can build up in a bird's body and cause it to die.

Fruit can be served year-round, either fresh or frozen. Freeze some less-than-perfect fruit from summer, then thaw and serve it at your feeders during winter for a special treat.

Make sure to clean up the feeder area after the fruit is served to maintain the health of the visiting birds and also to cut down on possible infestations from ants and other pests that might be attracted by sticky, sweet fruit pulp.

To Buy or to Build?

Whether you purchase a bird feeder or build one yourself is entirely up to you. Some clever and attractive feeders can be assembled using scrap wood and some common household items, such as an empty 2-liter soda bottle or an empty peanut butter or spaghetti sauce jar. If you're handy with tools and enjoy building, a homemade bird feeder may be just the ticket for you. Plans for these projects can be found in home improvement books and magazines or by searching online for "bird feeder plans."

If you aren't particularly handy or don't have the time to construct a feeder from scratch, visit your local discount or bird specialty store. You may find the feeder that's just right for you, as well as some good advice from the staff about the birds you're likely to see once you're ready to start serving meals at your fly-in restaurant.

Feeder Cleaning and Maintenance

To get the most out of your bird-feeding experience, make cleaning and maintenance a part of your regular routine. By incorporating a cleaning regimen into your plan from the start, you'll be able to manage debris from your feathered diners more efficiently, which means your yard will look better and your feathered visitors will be healthier.

You can help keep things clean in your feeders by offering fresh seed at all times. Your feeders will be more attractive to wild birds when filled with the freshest seed possible, so empty and refill your feeders after heavy rains or if you notice sick birds at your feeder. Disinfect the feeders before refilling them if you have had sick birds feeding at them to reduce the chance of spreading disease. A few tools will help make feeder cleanup quicker and easier. These include a stiff-bristled brush, a scraper, a regular scrub brush, and a bottlebrush (for cleaning nectar feeders).

When you routinely refill your bird feeders, take a few minutes before you add the fresh seed to scrub the feeder with a stiff-bristled brush, or hose it off quickly. This will remove bird droppings, loose feathers, and other stuck-on debris. Remove any seed that's stuck in the feeder, and make sure the feeder is dry inside before refilling it with seed.

You should plan on taking the feeders apart completely and cleaning them thoroughly about once a month if your feeders get a lot of activity. Scrub off any caked-on material with a stiff-bristled brush, then let the feeder parts soak in a bleach-and-water solution for about 3 minutes. After soaking, rinse the parts thoroughly and let them dry before putting them back together and refilling the feeder.

Feeder maintenance is less scheduled than your cleanup routine, but it's just as important. When you refill your feeders, make sure they don't have any holes or loose hooks in them and that

Take feeders apart and clean them thoroughly each month to ensure the health of visiting birds.

the glass panes around the hopper aren't cracked. If you notice any problems with your feeder, take the time to fix them as soon as possible to keep them from becoming worse.

Also, plan on "feeder tune-up" in late summer or early fall to ensure that your feeders are ready for the seasons ahead. Make sure all the perches on all your feeders are secure, for instance, and that all the hanging hooks and chains are in top condition. Repair or replace those feeders that aren't ready for the busy feeding season, then fill them up and get ready for your fall and winter visitors.

Making Treats for Birds

Making treats for the wild birds that visit your yard is a great way to get your children (or grandchildren) interested in bird watching. This family activity gives you time to share your bird-watching experiences with the children and explain to them about the different bird species that visit your feeders.

Here are a few simple treats to try:

Pinecone Feeder: Find or purchase several medium-sized pinecones that are open. Combine 1/2 cup of peanut butter, 1/2 cup of shortening, and 3 cups of cornmeal, and stir until mixture is sticky. Stuff the mixture in the openings of the pinecones using a spoon or a knife. Roll the coated pinecones in birdseed, or put the pinecones in a plastic food-storage bag and carefully pour seed over the cones so seeds stick to peanut butter mixture. Hang from trees with wire hangers, such as those you use for Christmas tree ornaments.

Orange Fruit Cups: Fill empty orange rinds with fruit pulp, dried fruit, or seeds. Hang from trees with natural (no dye) raffia, string, or wire hangers.

Snack Garlands: String whole peanuts or dried fruits to make garlands for your porch rail or backyard trees. (*Note:* Many wild birds don't see popped popcorn as a food source, so save the popcorn for your family when making a decorative garland.)

Cornbread Cornucopia: Make a loaf of cornbread using a premade mix. Add dried fruit, eggshells, nuts, or seeds to the mix. Bake and serve on a platform

It's fun and economical to make treats for birds, and then it's fun to watch them enjoy your offering.

feeder or crumble and toss on the ground for your feathered guests.

Birdie Bake Shop: If you serve day-old baked goods to the wild birds that visit your yard, occasionally offer peanut butter garnished with dried fruit or seeds on the bagels, bread, or doughnuts you provide. Spread the peanut butter on the baked goods, then roll them in seeds or sprinkle dried fruit on top of the peanut butter before setting them outside. (Never offer birds chocolate baked goods. Chocolate contains theobromine, a compound in the same class as caffeine and theophylline. It occurs naturally in cocoa and is dangerous for many animals, including birds and dogs, because they metabolize it at a different rate than humans.)

Storing Seeds

Successful seed storage requires that the seed remain cool and dry, and out of the reach of pests, from moths to mice. If you feed only a few birds, you can probably store seeds in a tin from snack foods on your back porch, but if you have a lot of feeders to fill, a galvanized metal trash can with a tight-fitting lid is likely your best storage solution. Store your seed in the garage to keep it cool and dry, and away from rodents.

Common Feeder Problems

One of the first and most noticeable problems you may encounter with your bird feeders is that no birds come to them. This problem can have a number of causes, including the fact that your feeder is new. If this is the case, you will need to be patient. In time, the birds will find your feeders.

Another situation may be that you have set out feeders in the wrong season. This is often true in summer when insect populations are high and other natural food sources are readily available. Again, be patient. As summer turns to fall and fall to winter, the birds in your area will turn to your feeders as a reliable secondary food source.

In some cases, birds may not visit your feeders because they are getting enough food from other feeders in your neighborhood. Ask your neighbors if they feed birds, and if they do, find out what they offer in their feeders. If they offer seeds only, put out some suet feeders in your yard, or offer dried fruits or other treats to attract a different group of birds than the neighbors are feeding.

Another situation that occurs at bird feeders is that certain "undesirable" birds are attracted. Such birds include starlings or grackles, which some people consider to be pests. If this becomes the case, you will need to change the type of feeders you have in your yard. Because starlings and grackles are unable to eat upside down or from short perches, provide a variety of tube feeders that are designed for finches, and the starlings and grackles should soon be on their way.

Predators can be another problem at bird feeders. Some feeders attract feral cats, whereas others may prove to be a haven for hawks. If you find furry or feathered predators hanging around your feeder, you can protect the birds from them by doing the following:

- Reduce the potential hiding places for cats by trimming bushes and setting up feeders in cleared locations or on posts.
- Move birdbaths into cleared areas, too, to protect visiting birds from cat ambushes.
- Erect fences around ground-feeding areas to protect those birds from cat attacks.
- Provide brush piles in your yard away from the feeders so birds will have hiding places to protect them from hawks.

A complaint some first-time bird feeders have is the mess that comes with the wild birds. Although we can't guarantee a mess-free feeding experience, here are some suggestions that will allow you to attract a neater class of eater at your feeders.

You're probably wondering what exactly a "neater eater" is. Wild birds that fall into this category are those birds that aren't attracted to traditional bird-feeder foods or that use the feeders as a stopping point to pick up a few seeds and fly away to eat them. These include woodpeckers, flickers, sapsuckers, blue jays, tufted titmice, hummingbirds, hawks, chickadees, nuthatches, orioles, and mockingbirds.

Somewhat neat eaters include cardinals, wrens, juncos, and mourning doves.

Birds that travel in flocks, including goldfinches, purple finches, pigeons, sparrows, starlings, crows, and grackles, fall into the category of "not-at-all neat" eaters.

Here are some steps you can take to attract the neater eaters and to discourage the messy ones:

- Offer selected seeds at your feeders, rather than a mix of seeds. When presented with mixed seeds, birds will pick through the mix until they find their favorites, scattering the unwanted discards as they go.
- Offer seeds other than sunflower at your feeders. Sunflower seeds can attract messier birds than niger, safflower, or other seed choices.
- Use the right type of feeder. Platform feeders offer a less-controlled dining experience than tube feeders because they can attract larger numbers of birds at a single sitting. Tube feeders are designed to feed a single bird at each perch, which cuts down on the number of visitors to your feeders.

- Offer whole peanuts in the shell. Many of the neater eaters relish whole peanuts, whereas messier birds don't care to bother with them.
- Let your feeders stand empty a day. Although many people will tell you that you need to keep feeders full at all times, you'll attract a more select dining crowd if you let the feeders empty completely about once a week. You'll also cut down on the chances of your seed getting moldy or rancid if you allow the feeders to empty because the seed won't be allowed to sit in the feeder long enough for it to spoil.
- Don't toss seed on the ground to attract ground-feeding birds, such as juncos, mourning doves, thrushes, larks, and towhees. Let these birds come to your yard to help clean up the seeds that spill from your platform and hopper feeders. They will help keep your yard cleaner.

Feeder Placement

One key to successful backyard bird feeding is to have your feeders placed correctly. You will need to keep a few factors in mind, including the location of nearby plants and shrubs to minimize predator attack and maximize protection; the height of feeders to ensure the birds feel comfortable while eating; the direction the wind blows; and the ease of feeder filling.

It's a given that you'll want to locate your feeders as close to the window you want to watch birds from as possible. Position feeders to coincide with daily activities. If you happen to have a garden window in your kitchen, for instance, set up a feeder or a birdbath near it so you can bird-watch as you prepare meals. If you have a breakfast nook with a bay window, locate another feeder near it so you can share a snack or a meal with the birds at the feeder.

Feeder height is an important, but sometimes overlooked, aspect of feeding success. Listed below are some levels that different birds prefer. Keep them in mind when setting up the feeders in your yard:

Placing a house or feeder on top of a pole can help minimize attacks from predators.

Ground level: Doves, pheasants, bobwhites, woodpeckers, towhees, sparrows, quail, and cowbirds

Low level: Juncos and robins

Medium level: Woodpeckers, tufted titmice, chickadees, buntings, cardinals, siskins, and nuthatches

High level: Hummingbirds, purple finches, and evening grosbeaks

Away from house: Blackbirds, starlings, and crows

The direction the wind blows is another factor many people don't take into consideration when setting up their bird feeders. Some of them get lucky and have feeding success, whereas others are unfortunate enough to have their feeders soaked by summer rains or frozen by blowing snow. Consider the wind direction before you install your feeders, and consider planting shrubs or other windbreaks to protect your feeders and the birds that will visit them from the harshest part of winter weather. Also consider placing the feeders on the side of the house most sheltered from the wind.

Year-round Feeding Tips

Different times of year call for different approaches to bird feeding. Use this chart for handy information on keeping your feeder properly stocked all year!

Winter

Things to Remember: Backyard bird feeders normally see increased traffic during winter because natural food sources are more difficult to locate. Keep feeders filled to accommodate the extra visitors, and offer a wider variety of foods—suet, table scraps, fruits, and nuts—than you might provide at other times of the year.

Things to Do: Keep water sources and birdbaths ice-free if you live in an area with snow. Keep feeders clear of snow.

Spring

Things to Remember: Traffic often remains high at backyard bird feeders in the early spring as migratory species return to their summer homes. Late frosts can affect feeder visitors, too, if the frost kills insects or damages budding flowers and trees. Provide mealworms after late frosts to feed insect eaters, and fill nectar feeders for hummingbirds and other returning nectar eaters.

Things to Do: Offer crushed eggshells near your feeders so female birds that are about to go to nest can supplement the calcium levels in their bloodstreams. Watch for behavioral changes that indicate males in search of mates, such as jousting or singing, and note any special spring plumages you see.

Summer

Things to Remember: Summer may be an ideal time to slightly reduce the amount of food you offer at your feeders. Birds are least likely to visit feeders during the summer because their natural food sources are abundant and they are busy raising their chicks.

Things to Do: Remember that suet melts more quickly in warm weather, so take steps to ensure that your suet feeders are in good shape. Clean seed feeders regularly to reduce the chance of the seeds becoming contaminated by molds or moths. Repair and replace feeders in time for the fall feeding season.

Fall

Things to Remember: Fall is the beginning of the busy time at your backyard bird feeders, so be sure you're prepared for your visitors! Have plenty of nutritious seeds and other foods on hand to keep your feeders stocked so migrating birds will be able to leave your yard well fed and ready for their journeys.

Things to Do: Notice which birds at your feeders have molted from their special spring plumage into less colorful feathers for fall. Provide nectar feeders for hummingbirds and other nectar-eating migrants. Add feeders if the traffic in your yard indicates that you need additional feeding sites.

Autumn can be a great time for bird-watching!

Calling All Migrants!

It takes a great deal of energy to fly the long distances some migrants must travel. According to one Princeton University researcher, Martin Wikelski, migratory birds expend more energy looking for food and shelter than they do when flying. That means bird-watchers must help them by providing a reliable source of the food they eat, as well as clean water and brush piles, trees, bushes, and other suitable resting spots. You can see the full report at *www.princeton.edu/pr/home/03/0620_birds/hmcap.html.*

If you live in areas with snow and ice, be sure to keep ice from forming on the water supply. You can do this by using the various heated waterbowls available on the Internet and in local specialty stores, as well as through specialty catalogs.

According to an ABC news report, Chicago opened a new "rest stop on the city's lakefront ... for migrating birds. ... The six-acre rest stop ... is planted with a variety of plants intended to attract the insects many of the birds prefer to eat. It also has a large birdbath and part of the land is fenced to protect birds from predators." Perhaps you can convince your city to do something similar.

Following is a list of many of the migratory species that come through your area of the country. In Chapter 7, we've listed those plants that migrants depend on that you could put in your yard, some of which attract insects and some of which bear fruit. Remember to offer supplements to purple martins that may have arrived before there are enough flying insects to keep them alive. Visit the Purple Martin Association Conservation Web site at *www.purplemartin.org.*

Check the following list of birds against the table starting on page 79 that names the foods that each bird prefers. Unlisted birds eat insects and will need only a secure resting spot and water. For a map of generalized flyways that migratory birds use, go to *www.birdnature.com/flyways.html.*

United States

Pacific

(Alaska, Washington, Oregon, California, Nevada, and Hawaii) Common loon, yellow-billed loon (Alaska only), great egret, cattle egret, dark ibis, tundra swan, Canada goose, snow goose, Ross's goose, blue-winged teal, red-breasted merganser, Pacific golden plover, American golden plover, semipalmated plover, greater yellowlegs, lesser yellowlegs, western sandpiper, long-billed dowitcher, Vaux's swift, black swift, black-chinned hummingbird, calliope hummingbird, rufous hummingbird, willow flycatcher, Hammond's flycatcher, dusky flycatcher, gray flycatcher, bank swallow, barn swallow, Swainson's thrush, Nashville warbler, yellow-rumped warbler, Townsend's warbler, hermit warbler, Wilson's warbler, yellow-breasted chat, western tanager, lark sparrow

Mountain

(Idaho, Montana, Wyoming, Colorado, Utah, Arizona, and New Mexico) Common loon, American white pelican, double-crested cormorant, great blue heron, great egret, green heron, black-crowned night-heron, dark ibis, tundra swan, Ross's goose, wood duck,

The yellowbellied sapsucker.

American wigeon, northern shoveler, canvasback, ring-necked duck, lesser scaup, hooded merganser, red-breasted merganser, sandhill crane, American avocet, greater yellowlegs, lesser yellowlegs, long-billed dowitcher, black-chinned hummingbird, calliope hummingbird, rufous hummingbird, Lewis's woodpecker, red-naped sapsucker, western wood-pewee, willow flycatcher, Cassin's kingbird, Cassin's vireo, purple martin, bank swallow, marsh wren, western bluebird, American pipit, Tennessee warbler, Nashville warbler, yellow-rumped warbler, Townsend's warbler, blackpoll warbler, black-and-white warbler, American redstart, Wilson's warbler, western tanager, rose-breasted grosbeak, lazuli bunting, green-tailed towhee, Brewer's sparrow, clay-colored sparrow, chipping sparrow, Savannah sparrow, vesper sparrow, lark bunting, Harris's sparrow, white-throated sparrow, fox sparrow, Lincoln's sparrow, dark-eyed junco, McCown's longspur, chestnut-collared longspur

West North Central

(North Dakota, South Dakota, Minnesota, Iowa, Missouri, Nebraska, and Kansas) Eared grebe, American white pelican, snowy egret, little blue heron, yellow-crowned night-heron, Canada goose, greater white-fronted goose, Ross's goose, snow goose, American wigeon, northern shoveler, ring-necked duck, greater scaup, lesser scaup, bufflehead, hooded merganser, red-breasted merganser, sandhill crane, American golden plover, semipalmated plover, greater yellowlegs, lesser yellowlegs, solitary sandpiper, dunlin, pectoral sandpiper, white-rumped sandpiper, Baird's sandpiper, semi-palmated sandpiper, least sandpiper, stilt sandpiper, yellow-bellied sapsucker, olive-sided flycatcher, alder flycatcher, least flycatcher, Philadelphia vireo, blue-headed vireo, purple martin, bank swallow, golden-crowned kinglet, ruby-crowned kinglet, mountain bluebird, veery, Swainson's thrush, gray-cheeked thrush, hermit thrush, Sprague's pipit, American pipit, orange-crowned warbler, Tennessee warbler, golden-winged warbler, yellow-rumped warbler, black-throated green warbler, palm warbler, bay-breasted warbler, blackpoll warbler, northern waterthrush, mourning warbler, Wilson's warbler, Canada warbler, rose-breasted grosbeak, Brewer's sparrow, clay-colored sparrow, Le Conte's sparrow, Harris's sparrow, white-throated sparrow, white-crowned sparrow, fox sparrow, Lincoln's sparrow, swamp sparrow, Smith's longspur, Lapland longspur

West South Central

(Oklahoma, Texas, Arkansas, and Louisiana) Common loon, horned grebe, eared grebe, western grebe, American bittern, great egret, snowy egret, little blue heron, cattle egret, green heron, black night-crowned night heron, yellow-crowned night heron, white ibis, dark ibis, wood stork, greater white-fronted goose, cinnamon teal, hooded merganser, red-breasted merganser, ruddy duck, sora, sandhill crane, American golden plover, American avocet, dunlin, black-necked stilt, greater yellowlegs, lesser yellowlegs, solitary sandpiper, spotted sandpiper, upland sandpiper, pectoral sandpiper, white-rumped sandpiper, Baird's sandpiper, western sandpiper, semipalmated sandpiper, stilt sandpiper, black-billed cuckoo, whip-poor-will, chimney swift, ruby-throated hummingbird, broad-tailed hummingbird, olive-sided flycatcher, yellow-bellied flycatcher, willow flycatcher, alder flycatcher, least flycatcher, eastern kingbird, red-eyed vireo, warbling vireo, Philadelphia vireo, blue-headed vireo, purple martin, tree swallow, sedge wren, marsh wren, ruby-crowned kinglet, wood thrush, veery, Swainson's thrush, gray-cheeked thrush, gray catbird, Sprague's pipit, northern parula, orange-crowned warbler, Tennessee warbler, blue-winged warbler, golden-winged warbler, Nashville warbler, yellow warbler, chestnut-sided warbler, magnolia warbler, Blackburnian warbler, black-throated green warbler, black and white warbler, American redstart, ovenbird, northern waterthrush, Louisiana waterthrush, mourning warbler, common yellowthroat, Wilson's warbler, Canada warbler, yellow-breasted chat, western tanager, scarlet tanager, rose-breasted grosbeak, lazuli bunting, indigo bunting, green-tailed towhee, Brewer's sparrow, clay-colored sparrow, chipping sparrow, Le Conte's sparrow, Nelson's sharp-tailed sparrow, Savannah sparrow, vesper sparrow, Lincoln's sparrow, swamp sparrow, chestnut-collared longspur, bobolink, Baltimore oriole

East North Central

(Wisconsin, Illinois, Indiana, Ohio, and Michigan) Common loon, horned grebe, American pelican, double-crested cormorant, great blue heron, cattle egret, tundra swan, northern shoveler, Green-winged teal, canvasback, ring-necked duck, lesser scaup, red-breasted merganser, ruddy duck, semi-palmated plover, greater yellowlegs, lesser yellowlegs, solitary sandpiper, dunlin, pectoral sandpiper, white-rumped sandpiper, semipalmated sandpiper, least sandpiper, stilt sandpiper, olive-sided flycatcher, yellow-bellied flycatcher, blue-headed vireo, winter wren, ruby-crowned kinglet, Swainson's thrush, gray-cheeked thrush, American pipit, orange-crowned warbler, Tennessee warbler, Nashville warbler, black-throated green warbler, palm warbler, bay-breasted warbler, blackpoll warbler, Connecticut warbler, Wilson's warbler, Nelson's sharp-tailed sparrow, Lapland longspur

The steller's jay is a shy bird that eats a wide variety of things including other animals, insects, nuts, and grains.

East South Central

(Mississippi, Alabama, Tennessee, and Kentucky) Common loon, horned grebe, double-crested cormorant, white ibis, northern shoveler, blue-winged teal, greater scaup, red-breasted merganser, sora, semipalmated plover, greater yellowlegs, lesser yellowlegs, solitary sandpiper, spotted sandpiper, upland sandpiper, dunlin, pectoral sandpiper, white-rumped sandpiper, stilt sandpiper, black-billed cuckoo, whip-poor-will, least flycatcher, Philadelphia vireo, blue-headed vireo, tree swallow, sedge wren, marsh wren, veery, Swainson's thrush, gray-cheeked thrush, Tennessee warbler, blue-winged warbler, golden-winged warbler, Nashville warbler, chestnut-sided warbler, magnolia warbler, Cape May warbler, black-throated blue warbler, cerulean warbler, Blackburnian warbler, black-throated green warbler, palm warbler, bay-breasted warbler, blackpoll warbler, northern waterthrush, Wilson's warbler, Canada warbler, rose-breasted grosbeak, Le Conte's sparrow, bobolink, Baltimore oriole

Middle Atlantic

(New York, New Jersey, and Pennsylvania) Red-throated loon, common loon, double-crested cormorant, gadwall, American wigeon, northern shoveler, canvasback, ring-necked duck, long-tailed duck, surf scoter, white-winged scoter, bufflehead, red-breasted merganser, ruddy duck, American golden plover, semipalmated plover, greater yellowlegs, lesser yellowlegs, solitary sandpiper, dunlin, pectoral sandpiper, white-rumped sandpiper, semipalmated sandpiper, least sandpiper, stilt sandpiper, long-billed dowitcher, gray-cheeked thrush, American pipit, orange-crowned warbler, Tennessee warbler, palm warbler, bay-breasted warbler, blackpoll warbler, Wilson's warbler, fox sparrow, Lincoln's sparrow

South Atlantic

(Delaware, Maryland, Virginia, West Virginia, North Carolina, South Carolina, Georgia, and Florida) Common loon, double-crested cormorant, great blue heron, little blue heron, white ibis, wood stork, gadwall, American wigeon, red-breasted merganser, sora, American golden plover, greater yellowlegs, lesser yellowlegs, solitary sandpiper, spotted sandpiper, upland sandpiper, dunlin, pectoral sandpiper, white-rumped sandpiper, semi-palmated sandpiper, stilt sandpiper, long-billed dowitcher, whip-poor-will, least flycatcher, blue-headed vireo, cliff swallow, marsh wren, veery, Swainson's thrush, gray-cheeked thrush, Bicknell's thrush, Tennessee warbler, Nashville warbler, yellow warbler, chestnut-sided warbler, magnolia warbler, Cape May warbler, black-throated green warbler, palm warbler, bay-breasted warbler, northern waterthrush, Connecticut warbler, Wilson's warbler, scarlet tanager, rose-breasted grosbeak, painted bunting, bobolink, Baltimore oriole

The black-capped chickadee.

Canada

British Columbia:

Red-throated loon, Pacific loon, common loon, yellow-billed loon, pied-billed grebe, horned grebe, red-necked grebe, western grebe, double-crested cormorant, pelagic cormorant, American bittern, great blue heron, green heron, black-crowned night heron, mute swan, snow goose, greater white-fronted goose, brant, Canada goose, wood duck, Eurasian wigeon, blue-winged teal, green-winged teal, cinnamon teal, canvasback, mallard, northern pintail, northern shoveler, American widgeon, greater scaup, lesser scaup, harlequin duck, surf scoter, white-winged scoter, common goldeneye, bufflehead, hooded merganser, common merganser, red-breasted merganser, turkey vulture, osprey, bald eagle, Cooper's hawk, red-tailed hawk, northern harrier, sharp-shinned hawk, rough-legged hawk, merlin, peregrine falcon, ring-necked pheasant, Virginia rail, California quail, semi-palmated plover, killdeer, black oystercatcher, greater yellowlegs, whimbrel, solitary sandpiper, spotted sandpiper, semi-palmated sandpiper, Baird's sandpiper, pectoral sandpiper, sharp-tailed sandpiper, western sandpiper, least sandpiper, common snipe, dunlin, mew gull, ring-billed gull, California gull, western gull, glaucous-winged gull, Caspian tern, pigeon guillemot, marbled murrelet, rhinocerus auklet, rock dove, band-tailed pigeon, mourning dove, great horned owl, snowy owl, barred owl, long-eared owl, short-eared owl, northern saw-whet owl, Vaux's swift, rufous hummingbird, belted king-fisher, downy woodpecker, northern flicker, pileated woodpecker, Pacific slope flycatcher, willow flycatcher, olive-sided flycatcher, western wood-pewee, violet-green swallow, barn swallow, tree swallow, northern rough-winged swallow, bank swallow, cliff swallow, Stellar's jay, north-western crow, common raven, chestnut-backed chickadee, black-capped chickadee, mountain chickadee, bushtit, red-breasted nuthatch, brown creeper, Bewick's wren, winter wren, marsh wren, golden-crowned kinglet, ruby-crowned kinglet, Townsend's solitaire, American robin, American pipit, Swainson's thrush, hermit thrush, varied thrush, European starling, northern shrike, solitary vireo, Hutton's vireo, warbling vireo, American pipit, cedar waxwing, orange-crowned warbler, yellow-rumped warbler, black-throated gray warbler, Townsend's warbler, MacGillivray's warbler, common yellowthroat, Wilson's warbler, western tanager, spotted towhee, chipping sparrow, savannah sparrow, fox sparrow, Lincoln's sparrow, song sparrow, golden-crowned sparrow, white-crowned

Many birds eat berries, which makes fruit-bearing plants a good choice for a created habitat.

An American robin in a nest.

common nighthawk, northern flicker, eastern kingbird, eastern phoebe, alder flycatcher, least flycatcher, western wood peewee, olive-sided flycatcher, tree swallow, gray jay, common raven, black-capped chickadee, American robin, hermit thrush, Swainson's thrush, ruby-crowned kinglet, cedar waxwing, Philadelphia vireo, solitary vireo, red-eyed vireo, orange-crowned warbler, black-and-white warbler, Tennessee warbler, yellow warbler, yellow-rumped warbler, palm warbler, magnolia warbler, black-throated green warbler, ovenbird, Wilson's warbler, Canada warbler, northern waterthrush, American redstart, yellow-headed blackbird, red-winged blackbird, rusty blackbird, common grackle, western tanager, chipping sparrow, white-winged crossbill, dark-eyed junco, Nelson's sharp-tailed sparrow, fox sparrow, white-crowned sparrow, clay-colored sparrow, white-throated sparrow, Lincoln's sparrow, swamp sparrow, song sparrow

sparrow, dark-eyed junco, red-winged black-bird, Brewer's blackbird, brown-headed cowbird, purple finch, house finch, red cross-bill, pine siskin, American goldfinch, evening grosbeak, black-headed grosbeak, house sparrow

Alberta

American white pelican, American bittern, Canada goose, mallard, green-winged teal, blue-winged teal, cinnamon teal, northern shoveler, American wigeon, ring-necked duck, canvasback, lesser scaup, common goldeneye, bufflehead, ruddy duck, golden eagle, bald eagle, northern harrier, American kestrel, ruffed grouse, sandhill crane, sora, American coot, greater yellowlegs, lesser yellowlegs, spotted sandpiper, common snipe, Franklin's gull, Bonaparte's gull, common tern, black tern,

Saskatchewan

Common loon, pied-billed grebe, horned grebe, red-necked grebe, eared grebe, western grebe, American white pelican, double-crested cormorant, great blue heron, black-crowned night heron, American bittern, tundra swan, Canada goose, greater white-fronted goose, snow goose, Ross's goose, mallard, American black duck, gadwall, northern pintail, green-winged teal, blue-winged teal, cinnamon teal, northern shoveler, American wigeon, Eurasian wigeon, redhead, ring-necked duck, canvasback, lesser scaup, common goldeneye, bufflehead, white-winged scoter, harlequin duck, ruddy duck, hooded merganser, common merganser, red-breasted merganser, turkey vulture, sharp-shinned hawk, Cooper's hawk, red-tailed hawk, Swainson's hawk, rough-legged hawk, bald eagle, northern harrier, American kestrel, merlin, peregrine falcon, ruffed grouse, sharp-tailed grouse, gray partridge, whooping crane, sandhill crane, sora, American coot, American avocet, semi-palmated plover, piping plover, killdeer, lesser golden plover, black-bellied plover, Hudsonian godwit, marbled godwit, whimbrel, long-billed curlew, upland sandpiper, greater yellowlegs, lesser yellowlegs, solitary sandpiper, willet, spotted sandpiper, ruddy turnstone, Wilson's phalarope, red-necked phalarope, common snipe, long-billed dowitcher, red knot, sanderling, semi-palmated sandpiper, least sandpiper, white-rumped sandpiper, Baird's sandpiper, pectoral sandpiper, stilt sandpiper, herring gull, California gull, ring-billed gull, Franklin's gull, Bonaparte's gull, Forster's tern, common tern, black tern, rock dove, mourning dove, black-billed cuckoo, great horned owl, snowy owl, common nighthawk, ruby-throated hummingbird, belted kingfisher, northern flicker, yellow-bellied sapsucker, hairy woodpecker, downy woodpecker, eastern king-bird, western kingbird, great-crested flycatcher, eastern phoebe, alder flycatcher, least flycatcher, western wood peewee, horned lark, tree swallow, bank swallow, northern rough-winged swallow, barn swallow, cliff swallow, purple martin, blue jay, black-billed magpie, common raven, American crow, black-capped chickadee, red-breasted nuthatch, house wren, marsh wren, grey catbird, brown thrasher, American robin, Swainson's thrush, veery, mountain bluebird, Sprague's pipit, Bohemian waxwing, cedar waxwing, loggerhead shrike, northern shrike, European starling, red-eyed vireo, warbling vireo, black-and-white warbler, Tennessee warbler, orange-crowned warbler, Nashville warbler, yellow warbler, yellow-rumped warbler, blackpoll warbler, palm warbler, northern waterthrush, mourning warbler, Cape May warbler, common yellowthroat, ovenbird, American redstart, house sparrow, western meadowlark, yellow-headed blackbird, red-winged blackbird, northern oriole, Brewer's blackbird, common grackle, brown-headed cowbird, western tanager, scarlet tanager, rose-breasted grosbeak, purple finch, pine grosbeak, common redpoll, pine siskin, American goldfinch, rufous-sided towhee, savannah sparrow, grasshopper sparrow, Baird's sparrow, Leconte's sparrow, sharp-tailed sparrow, vesper sparrow, lark sparrow, American tree sparrow, chipping sparrow, clay-colored sparrow, Harris' sparrow, white-crowned sparrow, white-throated sparrow, Lincoln's sparrow, song sparrow, Lapland longspur, snow bunting

Manitoba

Pacific loon, horned grebe, pied-billed grebe, western grebe, American white pelican, double-crested cormorant, American bittern, great blue heron, black-crowned night-heron, tundra swan, Canada goose, snow goose, American black duck, American wigeon, green-winged teal, mallard, northern pintail, black scoter, common eider, greater scaup, oldsquaw, surf scoter, white-winged scoter, gadwall, blue-winged teal, northern shoveler, canvasback, redhead, ring-necked duck, bufflehead, common goldeneye, Barrow's goldeneye, common merganser, red-breasted merganser, ruddy duck, northern harrier, sharp-shinned hawk, red-tailed hawk, American kestrel, merlin, rock ptarmigan, willow ptarmigan, sora, sandhill crane, American golden plover, semi-palmated plover, killdeer, greater yellowlegs, lesser yellowlegs, sanderling, semi-palmated sandpiper, common snipe, dunlin, least sandpiper, Hudsonian godwit, lesser yellowlegs, red-necked phalarope, sanderling, short-billed dowitcher, spotted sandpiper, stilt sandpiper, whimbrel, white-rumped sandpiper, Franklin's gull, Bonaparte's gull, ring-billed gull, glaucous gull, herring gull, Forster's tern, arctic tern, mourning dove, snowy owl, downy wood-pecker, hairy woodpecker, northern flicker, eastern kingbird, warbling vireo, horned lark, tree swallow, bank swallow, barn swallow, American crow, common raven, gray jay, boreal chickadee, house wren, sedge wren, marsh wren, ruby-crowned kinglet, Swainson's thrush, hermit thrush, American robin, gray catbird, American pipit, cedar waxwing, Tennessee warbler, yellow warbler, yellow-rumped warbler, American tree sparrow, American redstart, common yellowthroat, savannah sparrow, song sparrow, white-throated sparrow, dark-eyed junco, Harris' sparrow, Lapland longspur, Smith's longspur, swamp sparrow, white-crowned sparrow, snow bunting, brown-headed cowbird, rusty blackbird, Baltimore oriole, common redpoll, hoary redpoll, pine grosbeak, house sparrow

A chipping sparrow.

Ontario

Common loon, pied-billed grebe, double-crested cormorant, great blue heron, black-crowned night heron, green heron, American bittern, least bittern, Canada goose, brant, snow goose, Ross' goose, mallard, American black duck, gadwall, northern pintail, green-winged teal, blue-winged teal, American wigeon, northern shoveler, wood duck, ring-necked duck, greater scaup, lesser scaup, common goldeneye, buffle-head, oldsquaw, white-winged scoter, ruddy duck, hooded merganser, common merganser, red-breasted merganser, turkey vulture, northern goshawk, sharp-shinned hawk, red-tailed hawk, red-shouldered hawk, broad-winged hawk, rough-legged hawk, bald eagle, northern harrier, osprey, American kestrel, wild turkey, ruffed grouse, ring-necked pheasant, gray partridge, Virginia rail, sora, yellow rail, common moorhen, American coot, semi-palmated plover, killdeer, lesser golden plover, black-bellied plover, upland sandpiper, greater yellowlegs, lesser yellowlegs, solitary sandpiper, willet, spotted sandpiper, ruddy turnstone, American woodcock, common snipe, short-billed dowitcher, sanderling, least sandpiper, dunlin, great black-backed gull, herring gull, ring-billed gull, Bonaparte's gull, common tern, rock dove, mourning dove, yellow-billed cuckoo, black-billed cuckoo, eastern screech owl, great-horned owl, snowy owl, barred owl, long-eared owl, short-eared owl, northern saw-whet owl, whip-poor-will, common nighthawk, ruby-throated humming-bird, belted kingfisher, northern flicker, pileated woodpecker, red-headed woodpecker, yellow-bellied sapsucker, hairy woodpecker, downy woodpecker, horned lark, eastern kingbird, great-crested flycatcher, eastern phoebe, willow flycatcher, olive-sided flycatcher, alder flycatcher, least flycatcher, eastern wood peewee, Bohemian waxwing, cedar waxwing, chimney swift, tree swallow, bank swallow, north rough-winged swallow, barn swallow, cliff swallow, blue jay, American crow, black-capped chickadee, white-breasted nuthatch, red-breasted nuthatch, brown creeper, house wren, winter wren, marsh wren, sedge wren, gray catbird, brown thrasher, American robin, wood thrush, hermit thrush, Swainson's thrush, veery, eastern bluebird, blue-gray gnatcatcher, golden-crowned kinglet, ruby-crowned kinglet, northern shrike, logger-head shrike, yellow-throated vireo, solitary vireo, red-eyed vireo, Philadelphia vireo, warbling vireo, black-and-white warbler, prothonotary warbler, golden-winged warbler, Nashville warbler, yellow warbler, magnolia warbler, black-throated blue warbler, yellow-rumped warbler, black-throated green warbler, cerulean warbler, blackburnian warbler, chestnut-sided warbler, bay-breasted warbler, blackpoll warbler, palm warbler, ovenbird, northern waterthrush, mourning warbler, common yellowthroat, hooded warbler, Canada warbler, American redstart, bobolink, eastern meadow lark, red-winged blackbird, northern oriole, common grackle, brown-headed cowbird, European starling, scarlet tanager, northern cardinal, indigo bunting, rose-breasted grosbeak, evening grosbeak, pine grosbeak, purple finch, house finch, common redpoll, pine siskin, American goldfinch, rufous-sided towhee, savannah sparrow, vesper sparrow, dark-eyed junco, American tree sparrow, chipping sparrow, field sparrow, white-crowned sparrow, white-throated sparrow, fox sparrow, swamp sparrow, song sparrow, snow bunting, house sparrow

Québec

Grèbe à bec bigarré (pied-billed grebe), grèbe jougris (red-necked grebe), grèbe esclavon (horned grebe), plongeon catmarin (red-throated loon), plongeon huard (common loon), plongeon à bec blanc (yellow-billed loon), albatros à nez jaune (yellow-nosed albatross), fulmar boréal (northern fulmar), puffin cendré (Cory's shear-water), puffin majeur (great shearwater), puffin fuligineux (sooty shearwater), océanite de Wilson (Wilson's storm-petrel), océanite cul-blanc (Leach's storm-petrel), fou de bassan (northern gannet), cormoran à aigrettes (double-crested cormorant), grande aigrette (great egret), héron vert (green heron), bihoreau gris (black-crowned night-heron), petit blongios (least bittern), butor d'Amérique (American bittern), urubu à tête rouge (turkey vulture), érismature rousse (ruddy duck), cygne tuberculé (mute swan), cygne siffleur (tundra swan), oie des neiges (snow goose), oie de Ross (Ross' goose), bernache cravant (brant), canard branchu (wood duck), canard d'Amérique (American wigeon), canard chipeau (gadwall), sarcelle d'hiver (race crecca) (common teal), sarcelle d'hiver (green-winged teal), sarcelle à ailes bleues (blue-winged teal), canard souchet (northern shoveler), fuligule à dos blanc (canvasback), fuligule à tête rouge (redhead), fuligule à collier (ring-necked duck), fuligule milouinan (greater scaup), petit fuligule (lesser scaup), eider à duvet (common eider), eider à tête grise (king eider), arlequin plongeur (harle-quin duck), harelde kakawi (long-tailed duck), macreuse noire (black scoter), macreuse à front blanc (surf scoter), macreuse brune (white-winged scoter) garrot d'islande (Barrow's golden-eye), petit garrot (bufflehead), harle couronné (hooded merganser), harle huppé (red-breasted merganser), grand harle (common merganser), balbuzard pêcheur (osprey), pygargue à tête blanche (bald eagle) busard Saint-Martin (northern harrier), épervier brun (sharp-shinned hawk), épervier de Cooper (Cooper's hawk), buse à épaulettes (red-shouldered hawk), petite buse (broad-winged hawk), buse à queue rousse (red-tailed hawk), aigle royal (golden eagle), crécerelle d'Amérique (American kestrel), faucon émerillon (merlin), faucon pèlerin (peregrine falcon), dindon sauvage (wild turkey), lagopède des saules (willow ptarmigan), tétras à queue fine (sharp-tailed grouse), râle jauné (yellow rail), râle de Virginie (Virginia rail), marouette de caroline (sora), gallinule poule-d'eau (common moorhen), foulque d'Amérique (American coot), grue du Canada (sandhill crane), bécasse d'amérique (American woodcock), barge hudsonienne (Hudsonian godwit), courlis corlieu (whimbrel), maubèche des champs (upland sandpiper), grand chevalier (greater yellowlegs), petit chevalier (lesser yellowlegs), chevalier solitaire (solitary sandpiper), chevalier grivelé (spotted sandpiper), chevalier semipalmé (willet), tournepierre à collier (ruddy turnstone), bécassin roux (short-billed dowitcher), bécassin à long bec (long-billed dowitcher), bécasseau maubèche (red knot), bécasseau sanderling (sanderling), bécasseau semipalmé (semi-palmated sandpiper), bécasseau d'Alaska (western sandpiper), bécasseau minuscule (least sandpiper), bécasseau à croupion blanc (white-rumped sandpiper), bécasseau de baird (Baird's sandpiper), bécasseau à poitrine cendrée (pectoral sandpiper), bécasseau violet (purple sandpiper), bécasseau variable (dunlin),

The common screech owl.

bécasseau à échasses (stilt sandpiper), bécasseau roussâtre (buff-breasted sandpiper), phalarope de Wilson (Wilson's phalarope), phalarope à bec étroit (red-necked phalarope), phalarope à bec large (red phalarope), pluvier bronzé (American golden plover), pluvier argenté (grey plover), pluvier semipalmé (semi-palmated plover), pluvier kildir (killdeer), pluvier siffleur (piping plover), labbe pomarin (pomarine jaeger), labbe parasite (parasitic jaeger), labbe à longue queue (long-tailed jaeger), goéland à bec cerclé (ring-billed gull), mouette rieuse (black-headed gull), mouette de bonaparte (Bonaparte's gull), mouette pygmée (little gull), mouette tridactyle (black-legged kittiwake), sterne caspienne (Caspian tern), sterne de dougall (roseate tern), sterne pierregarin (common tern), sterne arctique (arctic tern), guifette leucoptère (white-winged tern), guifette noire (black tern), guillemot marbré (marbled murrelet), guillemot à cou blanc (ancient murrelet), macareux moine (Atlantic puffin), coulicou à bec noir (black-billed cuckoo), coulicou à bec jaune (yellow-billed cuckoo), engoulevent d'amérique (common nighthawk), engoulevent bois-pourri (whip-poor-will), martinet ramoneur (chimney swift), colibri à gorge rubis (ruby-throated humming-bird), pic à tête rouge (red-headed woodpecker), pic maculé (yellow-bellied sapsucker), moucherolle à côtés olive (olive-sided flycatcher), pioui de l'est (eastern wood-pewee), moucherolle à ventre jaune (yellow-bellied flycatcher), moucherolle des aulnes (alder flycatcher), moucherolle des saules (willow flycatcher), moucherolle tchébec (least flycatcher), moucherolle phébi (eastern phoebe), tyran huppé (great crested flycatcher), tyran tritri (eastern kingbird), pie-grièche migratrice (loggerhead shrike), viréo à tête bleue (blue-headed vireo), viréo à gorge jaune (yellow-throated vireo), viréo de Philadelphie (Philadelphia vireo), viréo aux yeux rouges (red-eyed vireo), viréo mélodieux (eastern warbling-vireo), merlebleu de l'est (eastern bluebird), grive fauve (veery), grive à joues grises (grey-cheeked thrush), grive de Bicknell (Bicknell's thrush), grive à dos olive (Swainson's thrush), grive des bois (wood thrush), merle d'Amérique (American robin), traquet motteux (northern wheatear), moqueur chat (grey catbird), moqueur roux (brown thrasher), troglodyte à bec court (sedge wren), troglodyte des marais (marsh wren), troglodyte mignon (winter wren), troglodyte familier (house wren), gobemoucheron gris-bleu (blue-grey gnatcatcher), hirondelle bicolore (tree swallow), hirondelle noire (purple martin), hirondelle à ailes hérissées (northern rough-winged swallow), hirondelle de rivage (sand martin), hirondelle rustique (barn swallow), hirondelle à front blanc (cliff swallow), roitelet à couronne rubis (ruby-crowned kinglet), alouette hausse-col (horned lark), Pipit d'Amérique (American pipit), bruant fauve (fox sparrow), bruant de Lincoln (Lincoln's sparrow), bruant des marais (swamp sparrow), bruant à couronne blanche (white-crowned sparrow), bruant des prés (savannah sparrow), bruant de Nelson (Nelson's sharp-tailed sparrow), bruant de Le Conte (Le Conte's sparrow), bruant sauterelle (grasshopper sparrow), bruant familier (chipping sparrow), bruant des plaines (clay-colored sparrow), bruant des champs (field sparrow), bruant vespéral (vesper sparrow), paruline à ailes dorées (golden-winged warbler), paruline obscure (Tennessee warbler), paruline verdâtre (orange-crowned warbler), paruline à joues grises (Nashville warbler), paruline à collier (northern parula), paruline jaune (yellow warbler), paruline à flancs marron (chestnut-sided warbler), paruline à tête cendrée (magnolia warbler), paruline tigrée (Cape May warbler), paruline bleue (black-throated blue warbler), paruline à gorge noire (black-throated green warbler), paruline à gorge orangée (blackburnian warbler), paruline des pins (pine warbler), paruline à

couronne rousse (palm warbler), paruline à poitrine baie (bay-breasted warbler), paruline rayée (blackpoll warbler), paruline azurée (cerulean warbler), paruline noir et blanc (black-and-white warbler), paruline flamboyante (American redstart), paruline couronnée (ovenbird), paruline des ruisseaux (northern waterthrush), paruline à gorge grise (Connecticut warbler), paruline triste (mourning warbler), paruline masquée (common yellowthroat), paruline à calotte noire (Wilson's warbler), paruline du Canada (Canada warbler), tangara écarlate (scarlet tanager), cardinal à poitrine rose (rose-breasted grosbeak), passerin indigo (indigo bunting), oriole de Baltimore (Baltimore oriole), sturnelle de l'ouest (western meadowlark), quiscale bronzé (common grackle), quiscale rouilleux (rusty blackbird), goglu des prés (bobolink)

New Brunswick

Red-throated loon, horned grebe, red-necked grebe, northern fulmar, greater shearwater, sooty shearwater, Manx shearwater, Wilson's storm-petrel, northern gannet, great cormorant, least bittern, great egret, snowy egret, little blue heron, cattle egret, glossy ibis, snow goose, brant, gadwall, Eurasian wigeon, lesser scaup, king eider, harlequin duck, surf scoter, white-winged scoter, black scoter, long-tailed duck, bufflehead, Barrow's goldeneye, ruddy duck, rough-legged hawk, golden eagle, gyrfalcon, peregrine falcon, American coot, black-bellied plover, American golden plover, semi-palmated plover, greater yellowlegs, lesser yellowlegs, solitary sandpiper, whimbrel, Hudsonian godwit, ruddy turnstone, red knot, sanderling, semi-palmated sandpiper, western sandpiper, least sandpiper, white-rumped sandpiper, Baird's sandpiper, pectoral sandpiper, purple sandpiper, dunlin, stilt sandpiper, buff-breasted sandpiper, short-billed dowitcher, long-billed dowitcher, red-necked phalarope, red phalarope, pomarine jaeger, parasitic jaeger, laughing gull, little gull, black-headed gull, Bonaparte's gull, Iceland gull, lesser black-backed gull, glaucous gull, Caspian tern, dovekie, thick-billed murre, yellow-billed cuckoo, snowy owl, northern hawk owl, boreal owl, red-headed woodpecker, red-bellied woodpecker, western kingbird, northern shrike, house wren, blue-gray gnatcatcher, gray-cheeked thrush, American pipit, Bohemian waxwing, blue-winged warbler, orange-crowned warbler, prairie warbler, yellow-breasted chat, summer tanager, American tree sparrow, clay-colored sparrow, field sparrow, white-crowned sparrow, Lapland longspur, snow bunting, blue grosbeak, dickcissel, yellow-headed blackbird, orchard oriole, common redpoll

Nova Scotia

Red-throated loon, common loon, northern fulmar, greater shearwater, sooty shearwater, Wilson's storm-petrel, Leach's storm-petrel, northern gannet, double-crested cormorant, great blue heron, brant, Canada goose, green-winged teal, mallard, northern pintail, blue-winged teal, ring-necked duck, greater scaup, common eider, black scoter, surf scoter, white-winged scoter, common goldeneye, bufflehead, common merganser, red-breasted merganser, osprey, northern harrier, sharp-shinned hawk, broad-winged hawk, American kestrel, merlin, peregrine falcon, black-bellied plover, lesser golden plover, semi-palmated plover, killdeer, greater yellowlegs, lesser yellowlegs, willet, ruddy turnstone, red knot, sanderling, semi-palmated sandpiper, least sandpiper, white-rumped sandpiper, pectoral sandpiper, dunlin, short-billed dowitcher, common snipe, American woodcock, red-necked phalarope, red phalarope, ring-billed gull, common tern, Arctic tern, mourning dove, common

nighthawk, ruby-throated hummingbird, belted kingfisher, yellow-bellied sapsucker, northern flicker, olive-sided flycatcher, eastern wood pee-wee, yellow-bellied flycatcher, alder flycatcher, least flycatcher, eastern kingbird, horned lark, tree swallow, bank swallow, barn swallow, ruby-crowned kinglet, veery, Swainson's thrush, hermit thrush, American robin, gray catbird, water pipit, cedar waxwing, Tennessee warbler, Nashville warbler, northern parula, chestnut-sided warbler, magnolia warbler, yellow warbler, Cape May warbler, yellow-rumped warbler, black-throated green warbler, palm warbler, bay-breasted warbler, blackpoll warbler, black-and-white warbler, American redstart, ovenbird, northern waterthrush, common yellowthroat, Wilson's warbler, Canada warbler, rose-breasted grosbeak, American tree sparrow, chipping sparrow, savannah sparrow, sharp-tailed sparrow, song sparrow, swamp sparrow, white-throated sparrow, dark-eyed junco, Lapland longspur, bobolink, red-winged blackbird, rusty blackbird, common grackle, purple finch

Prince Edward Island

Red-throated loon, common loon, pied-billed grebe, northern gannet, double-crested cormorant, great cormorant, American bittern, great blue heron, Canada goose, brant, wood duck, gadwall, American wigeon, American black duck, mallard, blue-winged teal, northern shoveler, northern pintail,

The male broad-billed hummingbird.

green-winged teal, ring-necked duck, greater scaup, common eider, surf scoter, white-winged scoter, black scoter, long-tailed duck, bufflehead, common goldeneye, Barrow's goldeneye, hooded merganser, common merganser, red-breasted merganser, osprey, bald eagle, northern harrier, sharp-shinned hawk, American kestrel, merlin, gray partridge, ruffed grouse, sora, black-bellied plover, American golden plover, semi-palmated plover, piping plover, killdeer, greater yellowlegs, lesser yellowlegs, willet, spotted sandpiper, whimbrel, Hudsonian godwit, ruddy turnstone, red knot, sanderling, semi-palmated sandpiper, least sandpiper, white-rumped sandpiper, pectoral sandpiper, dunlin, short-billed dowitcher, common snipe, American woodcock, red-necked phalarope, Bonaparte's gull, ring-billed gull, herring gull, Iceland gull, great black-backed gull, Caspian tern, common tern, arctic tern, black guillemot, rock dove, mourning dove, great horned owl, barred owl, northern saw-whet owl, ruby-throated hummingbird, belted kingfisher, yellow-bellied sapsucker, downy woodpecker, hairy woodpecker, northern flicker, eastern wood-peewee, alder flycatcher, least flycatcher, eastern kingbird, blue-headed vireo, red-eyed vireo, blue jay, American crow, common raven, horned lark, tree swallow, bank swallow, barn swallow, boreal chickadee, black-capped chickadee, red-breasted nuthatch, brown creeper, winter wren, golden-crowned kinglet, ruby-crowned kinglet, Swainson's thrush, hermit thrush, American robin, European starling, cedar waxwing, Tennessee warbler, Nashville warbler, northern parula, yellow warbler, chestnut-sided warbler, magnolia warbler, Cape May warbler, black-throated blue warbler, yellow-rumped warbler, black-throated green warbler, blackburnian warbler, bay-breasted warbler, black-and-white warbler,

American redstart, ovenbird, northern waterthrush, mourning warbler, common yellowthroat, chipping sparrow, savannah sparrow, Nelson's sharp-tailed sparrow, song sparrow, Lincoln's sparrow, swamp sparrow, white-throated sparrow, dark-eyed junco, Lapland longspur, snow bunting, rose-breasted grosbeak, bobolink, red-winged blackbird, rusty blackbird, common grackle, brown-headed cowbird, purple finch, common redpoll, pine siskin, American goldfinch, evening grosbeak, house sparrow

Newfoundland

Canada goose, American black duck, green-winged teal, ring-necked duck, common eider, long-tailed duck, common goldeneye, red-breasted merganser, common loon, northern fulmar, greater shearwater, sooty shearwater, Leach's storm-petrel, northern gannet, osprey, black-bellied plover, semi-palmated plover, greater yellowlegs, spotted sandpiper, ruddy turnstone, sanderling, semi-palmated sandpiper, least sandpiper, white-rumped sandpiper, common snipe, Wilson's snipe, pomarine jaeger, parasitic jaeger, ring-billed gull, Iceland gull, glaucous gull, common tern, arctic tern, dovekie, razorbill, Atlantic puffin, belted kingfisher, northern flicker, yellow-bellied flycatcher, horned lark, tree swallow, ruby-crowned kinglet, gray-cheeked thrush, Swainson's thrush, hermit thrush, American robin, American pipit, Tennessee warbler, yellow warbler, magnolia warbler, yellow-rumped warbler, black-throated green warbler, blackpoll warbler, black-and-white warbler, American redstart, ovenbird, northern waterthrush, common yellowthroat, American redstart, mourning warbler, Wilson's warbler, savannah sparrow, fox sparrow, song sparrow, Lincoln's sparrow, swamp sparrow, white-throated sparrow, snow bunting

Yukon Territory

Pacific loon, horned grebe, red-necked grebe, tundra swan, trumpeter swan, greater white-fronted goose, Canada goose, American wigeon, mallard, northern shoveler, northern pintail, green-winged teal, mallard, northern pintail, blue-winged teal, northern shoveler, gadwall, Eurasian wigeon, American wigeon, canvasback, redhead, ring-necked duck, greater scaup, lesser scaup, surf scoter, Barrow's goldeneye, buffle-head, bald eagle, sandhill crane, semi-palmated plover, solitary sandpiper, lesser yellowlegs, spotted sandpiper, semi-palmated sandpiper, least sandpiper, Baird's sandpiper, pectoral sandpiper, common snipe, Bonaparte's gull, mew gull, herring gull, arctic tern, northern flicker, alder flycatcher, gray jay, common raven, tree swallow, violet-green swallow, bank swallow, cliff swallow, black-capped chickadee, boreal chickadee, ruby-crowned kinglet, Swainson's thrush, hermit thrush, American robin, American pipit, yellow warbler, yellow-rumped warbler, Wilson's warbler, savannah sparrow, Lincoln's sparrow, white-crowned sparrow, dark-eyed junco, Lapland longspur, snow bunting, rusty blackbird, pine grosbeak, white-winged crossbill, common redpoll

Northwest Territories

Whooping crane, sandhill crane, tundra swan, snow goose, Canada goose, semi-palmated plover, American golden plover, long-billed dowitcher, sanderling, least sandpiper, semi-palmated sandpiper, western sandpiper, pectoral sandpiper, bald eagle, peregrine falcon, American pipit, Lapland longspur, snow bunting

Nunavut

Common loon, yellow-billed loon, arctic loon, red-throated loon, whistling swan, Canada goose, brant, white-fronted goose, snow goose, pintail, green-winged teal, American widgeon (baldpate), greater scaup, lesser scaup, old squaw, common eider, king eider, white-winged scoter, surf scoter, common scoter, common merganser, red-breasted merganser, rough-legged hawk, golden eagle, bald eagle, gyrfalcon, peregrine falcon, willow ptarmigan, rock ptarmigan, sandhill crane, sora, semi-palmated plover, American golden plover, black-bellied plover, ruddy turnstone, common (Wilson's) snipe, spotted sandpiper, lesser yellowlegs, knot, pectoral sandpiper, Baird's sandpiper, sanderling, red phalarope, northern phalarope, pomarine jaeger, parasitic jaeger, long-tailed jaeger, glaucous gull, Iceland gull, herring gull, Thayer's gull, mew (short-billed) gull, Sabine's gull, arctic tern, snowy owl, short-eared hawk, nighthawk, eastern kingbird, western kingbird, horned lark, tree swallow, bank swallow, barn swallow, cliff swallow, common raven, northern mockingbird, brown thrasher, American robin, gray-cheeked thrush, water pipit, yellow warbler, myrtle (yellow-rumped) warbler, black-polled warbler, brown-headed cowbird, purple finch, hoary redpoll, common redpoll, savannah sparrow, slate-colored junco, tree sparrow, Harris' sparrow, white-crested sparrow, Lincoln's sparrow, Lapland longspur, Smith's longspur, snow bunting

An American goldfinch.

6 Problems in Paradise

As you fill your yard with feeders and birdhouses, you will notice that you've also attracted some unwanted creatures to the habitat you've created. To help you put them into perspective, we've divided them into two categories. *Pests* may be undesirable from your perspective, but they won't eat eggs, chicks, or adult birds you've attracted to your little Eden. They may, however, eat the food you've put out or destroy food containers or nest boxes. *Predators* take things one step further, actually eating eggs, chicks, or adult birds.

In some instances, animals that are normally considered pests in one part of the country are predators in another. For example, although many types of ants are undesirable and we do what we can to keep them away from feeders, fire ants, which are common in the American South and Southwest, will attack in force and kill animals as large as young deer—or as small as hatchling birds.

In the habitat you create, we recommend that you pick your battles and realize that when nature works as it should, a healthy predator-prey cycle is in effect as long as the animals involved are native to the area.

As a general principle, the best way to get rid of overzealous pests or predators is to determine what has attracted them and, if possible, get rid of it or contain it so the undesirable animal can't get to it. Often this is food. Any animal, predators included, will choose the most easily accessible food—a young, injured, or lame animal over one that can run or fly well, for example, or easily accessible large quantities of seed or pelleted food intended for the birds you want to feed in your backyard. We will point out potential problems as we discuss each pest or predator animal.

Pests

Ants

Your biggest problem may be keeping ants out of your hummingbird feeders. Hummingbirds don't like to share their feeders with ants.

Commercial barriers are available that may help this problem. Most rely on you to keep them filled with clean water. If the water sits still for a while, the ants may learn to walk on it—the surface tension is just enough to allow them to do it. Keep the water free from debris because ants can learn to march across that, too. Although some recommend such barriers as motor oil, we recommend against it because it's toxic. Petroleum jelly and cooking oil may work if you coat a metal pole, but you will need to clean the poles and re-apply often.

If you have set up nest boxes, make sure ants don't invade them. This might make parents leave a nest. Also, watch for them at feeding stations where you offer bread and fruit. To rid your station or nest box of these pests, look for a trail to find their nest. Use an organic pesticide, such as one based on pyrethrums, a by-product of chrysanthemums, on the ant nests. (Pyrethrins are a chemical imitation of the natural product. We rec-

Hummingbirds will not drink from feeders used by ants. You will have to be persistent to rid the area of ants in a safe way.

ommend you use the natural product whenever possible.) Also, look for commercial ant bait. Use only those with pesticide inside a container. You can find these at hardware stores.

If you live in the south or southeast, you may have fire ants. (See sidebar, page 125.) These pests often need commercial control. Discuss with various contractors in your area the methods they use, then decide on one that is the least harmful to the environment. Some new ones on the market are based on essence of orange.

Bats

It's hard for us to consider bats a pest because they are so beneficial, but nectar-eating bats, common in the American Southwest, can quickly drain hummingbird feeders. You can either put up with them or remove the feeders at sunset and replace them in the early morning hours when the nocturnal bats have checked into their sleeping spots. Consider leaving the feeders out 24-hours a day and observing the bats as they arrive at your feeders in the evening.

Bees and Wasps

Almost every garden bird habitat will have bees and wasps, attracted either by the flowers you've planted to attract birds or the food you've left out in the feeders, such as fruit or nectar. More often than not, they don't pose a serious problem because they don't kill birds. They can clog up a hummingbird feeder or make it scary for you to refill feeders. Bee guards—available at many chain pet stores, online, or at specialty bird stores—can keep them out of your nectar feeders. Also available are traps that contain syrup that attracts flies, wasps, and bees. Once inside, they cannot get out, so they die.

Wasps and bees may invade bird nest boxes. If you use insecticides to kill these bugs, discard the nest boxes because residual insecticides can harm birds.

Because bees are so beneficial, we recommend against this last option. If you have a big problem and you must get rid of the bees and wasps, remove all attractive food for a week or two. By that time, they'll have found a new food source.

Watch, too, for wasps that might try to take over a home you've built for birds. If you must use pesticide to get rid of wasps in a birdhouse, don't use the house afterward for birds, no matter how well you clean it. Birds are especially sensitive to chemicals, including those considered relatively benign. Even those based on pyrethrums could kill birds in houses where the fumes can concentrate.

Other Birds

Although we like to see any and all avian comers at our bird feeders, we recognize that some people want to attract certain birds and ward off others, such as house sparrows, pigeons, crows, jays, grackles, blackbirds, and magpies. Generally the problem is that these birds may eat more of the food you provide than you believe is their share or some, such as grackles and blackbirds, may arrive in such huge flocks that they scare away other birds. We've heard of "solutions" that range from shooting them to shooting in the air to scare them or setting off firecrackers. Not only will these methods not work, but they are most likely illegal where you live.

The best solution is to remove the nest-box styles and the feeder type these birds prefer. Hanging feeders will sometimes discourage house sparrows, grackles, jays, blackbirds, pigeons, crows, and other heavy birds, which prefer to eat on a flat surface, preferably the ground. Many feeders are designed for small birds with a heavy wire mesh with openings large enough for finches, chickadees, siskins, and other tiny birds. Also effective are feeders with a weighted perch that will snap the feeder tray shut when a heavy bird, such as a jay, lands on it.

If you put up nest boxes, choose only those with holes that will allow in the size bird you want to attract. Also, pay attention to the exact requirements of the birds you want. For instance, purple martins interest many people because they eat mosquitoes.

According to information on the Purple Martin Conservation Association Web site, "A martin house must have compartments whose floor dimensions measure at least 6 by 6 inches (15.24 cm x 15.24 cm), but compartments measuring 7 by 12 inches (17 cm x 30.48 cm) are far superior. The entrance hole should be placed about 1 inch above the floor and have a diameter in the range of 2 to $2^{1}/_{4}$ inches (5.08 cm to 6.35 cm) although martins are known to use holes as small as $1^{3}/_{4}$ inches (4.45 cm). If your martin house does not have at least a 6- by 6-inch (15.24 cm x 15.24 cm) floor and at least a $1^{3}/_{4}$-inch (4.45-cm) entrance hole, modify it." It must also be accessible enough to clean after the martins have left for the year. It must offer protection (depth of box helps, as does the small size and shape of the openings). It must be white and expandable. For more information on the requirements of these most desirable birds, check *www.purplemartin.org*.

Following are some pest birds and what you can do to discourage them.

Blackbirds: These birds can become pests because they tend to live in huge flocks. If they discover a constant source of their favorite foods in your yard, they will hang around. Their aggression and the food consumption of such a large group of birds will discourage other birds you might prefer. To deter them, don't offer their favorite foods: cracked corn and baked goods, such as bread of any sort. Many don't like niger seed or food offered in hanging feeders.

Grackles are an annoyance because they live in large groups and are noisy and messy. Removing their favorite food for a week or so may cause them to seek it elsewhere. If they roost in your yard, use a strong water gun to scare them away.

Blue jays: These birds are aggressive. You can discourage them from bullying smaller birds at your feeder by offering their favorite foods, peanuts and sunflower seeds, at separate feeders. They don't eat at hanging feeders and will not eat niger seed. On a positive note, when a jay is around, it will give an alarm cry when a predator comes on the scene.

Grackles: Similar to blackbirds, these birds hang out in large groups and can be quite a mess. In addition, if they decide to nest in trees in your yard, you'll have a hard time getting rid of them, even if they don't eat there. If they start, use noise-makers or water blasters to get rid of them, but you'll have to be persistent. Many don't eat at hanging feeders and they prefer cracked corn. They may eat chicks of smaller species.

House sparrows: Some people consider these birds "junk birds" because they are not native to this country and they can dominate backyard feeders by their sheer numbers. On the up side, however, they usually present no aggressive danger to other birds, except for the occasional nest-box attack. They do eat a lot of seed and will tolerate hanging feeders.

Starlings: These medium-sized birds are considered pests because they will dominate feeders that hold suet, their favorite food. Unfortunately, various woodpeckers also prefer this food. Starlings may also dominate nest boxes intended for birds attracted to a 4-inch (10.16-cm) entry hole. They've also been known to kill and eat chicks of smaller bird species. Starlings are a nonnative species and are not covered by laws concerning native and migratory birds.

Woodpeckers: Some homeowners consider these birds pests because they can persistently peck nest holes or go after bugs in the wood of homes. In general, if they are banging away at your home to make a nest hole, it's because they've found what looked like an invitation, either a knothole that fell out and attracted the bird or inviting circular air holes in the fascia that your builder put in. Cover such holes with metal to discourage these birds.

If other birds become, in your eyes, pests, stop offering their favorite food for a while. They'll find another source and leave your yard. (See our specific information on food preferences for different species in Chapter 5.) Adding baffles on birdhouses and bird feeders can also work, as can greasing any pole with petroleum jelly, but you will have to keep the petroleum jelly fresh, at least weekly; as the squirrels paw at it to get up the greased pole, they will add grit to the mixture, which will give them traction. They'll keep at it until they can scamper up the pole. (See the section on feeder placement starting on page 95 for more detailed information.)

Chipmunks

Closely related to squirrels, these animals fall into the "almost too cute to be true" category; however, they do eat a lot and can decimate a seed supply. What's more after one finds your feeders, more will follow. Their preferred foods are acorns, nuts, berries, cherries, and other fruit (especially if you plant it and are looking forward to eating it) and any kind of seed. They do slow down in winter, though they don't actually hibernate. Trapping them will only allow other, perhaps less-dominant, animals in the area to take over the "territory."

If you trap them, do not kill them. Move them to another area. You could help solve the problem and reduce your stress by setting up a chipmunk feeder station near your viewing area. Use a flat surface. Just keep in mind they aren't as agile as squirrels and won't enjoy the mind games squirrels seem to thrive on.

Opossums/Possums

Even if they live in your area, you will rarely see these shy, pouched mammals. The chief problem with them is that they eat seeds, as well as leaves, shoots, buds, and insects. What's more, they are very prolific, with as many as 14 in a litter and a gestation of just 13 days. In about 4 months the young are self-sufficient. They don't eat from hanging feeders. To prevent problems, store all birdseed in metal containers with firm lids in a closed-up garage so they can't gain access to it.

Squirrels

These mammals can be frustrating and interesting. They are among the wiliest of the pests in your habitat. They will not only eat much of the food intended for your birds but also damage many feeders. Gray squirrels seem more daring and persistent than red squirrels. We've read many solutions to the squirrel problem, but most don't work.

Trapping them and removing them only allows younger squirrels to fill the void left by the more dominant one that had claimed your yard as its territory. Again, we recommend against destroying them in any way, including shooting them.

You can buy several squirrel-repelling products that contain capsicum (peppers). In theory, squirrels don't like the hot taste. Birds either like it or don't notice it, and it will add nutrients to the feed. Some come suspended in cooking oil. Putting this on the seed in our feeders doesn't seem to

Squirrels are among the smartest of the pests in your yard. Considering they will go to great lengths to get seed, you might as well make a game of it and set up complicated feeders for them. Remember, though, you can't beat them, so you may as well enjoy them.

work and can be a big mess to clean. Other manufacturers put out small amounts of ground red pepper. Because it would take a lot of this to mix with seed to be effective, try buying dried red peppers at your grocery store and grinding them in your blender until you have pepper dust. Take care not to remove the blender cover until the dust has settled; it will irritate your eyes. To prevent irritation, wear disposable gloves when handling a capsicum product, and remember to wash your hands thoroughly afterward. Also, never touch your face, especially your eyes and lips when handling capsicum.

If you live near a forest, you could be the potential host to many, many squirrels. Numerous squirrel baffles are on the market to put over and under bird feeders that mount on poles. If you have trees in your yard or if your home is near the pole, the squirrels can jump to the top of the feeder so the baffle must be big enough that the squirrel can't lean over and then grab hold of a perch. Once it gets a perch, it has gained access.

As with large birds, you can use feeders with weighted perches that will close the feeder when the squirrel jumps or climbs on.

The most effective product we've used gave the squirrel a mild shock when it made contact with two feet, but it jumped off quickly. In about a year's time, however, the product no longer worked. We found out when we noticed squirrels feeding at will. It had been expensive, and we didn't replace it.

In the end, we just decided to enjoy the squirrels, setting up feeding stations away from the bird feeders with dried corn, peanuts, and sunflower seeds. It helped, but it didn't draw them entirely away from the feeders. Other people have set up elaborate obstacle courses that squirrels must learn to maneuver to get to acorns and other nuts. The squirrels seem to enjoy the challenge.

Predators

Animals in the predator class go beyond pesky. Many of them can seriously decimate the bird population not only in your yard but also beyond. As the creator and guardian of the habitat in your yard, you'll have to be the judge about whether each constitutes a serious threat or something you will have to remove.

Other Birds

Although you may not think of birds as predators, eagles, jaegers, hawks, kestrels, shrikes, loggerheads, and owls are among the many birds that eat other birds. By and large, these birds will catch the mostly unaware or sickest of the bunch that gathers around your feeders. These predators won't hang out there on a regular basis and pose the least threat to peace in your backyard. We know of many people with successful backyard feeders who have hawks and owls living nearby.

Do not attempt to kill these hunting birds. It's not only illegal but also disruptive to the natural order of life in your area. Predatory birds kill many rodents and reptiles that you may find far more alarming.

Some small birds, such as sparrows, purple martins, and cowbirds, have been known to kill the chicks of other birds. Consider this a part of nature. There is really nothing you can do about it that will not damage the natural order of things.

This is the sad part of setting up a bird-feeding and -nesting area, but you will have front seat to the natural cycle in which you will see life begin and end.

Owls are fun to watch, but they do have a tendency to kill smaller birds. Our role as bird-watchers is to observe nature in action, although it may seem cruel. We can, however, set up feeding stations and bird-houses in more sheltered areas where large birds cannot easily target smaller birds.

Wild birds have a short life span because of predation, loss of habitat, environmental poisoning, weather, and lack of food. You can help by providing food and water in winter and drought and nesting places in which they will, largely, find safety if you build and place the nesting sites correctly.

Cats

As a rule, we consider cats the worst animal danger to a backyard habitat. Housecats are native to Africa and Asia. They first came to North America in the 1800s. Because housecats are not native to this country, indigenous birds do not have the instinctive awareness to help protect themselves against these cunning hunting animals.

If you have cats, keep them indoors. This will keep them safe from diseases they can contract from outside sources. Cats that reside exclusively inside a home live longer than outside cats. If you believe a cat has a right to come and go outside, do not feed birds in your backyard. Putting a bell on a cat will not help birds. By the time a bird hears a bell activated by a cat that has hidden in bushes, it will be too late.

If you have stray cats that come into your yard, trap them. Take them to an animal shelter. Do not turn them loose in another area; they will kill birds there. Do not feed stray cats or encourage your neighbors to do so. Feeding a feral cat will give it a health advantage the birds it will hunt do not have.

According to Al Manville, of the U.S. Fish and Wildlife Services Migratory Bird Management Office (as reported in *National Wildlife*, April/May 2003 by Heidi Ridgley), feral (undomesticated) cats "could easily kill 100 million songbirds a year." That's a conservative estimate, apparent when you consider a University of Wisconsin study done in the early 1990s, as reported by Ridgley, that says about 1.4 to 2 million cats "range freely in that state [and] kill 31.4 million small mammals and 74.8 million birds a year—at a minimum."

Ridgley also wrote that an estimated 20 to 30 percent of the total kills that cats make comprises songbirds. In that issue, Ed Clark, director of the Wildlife Center of Virginia, the nation's largest wildlife hospital, says, "Cats compete with owls, hawks, weasels, and other important native predators that aren't subsidized by people and that need these creatures to survive." Many people trap cats, spay or neuter them, and take care of any health problems, then turn them loose and feed them, but allow the cats to roam freely. These cats pose a tremendous problem to wild birds. We recommend against the practice if you love birds. If you also love cats, trap them, spay or neuter them, recover their health—and keep them inside your home at all times.

Birds that survive a cat attack but sustain puncture wounds either from the cat's fangs or claws will likely die, even if taken to a veterinarian's office. Cat saliva contains many types of bacteria that will kill birds. Cats hunt day and night. They will hunt even if well fed because they are predators.

Feral cats kill millions of birds on this continent every year. It's best for both birds and cats if cats are kept indoors.

Dogs

Dogs can be a plus in a yard because they will scare away cats, snakes, squirrels, possums, raccoons, and other similar animals. If you have an aggressive dog that has killed a small animal, however, it may get into the habit of killing for sport. It happens, and it's up to you to know the habits and nature of your dog. If you suspect your neighbor's dog will kill birds, find out if it can get into your yard and either fix or erect a fence.

At the very least, a dog may harass the birds that want to feed or drink at the habitat you've set up. In which case, such an animal will prevent you from enjoying the company of any birds that might have come to your carefully constructed habitat. Know your dog. If you are unsure, set up a trial feeder and watch your dog carefully as birds come to eat. If necessary, you can fence off an area for the dog and another area for the birds.

In most instances, we recommend against setting up a feeding area in an unfenced area. By doing so, you are inviting birds into an area that they may come to trust as safe, making them easy prey for predatory animals.

> ### Keep Wild Animals Wild
>
> Never tame any wild animal to eat out of your hand: This could make it more aggressive with you than it should be, leading it to expect food from you and your home. Aggressive animals, such as raccoons, are determined and might break into your home when you aren't there. Taming a wild animal could also make it easy prey for a human who doesn't share your love of animals.
>
> In the United States, federal and state laws forbid the capturing, killing, or taming of most birds not covered under the Migratory Birds Convention Act of 1994. Exceptions include starlings and house sparrows, both introduced species.
>
> In Canada, check with the following Web sites for your province or an Environment Canada office near you: *migratorybirds.fws. gov/intrnltr/mbta/mbtintro. html* or *www. cws-scf.ec.gc.ca/enforce/contact_e. cfm*. Many birds in Canada are covered under the Migratory Birds Convention Act (1994).

Raccoons

Raccoons are aggressive animals. They feed on a variety of things, including nuts, fruit, seeds, corn, birds, and bird eggs. They don't pose a problem for most bird-watchers. Their main habitats include wooded areas near rivers and creeks or swamps. They are especially attracted to large quantities of seed. These clever mammals can open many locks intended to keep them out. Store seed in large metal containers inside a locked garage or secure outbuilding. Do not try to tame or feed raccoons from your hand, which will only encourage them to hang around your yard and could pose a danger to the birds nesting near your home. Do not shoot or otherwise harm these animals. Trapping and removing them will probably not work, unless you've already made the mistake of hand-feeding one that has become too aggressive.

Skunks

These animals, although potentially disagreeable, only marginally belong in the predator category. Skunks live under houses, in rock piles and heaps of wood. They do eat eggs, and if you've attracted ground-nesting birds, a skunk could eat the eggs, but skunks also eat berries, insects, and small rodents. If one lives on your property and becomes a pest, call an animal control officer to remove it to an uninhabited area. We recommend against trapping a skunk yourself. If you have one trapped from May (or early spring in your area) through fall, make sure to check for burrows containing a litter. Always relocate the litter with the mother.

Snakes

There are too many snakes across continental North America to name. We know that countless people are terrified of snakes and kill any they see. We recommend against this strategy. Although some snakes are venomous, they will want to avoid you as much as you want to be rid of them.

Snakes will eat bird eggs, and if hungry they will seek out nests. This is truly a case of knowing your predator. Which snakes are common in your area and what do they eat? Many snakes prefer rodents. Rodents are attracted to birdseed and other grains. If you keep your seed stores in sturdy, metal containers in a closed garage, you will have taken a huge step toward preventing rodents from accessing it. Rodents tend to multiply in relation to the readily available food supply. If you store your birdseed in an outbuilding in its original paper or plastic sack, you are, in effect, inviting mice and

Snakes will try to get into nests to eat eggs and young chicks. You can set up a wide baffle, but we recommend against using chemical repellant for snakes because it could kill birds.

rats to come and multiply. When that happens, you will also attract snakes to eat the rodents, and while they are there, the snakes may check out the birdhouses, too.

If you set up birdhouses on poles, set up baffles to prevent snakes from slithering up to the eggs and chicks. A baffle made of a circle of metal, suspended around the base of the tree, several feet up and filled with small wire mesh so the snake cannot get through it to proceed up the tree or pole will help keep any eggs safe. Although some products made to repel snakes will work, we recommend against them because they could kill a bird that walks through the powdered chemical. In the case of a pole, the taller the better. Fresh petroleum jelly on the pole, as you might apply it to repel squirrels, will also help keep snakes from climbing to the birdhouse.

Squirrels

These animals, largely in the pest category, will also occasionally eat bird eggs and chicks. Below the birdhouse, put a large downward

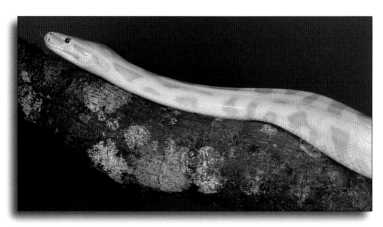

Snakes don't usually live in urban areas. If you live in a small town or rural area, though, you need to take precautions in the form of baffles and petroleum jelly to prevent them from eating eggs and chicks.

A well-placed baffle can prevent squirrels and snakes from gaining access to birdhouses and feeders.

curving baffle on the pole on which you will affix the house. Birdhouses in trees are easy for squirrels to access. Some birds are well able to fight off squirrels, snakes, and other predators. You will have to judge the predators and the birds likely to be attracted to your yard. If you judge a site too dangerous, locate any birdhouses on poles well away from trees; choose a place at least 12 feet away from the drip line or outer edge of the end of the branches of the closest tree or roofline. If you have only one tree in your yard, put several feet of smooth metal as a band around the base of the tree. If the squirrel can't jump from the roof to the tree, it can't access the nest.

Place any food for squirrels well away from the birdhouse, and keep it full of food. This will help keep squirrels from looking for eggs and chicks.

Trapping and removing squirrels is futile. More will simply fill the vacuum you've created.

Fire Ants

One pest that is marching steadily across the southern part of the United States is the fire ant. An introduced species from South America, it probably came in on a ship to a southern port, perhaps Alabama. It's hardy and travels in dirt and on equipment. It also flies to establish more colonies each time it's disturbed. Every colony has many queens, and when it rains, the queens take other ants with them, mate in the air with males, and then start their own colonies. Some queens will leave their colonies and form new ones nearby.

They swarm onto an animal that comes near their nest, or they pile quickly on an animal in its own nest so it cannot move. Ground nesting birds are at risk. Each ant bites repeatedly, injecting a strong toxin. They kill animals as large as young deer.

Fire ants are red with some black on the lower abdomen. There are native fire ants that don't pose the same problem because their natural enemies balance them. The introduced fire ants are the problem because they have no natural enemies in North America. The introduced fire ants are called RIFA.

Fire ants are difficult to kill because they won't eat anything that tastes bad. Neither gas nor water will kill them, nor will stomping on their nests (a risky proposition to the person doing the stomping). Check with your local agricultural agent to learn about the most environmentally safe and effective products. Agricultural colleges are also an excellent source of information on controlling fire ant infestations.

The following areas have known infestations:

East South Central   **Pacific**

Mountain   (not Hawaii or Alaska)

South Atlantic   **West South Central**

7 Creating a Backyard Habitat

What could be better than a yard full of birds singing, feeding, and nesting among beautiful trees, bushes, and flowers? Once you've established this kind of attractive habitat in your backyard, you'll learn it's calming to watch birds going about their lives. It's also enormously interesting—and addictive. You may begin to keep lists of the birds you see and recognize regular year-round individuals. However, first we'll help you create this habitat so you can begin to attract beautiful birds year-round.

When you first became interested in wild birds, you may have thrown some seed on the ground in your yard. Or you may have put up a feeder you bought in the supermarket along with a bag of generic wild birdseed. As your interest developed, however, you began to realize that you have various types of birds in your area and that you would like to attract as many as possible. How, you wondered, could you do that? The answer is simple: by creating a natural environment in easy, well-thought-out stages that suit the amount of time and space you have available and a budget you can work within.

Your backyard is a potential magnet for birds and other wildlife. By starting small and focusing on specific aspects, you can, step-by-step, achieve the balanced ecosystem that will provide wild birds with the basic needs they seek: shelter, water, and food.

The Benefits of a Small Wildlife Habitat

Creating a backyard ecosystem is good for the environment. As urban sprawl continues, it removes and changes the territory in which wild animals, including birds, thrive. By fashioning a wildlife refuge in your backyard, you can help keep many native plant and animal species alive. Even better: Convince your neighbors to do so, too. Seeing the increase in birds and other wildlife in your yard may win them over without further effort on your part, especially when they see that your workload tapers off as the seasons go by, while their lawn maintenance efforts and expense continue.

Neatness Doesn't Count!

By keeping things overly tidy, you can prevent your yard from attracting the birds you'd like to see. Some beautiful birds will thrive on seed heads of weeds and grasses, such as dandelions, echinacea (purple coneflowers), or sunflowers. They will also seek out parts of more desirable flowers, such as rose hips on multiflora vines—past their prime and seemingly in need of a trim. Others will look for insects on the brambles of climbing vines and in leaf litter. Letting the flower garden overgrow is healthy because it encourages insects to live out their life cycles, providing food for birds. The seed heads that eventually develop also feed the birds in your yard. Many birds need a variety of foods to flourish, including both insects and seed. Nectar eaters may also eat insects at some times of the year, or they may need them to feed to their young.

In the ideal bird habitat, aphids and spider mites may get out of your control and caterpillars may eat holes in the leaves of lovely flowers. Birds will eat some (but not all) of these animals. As it grows and develops, though, a healthy ecosystem will achieve a natural balance necessary for the benefit of the animals in it, even if not to the eye of a gardener whose goal is neatness and order.

The decrease in upkeep expense and reduced effort required by you may persuade your neighbors to create similar habitats. The larger such an area grows, the better for birds and other animals, including humans.

"Messy" areas in a yard give some birds a safe place to look for food and build secure nests. This is an easy way to attract wild birds.

Predators and Prey

By improving your yard to attract birds, you will create a habitat for many other animals, too, such as insects, arachnids, mammals, and reptiles, including many kinds of snakes. Although you don't necessarily want some of these critters around your home, they are essential to maintain a healthy backyard ecosystem. When you see a snake, simply leave it alone. If venomous snakes live in your area, never reach into logs, dense grasses, woodpiles, or holes. Make plenty of noise as you approach an area in which you plan to garden and swish a long stick through it. Snakes will readily retreat.

Predators like this young red-tailed hawk are constantly on the lookout for smaller birds.

Keep in mind that in every ecosystem, no matter how small, the daily battle for life and death takes place. Snakes, lizards, and other birds will eat some eggs and chicks. You can take measures to protect the nests and bird-feeding and -watering areas from predators, and we recommend many successful ways to do this. However, realize at the start that you cannot prevent nature from taking its course.

Owls, hawks, and other raptors are constantly on the lookout for smaller birds and mammals. Hawks, kestrels, and merlins hunt in the early morning and evening hours. Owls hunt for their prey at night. Thick hedges offer the best haven for small birds from larger birds.

In this benign view of the predator-prey relationship, we don't include pet cats, which we believe should be kept inside the owners' homes, where they, too, will be safer. If you have outside cats or your neighbors' cats come into your yard, consider carefully the amount of danger you will expose wild birds to if you create an appealing habitat. Avoid planting herbs that appeal to cats, such as catmint, or catnip. Set up feeding and watering stations for the birds with plenty of open area surrounding them, at least 10 feet from any low-growing ground cover or bushes. This will help prevent cats from sneaking up on birds. Belling a cat will not protect birds. They must see this danger to realize that they must flee. Their best means of escape is to fly, and to do that, they need room to take off.

Pest Control

A yard with a neat lawn and carefully tended flowerbeds is not the ideal home for birds. Such a yard was probably achieved by using pesticides and herbicides to control insect and weed populations. By killing insects and "weeds" (both of which birds eat) with chemicals, even natural varieties that contain pyrethrums derived from chrysanthemums, you will upset the natural balance of the ecosystem. Worse, because its effects are longer lasting, pesticides on plants can affect birds for many generations. When birds eat plants sprayed with pesticides or herbicides, those chemicals enter their systems. The chemicals may weaken the eggshells or affect the health of developing chicks. We know, for example, that the use of pesticides containing DDT nearly caused the extinction of brown pelicans, bald eagles, and peregrine falcons. Chemicals get into ground water, rivers, lakes, and oceans and then into food sources for many birds.

You may find this nonintervention policy difficult at first, but relax, observe, and enjoy your small piece of nature. You will notice that it seems some insects are out of control one year, but they'll be less noticeable the next.

One year in Houston, we carefully cultivated a passionflower vine. Its first year was a struggle, and it looked as if the vine wouldn't survive. The second year it grew and quickly covered our arbor with beautiful purple flowers. Soon we noticed clouds of butterflies hovering around the flowers and landing on the vine. Later, we watched in dismay, though, when hordes of caterpillars seemed to appear overnight. It seemed as if the voracious appetite of these caterpillars would destroy the passionflower vine. We gathered caterpillars and removed them to a nearby forest. Our chemical-free approach soon paid off, however, when we noticed an increase in birds in the yard eating many of the remaining caterpillars.

Later, we watched cocoons develop on the arbor, the house windows, and the fence. We waited eagerly to see what kind of butterflies would develop. We were rewarded again with swarms of the same beautiful butterflies that had eaten the vine.

The following spring, the passionflower vine came back more vigorous than ever, and we never saw the decimating hordes of caterpillars again. More important, the birds in the yard remained healthy.

Alternatives to Pesticides and Herbicides

An ideal bird garden uses organic techniques. We recommend using native plants, which are more disease- and insect-resistant than plants introduced to your area from another part of the continent or from another continent entirely. Introduced plants are usually referred to as exotics. Whereas some exotics are so delicate that they require a great deal of supportive care, others thrive—the weather and soil conditions suit them; they have no enemies; and they are of such an invasive nature that they crowd out native varieties. Neither is desirable in the kind of natural habitat best suited to birds. (See "Invading Plant Species" at the end of this chapter.)

Also, consider the sun and water requirements of any plants. Any tree, shrub, or ground cover that is underwatered or overwatered or that gets too much or too little light will become stressed. A stressed plant is more vulnerable to pests. A healthy

Seed-bearing flowers like sunflowers are important to birds because they provide food when they go to seed. When they go to seed, leave them alone for several weeks because they are also reseeding themselves and will grow again the following year.

plant getting the right amount of light and water will also have some pest problems, but will be more able to survive the attack without your intervention.

To help maintain the health of all of your plants, use an organic fertilizer. Mulch the base of your plants, but check the mulch for snails and slugs before you use it. To catch any slugs or snails that may escape your eye, put out a dish of beer every 10 feet or so. Snails and slugs are attracted to beer and will drown in it.

During the year, make visual checks of your plants. If you see heavily diseased branches, remove them. When you cut a branch from a tree, quickly spray the cut area with a matte, black paint (available for this purpose at hardware or garden stores). This will prevent insects that could kill your tree from entering the wound. Trees emit a scent for a few hours after being cut that would attract boring insects. The paint seals the cut and covers the odor.

Pick off excess numbers of caterpillars by hand. Check with your county agent or local Environment Canada office for the advisability of using nematodes, beneficial wasps or mites to kill a variety of insects, keeping in mind the delicate balance of nature. Either take a problem insect with you to show to the expert or be able to describe it in detail. Keep in mind that birds eat an astonishing amount of insects, especially when feeding chicks, and they will help maintain the necessary balance in your yard.

You can also buy ladybugs and praying mantises by mail or through your local garden center, but make sure they can thrive in your area of the country—or that you need them at all. Never buy any insect by mail that you haven't checked out with the local government expert; this will help you avoid importing a non-native species.

To prevent weeds from growing in areas you want to keep clear of growth, keep a thick layer of mulch on most of the exposed ground, which will prevent seeds from taking root. Learn the name of each weed that does appear in your garden to find out if it is one that birds like to eat. Never use preemergent herbicides, which can kill the plants you want to grow.

Your county extension agent or a knowledgeable employee of your local garden center can be the best source of information on how to help plants native to your area flourish without the use of chemicals.

Some Unusual Alternatives

Most gardeners, and we include ourselves, are dismayed by the fast and excess damage done by slugs and snails. We have some ways to lessen their numbers in quick (but deadly) ways that remain benign to birds and other animals. You could set out a pan of beer, which snails and slugs are attracted to, which will kill them.

The second method employs diatomaceous earth, a product you can find in gardening shops, on line, and in pool supply stores. This fine dust composed of tiny crystals slice their abdomens, and they dehydrate and die.

An Easy Beginning: Focus

Wild birds need hiding places to survive. You can begin your quest for a bird habitat by piling brush and rocks in a secluded back section of your yard, preferably a corner, which offers two-sided shelter from wind and rain. Birds will perch in these seemingly untidy areas, which give them some protection from predators and the weather. If the brush has thorns and the branches are tightly woven, the pile will offer the birds an even safer haven. Insects, lizards, and spiders will also seek refuge here, offering food for the birds.

Late in December through January, look for discarded Christmas trees. Stack them against your fence in the corner with the rest of the debris. In late winter and early spring when you and your neighbors prune trees and shrubs,

These plant shrubs have berries with branches that are tightly woven. Birds not only eat the berries, but also nest and hide from predators in these bushes.

gather and add branches to your brush or rock pile. If a tree dies in your yard, leave it. Woodpeckers will use it for nests and will seek insects in it. Add a log or two to your yard.

When trees lose their leaves, resist the temptation to rake and bag them. Leave them on the lawn as a breeding and hiding place for the insects and worms many backyard birds eat. If you sweep the leaves off patios or sidewalks, simply gather them and use them as mulch on top of the soil under existing trees and bushes. Earthworms, millipedes, and other small animals will seek shelter under this warming cover, where birds will look for them.

To avoid becoming overwhelmed with the task of creating a wild-bird habitat, start small. Choose a focus area. Where will you most likely watch the birds that come into your yard? From your kitchen or living room window? A sitting room?

Try to plant trees that are native to your area. They are exactly what birds that live in and migrate through your area need to find food: insects attracted to those trees or their fruit. What's more, these trees will grow without much effort from you.

Within easy viewing distance, locate the center of your project. As the yard develops, you may include other focus areas, but at first, plan on only one. Taking another tack, you may choose an existing element, such as a large, beautiful tree; a feeding area; or a creek, pond, or birdbath that attracts birds already. You could then set up a viewing area in your home that makes it easy to watch the spot and get the most enjoyment out of watching the birds without disturbing them.

Making a Plan

Although your layout will begin in your mind, put it on paper before you buy any plants. Make a rough drawing of your yard. Note fence or border areas, as well as existing plants and buildings. Watch your yard for birds for a few weeks. Note which plants they favor and the kinds of birds that come to your yard. You may want to list them. Now, using a guide for your area, find out which birds migrate through your area or live there year-round. Make a note of the ones you'd like to come to your yard, the foods they eat and the types of areas in which they nest. Use this as part of your guide to making your yard the habitat you have in mind. This can save you money, too, because a number of plants in your yard probably already draw birds there.

We recommend you plant your yard in layers: a low-cut area around the feeders and water source—a natural focus because they attract birds. Next plan for ground cover, shrubs, and trees. This will form a habitat that will look natural to birds, something like a meadow and forest would appear from the air, an appealing place for birds to investigate.

Take a careful look at your focal point. This should include an area of mowed grass about 10 feet from the center to any higher ground cover. Leave part of this as dirt that birds can use for a dust bath, or create an area surrounded by bricks to prevent grass from overgrowing it. Keep the bricks low—no higher than the level of the dirt. Use them only to prevent grass from growing over the area. (Wild birds need dust and water baths to maintain the health of their feathers. Dust may help wild birds rid themselves of parasites, such as mites.) Make sure the dust-bath area is located far from any ground cover, where a predator, such as a cat, could lurk. Birds are especially vulnerable while they bathe in water or dust. Make the area large enough for two medium-sized birds to bathe. Any larger and you will likely see sparrows squabbling with each other over the territory. You may also see birds sunbathing in this area, especially if they feel secure. Birds need sunlight to help their bodies absorb and properly use the nutrients in their food.

This low-cut area will help keep birds safe from predators and will allow you to watch them as they feed, drink, and bathe. In some regions you can plant grass that doesn't grow high, but birds are messy and will drop seeds from the feeders, which will eventually grow taller than any low-growing grass. Again, take the most relaxed approach and use whatever grass you already have in the area. If you've chosen a large tree as your focal point, you may already have a hard-packed dirt area in which grass won't grow. This will work into your plan as a good dust-bathing area.

Just outside the low-growing area, sketch in a section of "rough" grass that you won't mow. This can include low-growing herbs or grasses, such as buffalo grass, Indian grass, deer grass, blue oat grass, wild buckwheat, or reed grasses that you will let go to seed. These grasses are noninvasive—that is, they won't move aggressively into areas where you don't want them. Do not use Bermuda for this purpose because it's invasive: It quickly puts out runners with roots at the base of each clump of blades. This makes it a great grass for people who want manicured lawns that they will mow. It's tough and covers ground quickly, but it will also choke out other plants. In this area, too, you can sow birdseed. Just throw it on the surface and water it. The seeds will grow and develop seed pods the birds will love.

Add a few areas where you will either add soil to make hilly places, or you can dig into the soil in one place and move it to another. Add some rocks to the small hills. Plant grasses in these areas. This not only will add visual interest to your backyard but also will add places where birds will seek out the insects that will hide there. If you can find rocks alongside a country road, so much the better, but they are usually inexpensive at garden or specialty rock centers.

Berries are always a welcome sight to birds that are passing through.

The next layer would consist of low shrubs planted in clumps. To make it pleasing to your eye, you can make the overall shape of the border between grasses and shrubs somewhat asymmetrical, or uneven. Or, depending on your growing zone, you could choose low-growing, flowering ground cover, such as gazanias and periwinkles (vinca) that provide food for some birds as well as cover. In this area, too, you can sow wildflowers that will go to seed to feed birds and to help produce next year's crop. Flowering perennials to consider include lupines, wild lilac, scarlet monkeyflower, foothill penstemon, fuchsia, butterfly weed, coneflower, goldenrods, asters, black-eyed susans, bee balm, bergamot, columbine, and violets. The seeds and flowers on these plants will attract birds. Don't try to maintain neat borders or distinctive areas; you want to make it look as natural as possible.

Behind the ground cover, plant shrubs, especially those that will bear fruit. Again, a variety is most important. Make sure you have plants that flower and develop mature fruit at different times of the year. Among these shrubs include some evergreens to offer winter protection for birds that do not migrate. Plant some deciduous shrubs, too. Their dropped leaves will form a vital layer of mulch in winter and spring. Group them to create multiple levels. Depending on your area of the country, you might choose from the following: blueberry or huckleberry, currant, cranberry, raspberry, multiflora rose, chokecherry, juniper, yaupon holly (shrub variety), American holly, bayberry, winterberry, elderberry, hackberry (shrub variety), salal, sage, or wax myrtle. This is only a limited suggestion. (Before you plant holly, talk to an expert. Some female plants will not bear fruit unless a male tree is nearby to pollinate them.)

Behind the shrubs, near the perimeter of your yard, plant trees. Plan this section carefully. Before you plant any tree, take into account the width of its top when it matures. Don't plant any tree so close to another that the two will crowd each other.

If the existing trees are healthy, plant trees nearby that complement them. Be sure to allow enough room for everything to fit when you have a mature yard. Some evergreen trees make a good addition to your yard, again offering good year-round protection and varied limb size for perching and nesting. Among the trees that offer birds food, you might choose some of the following: oak, pine, dogwood, cottonwood, aspen, cherry, redbud, chokecherry, apple, plum, fig, yaupon holly (tree variety), birch, beech, hawthorn, or hackberry. Again, balance your choice with evergreen and deciduous trees. Plan for some that bear red fruit or have red leaves that surround the fruit because birds are especially attracted to red.

Some trees, such as hackberry, which grows in the southern and southeastern United States, are considered by some to be pest or trash trees because they grow so easily; however, birds eat the fruit of these trees and then spread the seeds in their droppings. These trees grow quickly and feed birds. In your area, temper any advice about local trash trees with information on the fruit they produce for wild animals and their ease of care.

Next to the edge of your yard, plant evergreens, such as Douglas fir, oak, or madrone, to give birds protection during cold or windy weather.

If you have a fence, consider adding vines that will cover it quickly and become a thicket. This will offer birds a safe place to nest and hide from predators. Vines to consider include bougainvillea, trumpet, blackberry, raspberry, wild grape, passionflower, and Virginia creeper. All offer food as well as protection for birds. Keep light requirements in mind before planting trees and vines near each other.

Evergreens can provide protection for birds during cold and windy weather.

In hot, dry climates, you may want to develop a garden that combines some native flowering plants and cactus. Low-growing cactus such as claretcup could be combined arid-tolerant shrubs, such as globemallow and dorri sage. Behind these, plant shrubs such as desert marigold, penstemon, ajamete, barberry, butterfly bush, and fairyduster. Taller plants could include ocotillo, saguaro, desert willow, mesquite, and Joshua trees.

Other Plant Considerations

Begin by listing each plant that you would like to put in your yard. Research the most extreme heat and cold levels, and rain cycles and rain levels possible for your area.

Look specifically at the water needs of each plant. How much water does the plant require and how does that meet with water availability in your area, especially in summer? Under drought conditions, some areas put in place heavy water-restriction regulations and either heavily fine people who ignore such ordinances or charge so much for water that taking care of thirsty plants becomes impractical or impossible.

Native plants are most likely to survive the normal drought, heavy rain cycles, and other weather conditions common to your region. Next, check the plant for hardiness to heat and cold. To make it easier on yourself, purchase perennials for the ground cover. Some will not only come back after a hard winter but also require a certain number of cold days to do well. Gardening books available at your local garden center can help you locate the zone you live in and give you information on plants native to your region.

If a plant can thrive in your area, check out its value as food for wildlife of all kinds. Does it bear edible fruit or berries? Will it produce seed heads attractive to birds? Does the plant draw insects that birds eat? Do the birds that live in or migrate through your area use the flowers or fruit of that plant for nutrition? (You can learn about bird migration patterns from some birding guides or online.)

When mature, will this plant fit well in your yard, or will it become too large and need to be removed? Can each of the lower-level plants do well in the amount of sun or shade in your yard once the taller trees and shrubs mature?

Using the advice of your county extension agent, Environment Canada expert, or garden center, sow enough plants so your yard will offer a food source to birds year-round. The more diversity you achieve in your yard, the better. You will then feed the maximum number of birds.

On your layout, plan for shade areas and plant shrubs there that will tolerate shade. When you go to the nursery or look in books for plants, you will notice that some are tolerant of full or partial shade. Such shrubs will grow well during the immature period of your garden and later when the large trees are fully grown. If you already have mature trees, plant only those shrubs and flowers under them that can tolerate shade conditions. Also, take into consideration the water needs of any tree already in the yard. Don't plant shrubs or flowers that need a lot of water under a tree with low water needs.

Birdscaping a Small Yard

If you live in an apartment or a condominium, you still need a plan, even if your yard is small. In fact, a plan may be most important for your yard because of the potential for plants to quickly overgrow the space you have.

Vines that become thick and tangled may offer you the best option to plant against fences. Many of these vines can offer birds protection from weather and predators, as well as good nesting sites and food. Take care, however, to choose a vine that won't take over your yard or your neighbors' yards. Trumpet vine is terrific for attracting hummingbirds, but it's also invasive and will quickly grow over a fence. It may soon become so heavy that it will break down the fence. It can also begin sprouting up all over your yard. Instead, you might find a multiflora climbing rose, clematis, honeysuckle, virgin's bower, or wild grape more suitable for your yard.

In small areas, comparatively diminutive pomegranate trees and dwarf fruit trees can add a focal point with shelter, food, and perching places with-

Brightly colored flowers, especially those that are red or orange, attract hummingbirds that may migrate through your area in spring and fall or live in your area all summer. Trumpet vine, although an aggressive plant, requires little or no care and attracts these tiny green gems. Its aggressive nature is a factor to consider, however.

out overpowering the available space. Other native shrubs to consider include the Labrador tea, red-berried elder, various dogwood shrubs, bearberry, black haw, dwarf sumac, swamp rose, sweet gale, or the northern gooseberry.

Plan for ground cover with care. Remember to give birds enough room to see and fly away from predators.

An Apartment Habitat

You can make an apartment balcony attractive to birds. At the same time, adding some plants, food, and water for birds can enhance your own living area. Large pots with flowering shrubs on the sides of a balcony can offer food for some birds, such as hummingbirds or small finches. Container gardening with some small evergreen trees and shrubs in pots can work well. Offer a variety with branches of differing sizes of plants native to your area. These can offer security to birds as they rest and also a haven in a cold wind or low temperatures.

Add to this a variety of feeding stations with seed. Also add nectar feeders for hummingbirds. A shallow birdbath will offer birds water to drink and a secure place to bathe. Birdhouses hung high on the sidewalls can offer shelter and nesting places for a variety of birds. (See Chapter 8.)

Birdbaths have the potential to add a problem to your yard: Since the advent of West Nile virus, mosquitoes are more than just a nuisance in North America. Change the water often and faithfully. In warm weather, mosquito eggs can develop into adult mosquitoes in just 2 days. Empty the water every day to avoid this problem. If you have a birdbath or small pond that's too large to empty regularly, add some pond fish, which will eat the eggs. For hardy fish, look in local ponds or creeks.

A trellis against one or both sidewalls of the patio could support attractive vines. Choose varieties that can survive in the light available to your balcony. Brightly flowering varieties are most likely to catch the attention of birds as they fly by.

If you have a small patio with a large glass window or sliding glass door, hang streamers that flutter in the breeze. These will help birds avoid flying into the glass. Stick-on pictures of hawks and owls don't work as well. Birds either get used to them or don't register the danger associated with them. Another goal is to make sure the windows don't reflect the sky well, which birds will react to as if it were open air. Reflecting windows, especially large windows, kill millions of birds every year.

Money, Money, Money

Don't forget cost. Set up a budget and stick to it. Consider that, with the exception of trees and larger shrubs, you should buy three to five of each plant to form natural-looking groupings. Depending on the area you need to cover and how far each plant spreads, you may need more than 10 ground-cover plants. Price the plants you'd love, but also list less-expensive alternatives that would serve birds just as well.

Although these plants cost money when you initially add them to your yard, that's largely a one-time cost. As the new plants thrive, you will not have to spend the time, money, and effort on your bird habitat that it now takes you to maintain a well-manicured yard. The chemicals, mowers, and trimmers you have used will be largely things of the past.

Plants to Attract Hummingbirds

Hummingbirds top many lists as the most interesting bird in any backyard. You can attract them to your yard with feeders to supplement your flowers, but flower nectar provides the best source of fuel. As they feed in your yard, watch them fly backward (they are the only bird that can do so) and fight with other hummingbirds to defend their territory. If you watch closely, you can see them rest on a small branch where they feel safe. The following is an abbreviated list of plants that attract hummingbirds. In general, they are drawn to red, orange, yellow, pink, and purple plants.

Flowers
Fuschia, geranium, phlox, bluebells, lupines, lilies, iris, columbine, mosquito plant, claretcup cactus, beardlip penstemon

Vines
Trumpet, honeysuckle

Shrubs
Flowering currant, chuparosa, desert lavender, red yucca, fuschia, ocotillo cactus, century plant, scarlet hedge nettle, scarlet monkeyflower, oleander

Trees
Desert willow, California buckeye

What About Water?

A vital part of your birdscaped yard should be a clean, dependable source of water for your feathered friends. This simple, basic need is often overlooked when planning a birdscaped yard, so make sure to include it from your first simple sketches as you come up with your plan. Birds need water to drink and to bathe in, and having a good water source can make your yard attractive to birds and other wildlife.

Having a water source in your yard will ensure that you attract a wide variety of birds, too. Among the species that flock to birdbaths and other backyard water sources are bluebirds, buntings, cardinals, flycatchers, goldfinches, hummingbirds, jays, mockingbirds, orioles, owls, quail, roadrunners, robins, sapsuckers, tanagers, thrushes, warblers, and woodcocks.

Why It's Important

Like all animals, birds have a physiologic need for water. They require water to digest food properly, to eliminate wastes from their bodies, and to maintain good health. Most birds can find enough water in their surroundings, but desert-dwelling birds face special challenges because of the dry climate in which they live. These birds obtain part of the water they need by consuming juicy insects. They may also take in water by eating cactus or other succulent plants.

According to Dr. Margaret Rowe, who wrote *Feathers, Flyways and Fast Food*, birds obtain water in three ways: from their food, from their drinking water, and from chemical processes that take place in their bodies.

Dr. Rowe added that birds economize on water by removing wastes from their bodies in semisolid form. For example, wastes containing nitrogen are removed in a paste containing uric acid. By contrast, mammals use more than 20 times as much water to remove the same amount of nitrogen-containing waste in the form of urine.

Make a plan before you begin planting your yard. Focus on a birdbath of water and a dust-bathing area. Remember to plan for cats by not planting bushy plants near the birdbath and feeders.

According to avian veterinarian Gerry Doerrestein, seed-eating birds have the greatest need for additional water in their diets. Nectar-, insect-, and fruit-eating birds receive much of the moisture they require from their diets, as do meat-eating raptors, but seed-eating birds need supplemental water sources because their basic diets are so dry.

In addition to the basic health needs fulfilled by water, some birds require water to obtain food. Ducks, geese, herons, egrets, gulls, and other shore birds depend on bodies of water for plants, insects, invertebrates, fish, and other food sources. A well-designed backyard pond or water garden can attract a wider variety of bird species than a simple birdbath, so consider which types of birds you want to attract as you add water to your birdscaping plans.

Still other types of birds need water to successfully build nests and raise young. The cliff swallow, for example, requires water to build its mud-based nests. The city of San Juan Capistrano, California relies on its annual visit from cliff swallows that nest in the eaves of the historic mission there to draw bird-loving tourists from around the world. This annual event is so popular that it spawned a popular song, "When the Swallows Come Back to Capistrano," in 1939. The birds, which have been returning to the town since the late 1700s, used to swarm the mission in large flocks. As the town and the surrounding farmlands have developed, though, the birds have had to seek other nest sites because water sources near the mission had dried up or been rerouted over time. After attention was drawn to the problem in the late 1990s, the city took steps to attract birds back to the mission by recreating water sources to provide the birds with the mud they require for nest building and by releasing insects that the birds enjoy eating near the mission.

How to Provide Water

In some cases, providing water for wild birds in your backyard is easy: Property owners who have an existing pond, stream, or other wetland on their properties should do their best to preserve it in as natural a state as possible.

Providing water for birds can be as simple as setting up and maintaining a birdbath.

If you aren't lucky enough to have a ready-made water source in your yard, don't worry. Many options, ranging from simple buckets to complex ponds and waterfalls, exist to add water to a backyard setting.

Providing water for wild birds can be as simple as leaving a soaker hose on in your yard during the day or turning on a sprinkler head in the evening for a half hour or so; it can be as ornate as an intricate birdbath with running water in summer or heated water in winter,

Try to change birdbath water every day to prevent mosquitoes from completing their life cycle.

or a garden pond with a shallow waterfall that contains rocks birds can stand on while they drink or bathe. The elaborateness of your finished design is up to you; we will provide different options from which you can choose, based on the size of your yard, your budget, and your plumbing and landscaping skills.

Make sure you provide water for wild birds in an area that's separate from the feeding stations in your yard. This will give the birds an opportunity to clean seeds and seed hulls off their feet before drinking or bathing, which will help keep the watering station relatively clean. A neighbor of ours has a low-lying birdbath that is placed too close to his feeding stations. The feeders (one full of seed, the other full of hummingbird nectar) receive a steady stream of visitors throughout the day, but the bath is only used immediately after he's dumped out the seed debris and refilled it with fresh, clean water.

If your birdbath is a busy place, it will quickly become fouled with feathers, seed, dirt, bird droppings, and other debris, so frequent cleaning will help keep feathered visitors healthy.

The simplest way to give birds in your yard a water source is to punch a small hole in the bottom of a bucket or a plastic gallon jug filled with water (if you recycle a milk jug, be sure to wash it thoroughly before using it as a bird waterer). Hang the bucket or jug by its handle over a stoneware plate or terra-cotta saucer, and wait to see what types of birds you attract. If the water doesn't seem to drip out fast enough to suit you or the birds, enlarge the hole or add more openings to the bucket or jug. Remember to refill the container often to provide a reliable water source.

This simple method of providing water not only gives birds a chance to drink and bathe, but also will help attract birds to your yard with its dripping sound. You can also attach a garden hose with a nozzle to the trunk of a tree with some garden twine tied at 1-foot intervals along the length of the hose and run the hose up to a sturdy limb. Suspend the nozzle from the limb, and let the water run just enough to create a steady drip on a flat surface, such as a large rock or a plate in an open part of your yard. Another simple solution is to fill a shallow saucer with water and place it out in an area of your yard that allows birds to drink safely without the fear of predators. If you choose this route, make sure to refill the saucer at least daily (more often in warmer weather) with clean water, and scrub the saucer with a clean wire brush and a solution of nine parts water to one part bleach weekly to keep the water (and the saucer) clean and fresh! Rinse the saucer thoroughly to remove all traces of the bleach before refilling it with water.

You could also provide water for wild birds in a birdbath. Your birdbath can be as simple as a glass pie plate full of water or a hose trickling into an upside-down garbage can lid anchored to the ground with a rock. You could provide an elab-

The sound of dripping water will attract birds for drinking and bathing. Make sure to keep the bucket filled.

orate ready-made bath with pedestal and circulating fountain. (If you provide a ground-level birdbath, make sure to locate it in a part of your yard that is free from shrubs and low-lying ground cover, where predators can lie in wait for wild birds.) Readers who live in areas that have long, cold winters should consider a heated birdbath. It's difficult for birds to find water during an extended freeze.

If you're handy with tools, you can construct your own birdbath using plans found in many do-it-yourself books, or you can design your own. On the other hand, if you aren't blessed with construction skills, you can choose from among a number of different birdbath designs at your local garden center or wild-bird specialty store.

Whatever type of bath you provide, make sure to set up an "island" in the middle of the birdbath for birds to sit on while drinking. You can invert a glass or metal pie plate or place some flat stones that are slightly higher than the water level of the birdbath for the birds to use as perches. Keep in mind that birds really only enjoy getting into the water at about knee level, so you'll have to take steps to ensure that the visitors to your bath can enjoy themselves in comfort!

Experts recommend a birdbath bowl that measures at least 12 inches across. (Larger is better, but your selection will depend on your budget and on the size of your yard.) It should range in depth from $1/2$ to 1 inch along the edges down to $2 1/2$ to 3 inches in the deepest part of the center to accommodate the needs of both smaller and larger birds. If you've chosen a pedestal-style bath, the pedestal should be at least 3 feet high to further protect bathing and drinking birds from cats and other predators.

Because birds like to wade into their baths from the edge of the bath, make sure the surface of the bath isn't too slippery for birds to walk on it when it's wet. Choose a birdbath that's sturdy and easy to clean, such as one made of concrete. If the birdbath you choose is made of plastic or another lightweight material, make sure to anchor it securely in the ground before birds begin to use it. Wobbly, unstable baths can be unsafe for people or pets in your yard, and they can also cause a mess if overturned.

Resist the temptation to purchase any wooden birdbaths you may encounter. Wooden birdbaths can be difficult to keep clean, and they can be prone to rot and other problems. Also, avoid any baths you may find that are lead-lined because harmful substances can over time leach out of the lead lining and harm the birds.

To protect the ground around your birdbath from being flooded at bath time, create a drainage area under the bath that will effectively remove water. To do this, dig a 4-inch-deep cavity under the bath and fill it with gravel. Extend the graveled area so it covers about 4 feet around the bath.

For something more complex, consider adding a garden pond to your yard. The level of detail is up to you: Some pond builders dig a hole and line it with heavy plastic or concrete, then add a pump, water, and some plants, whereas others prefer to install a ready-made fiberglass shell and add water and all the trimmings. Whatever level of pond building you undertake, use the soil you've dug to form banks and berms around your pond. Certain bird species, such as swallows or phoebes, need wet soil to build their nests, and other species, such as herons or egrets, may be attracted to the invertebrates and insects that end up calling your pond home.

As with a birdbath, remember to include some flat, smooth stones in your pond design that birds can stand on while drinking. Most birds aren't well suited for wading or swimming; they need something to perch on as they drink.

After you've built your pond, resist the temptation to fill it with chemicals to control algae or reduce the number of hatching mosquitoes or to keep it from freezing. Mosquitoes need still water to complete their breeding cycle (about 2 days in warm weather). If you have a small waterfall that keeps the water moving, it will help keep the pond from becoming a breeding area. If you have a still pond, add some goldfish or minnows, which will thrive on the mosquito larvae. The wild birds that come to your yard will depend on your pond as their water source, which means it needs to be clean and chemical-free!

To further enhance your birdbath or pond, add a mister or dripper to attract birds. Some companies also offer misters or drippers with recirculating pump systems to maximize water usage. Another way to enhance your water source is by adding a waterfall to your pond or birdbath. These are created by using a pump system hidden in a rocky outcrop. Ask your wild bird store or garden center for recommendations if you are interested in adding these features to the water source in your yard.

Pond Plants to Consider

As you plan your pond, you might want to include some of the following plants to add interest and variety to the area. This list is by no means conclusive; ask for suggestions at your local pond specialty store about which plants grow best in your area. Some of these plants provide food for birds.

In the pond: Waterweed, water milfoils, water lettuce, water hyacinth, water lilies, frogbit, duckweed, golden club, sweet flag, common buttonbush, arrowhead, and cattails.

At the water's edge: Umbrella and tufted sedge, soft rush, arrowheads, water lilies, Japanese iris, brilliant red cardinal flower, monkeyflowers, forget-me-nots, turtleheads, and marsh marigolds.

Controlling Algae

One drawback of having a backyard pond is the tendency toward algae growth, especially during warm weather. Although you may be tempted to try chemical solutions to an algae problem, keep in mind that when you kill algae with such methods, those chemicals can also harm the birds and other animals that drink from your pond.

To control algae effectively, first you must control materials that it can use for food in the pond. Because fish waste is the most common nutrient source for algae in a pond, you should stop feeding any fish you might have added to it until you've controlled the algae. Fish will survive on the algae, as well as insect larvae and other edible materials in the pond.

Plant fast-growing aquatic plants that will steal nutrients from the algae. Look for plants such as water celery, water hyacinth, and water mint at your pond specialty store. Plant them in a gravel bed that has water circulating through it to allow the plant roots to absorb nutrients more efficiently. In the case of floating plants, such as water hyacinth, place them in a spot where water can flow through the roots. Thin these plants regularly to ensure they don't overgrow the pond.

In addition to nutrients in the water, algae needs sunlight to grow; limit the amount of sunlight that falls onto your pond. You can do this by planting evergreen shade trees (deciduous trees are likely to drop leaves in the pond every fall) around the pond or by installing an umbrella or patio cover. You can also add a sufficient number of floating plants, such as duckweed or frogbit, to help shade your pond.

Aeration can also help reduce algae growth in a pond. Aerating the pond with a strong pump and filter system will help retard algae growth.

Biological clarifiers also help remove algae from a pond. These clarifiers break down waste materials in the pond and help remove it from the water more quickly. A recently rediscovered biological clarifier is barley straw. An average-size garden pond (not containing more than 1,200 gallons of water) needs one 8-ounce straw bundle in spring and one at the beginning of summer. As the straw begins to break down, it releases chemicals into the water that reduce the amount of algae growth. However, this process takes about a month to begin working effectively.

Where to Provide Water

Where you establish your watering site for wild birds is entirely up to you. A lot will depend on the design of your birdscaped yard and the location of your viewing window. Set up your watering station with the following tips in mind:

- Keep it near a hose for easy cleaning and refilling. Set yourself up to succeed in this endeavor by making it as easy as possible to keep the watering station full of fresh, clean water.
- Keep it in a clear area so predators can't sneak up on the birds as they drink and bathe. Make sure birds that come to the waterer have hiding places nearby that they can easily get to whether they are wet or dry. If your watering station is a birdbath, situate it in a spot in your yard that offers wet birds a refuge, such as a plant with thin, thorny branches that cannot support the weight of a cat, larger bird, or other predator.
- Unless a pond is your watering station, keep the water source off the ground to further protect birds from harm. You can do this in several ways, either by suspending the waterer from a sturdy tree branch or porch overhang or securely attaching it to a pedestal.

When to Provide Water

If you're going to provide water for wild birds in your yard, provide it all year. Birds need dependable water supplies throughout the year, but especially during extreme heat or cold, when natural water sources may not be available. (In summer, they can dry up, and in winter, they can freeze over.)

During warmer weather, birds need water to rehydrate themselves and to cool their bodies. Unlike people and other mammals, birds don't sweat. Having cool water in which to bathe can help them cool themselves, and it's fun to watch the birds fluff, dip, and bob in the water.

When the weather turns cold, birds need water, too. The National Audubon Society reports that it requires 12 times as much energy to obtain water from ice as to warm water from freezing point to body heat, so having access to running water is vital. Birds also need water in which to bathe during cold weather to maintain their feathers in tip-top shape.

To help provide water for wild birds during winter, add a small heater to your birdbath made for the purpose. (Ask for recommendations at your wild-bird store or garden center or order from one of the many catalogs devoted to the care of wild birds.) *Never* use chemicals or antifreeze in the birdbath because they can harm or kill birds.

Fruit- and Seed-bearing Plants That Attract Birds

Consider adding some of the following trees, shrubs, flowers, and vines to your landscaping. They are attractive to wild birds because of the fruit or seeds they produce.

Fruit Trees			
Name of Plant	**Suitable Regions**	**Flowers**	**Fruits/Seed**
Crabapple	West North Central, New England, East South Central, East North Central, Mountain, Middle Atlantic, South Atlantic, Pacific, West South Central British Columbia; western Yukon Territory; southern Alberta, Saskatchewan, Manitoba, Ontario, and Quebec; New Brunswick, Nova Scotia, and Prince Edward Island	Spring	Fall/winter
Dogwood	West North Central, New England, East South Central, East North Central, Mountain, Middle Atlantic, South Atlantic, Pacific, West South Central British Columbia; western Yukon Territory; southern Alberta, Saskatchewan, Manitoba, Ontario, and Quebec; New Brunswick, Nova Scotia, and Prince Edward Island	Spring	Summer/fall
Hackberry	West North Central, New England, East South Central, East North Central, Mountain, Middle Atlantic, South Atlantic, Pacific, West South Central British Columbia; western Yukon Territory; southern Alberta, Saskatchewan, Manitoba, Ontario, and Quebec; New Brunswick, Nova Scotia, and Prince Edward Island	Late spring	Fall

Fruit Trees *(continued)*			
Name of Plant	**Suitable Regions**	**Flowers**	**Fruits/Seed**
Hawthorn	West North Central, New England, East South Central, East North Central, Mountain, Middle Atlantic, South Atlantic, Pacific, West South Central British Columbia; western Yukon Territory; southern Alberta, Saskatchewan, Manitoba, Ontario, and Quebec; New Brunswick, Nova Scotia, and Prince Edward Island	Spring	Summer/fall
Persimmon	West North Central, New England, East South Central, East North Central, Mountain, Middle Atlantic, South Atlantic, Pacific, West South Central British Columbia; western Yukon Territory; southern Alberta, Saskatchewan, Manitoba, Ontario, and Quebec; New Brunswick, Nova Scotia, and Prince Edward Island	Summer	Fall/winter
Sumac	All areas of the United States (Avoid poison sumac, which is really not sumac but a relative of poison ivy.) British Columbia; western Yukon Territory; southern Alberta, Saskatchewan, Manitoba, Ontario, and Quebec; New Brunswick, Nova Scotia, and Prince Edward Island	Fall	
Mountain Ash (various species)	Mountains of East and West coasts of the continent	Spring	Fall

Fruit-bearing Shrubs			
Name of Plant	Suitable Regions	Flowers	Fruits/Seed
Alpine bearberry	Northwest Territory	Late spring	Summer
American Beautyberry	Eastern United States		Fall
Bayberry	East and Southeast of the United States, some along the West Coast into Alaska Far southern Ontario, all of Nova Scotia and Prince Edward Island		Fall
Blackberry	West North Central, New England, East South Central, East North Central, Mountain, Middle Atlantic, South Atlantic, Pacific, West South Central British Columbia; western Yukon Territory; southern Alberta, Saskatchewan, Manitoba, Ontario, and Quebec; New Brunswick, Nova Scotia, and Prince Edward Island	Summer	Summer
Cotoneaster	East South Central, Mountain, South Atlantic, Pacific, West South Central	Fall	Winter
Holly	East South Central, East North Central, Mountain, Middle Atlantic, South Atlantic, Pacific, West South Central British Columbia; western Yukon Territory; southern Alberta, Saskatchewan, Manitoba, Ontario, and Quebec; New Brunswick, Nova Scotia, and Prince Edward Island	Summer	Fall/winter

Fruit-bearing Shrubs *(continued)*			
Name of Plant	Suitable Regions	Flowers	Fruits/Seed
Hawthorns	Across the United States British Columbia; western Yukon Territory; southern Alberta, Saskatchewan, Manitoba, Ontario, and Quebec; New Brunswick, Nova Scotia, and Prince Edward Island	Summer	Fall
Pyracantha	East South Central, East North Central, Mountain, Middle Atlantic, South Atlantic, Pacific, West South Central British Columbia; western Yukon Territory; southern Alberta, Saskatchewan, Manitoba, Ontario, and Quebec; New Brunswick, Nova Scotia, and Prince Edward Island	Summer	Fall
Saltbush (four-winged)	Desert Southwest		Fall
Saskatoon Serviceberry (Juneberry, shadblow)	East North Central, Mountain, Middle Atlantic, Pacific, South Central British Columbia; western Yukon Territory; southern Alberta, Saskatchewan, Manitoba, Ontario, and Quebec; New Brunswick, Nova Scotia, and Prince Edward Island	Spring	Spring
Viburnum	East South Central, South Atlantic, West South Central United States		Fall
Yellow Rattle	Northwest Territories		Fall

Fruit-bearing Vines			
Name of Plant	Suitable Regions	Flowers	Fruits/Seed
Grape	West North Central, New England, East South Central, East North Central, Mountain, Middle Atlantic, South Atlantic, Pacific, West South Central British Columbia; western Yukon Territory; southern Alberta, Saskatchewan, Manitoba, Ontario, and Quebec; New Brunswick, Nova Scotia, and Prince Edward Island	Summer	Summer/fall
Wild Strawberry	West North Central, New England, East South Central, East North Central, Mountain, Middle Atlantic, South Atlantic, Pacific, West South Central British Columbia; western Yukon Territory; southern Alberta, Saskatchewan, Manitoba, Ontario, and Quebec; New Brunswick, Nova Scotia, and Prince Edward Island	Spring	Summer

Seed-bearing Trees			
Name of Plant	Suitable Regions	Flowers	Fruits/Seed
Aspen	Various species across the continent	Spring	
Hickory	West North Central, New England, East South Central, East North Central, Mountain, Middle Atlantic, South Atlantic, Pacific, West South Central Coastal British Columbia and Yukon Territory; Southern Alberta, Saskatchewan, Manitoba, Ontario, and Quebec; New Brunswick, Nova Scotia, and Prince Edward Island	n/a	Winter

Seed-bearing Trees *(continued)*			
Name of Plant	Suitable Regions	Flowers	Fruits/Seed
Oak	West North Central, New England, East South Central, East North Central, Mountain, Middle Atlantic, South Atlantic, Pacific, West South Central British Columbia; western Yukon Territory; southern Alberta, Saskatchewan, Manitoba, Ontario, and Quebec; New Brunswick, Nova Scotia, and Prince Edward Island	n/a	Summer/fall
Pecan	East South Central Mountain, South Atlantic, Pacific, West South Central	n/a	Fall
Poplar	Various species across the continent	Spring	Fall
Pine	Various species across the continent	Spring	Fall
Fir	Various species across the continent		Fall
Seed-bearing Shrubs and Flowers			
Name of Plant	Suitable Regions	Flowers	Fruits/Seed
Cosmos	West North Central, New England, East South Central, East North Central, Mountain, Middle Atlantic, South Atlantic, Pacific, West South Central British Columbia; western Yukon Territory; southern Alberta, Saskatchewan, Manitoba, Ontario, and Quebec; New Brunswick, Nova Scotia, and Prince Edward Island	Summer/fall	Fall/winter

Name of Plant	Suitable Regions	Flowers	Fruits/Seed
Marigold	West North Central, New England, East South Central, East North Central, Mountain, Middle Atlantic, South Atlantic, Pacific, West South Central British Columbia; western Yukon Territory; southern Alberta, Saskatchewan, Manitoba, Ontario, and Quebec; New Brunswick, Nova Scotia, and Prince Edward Island	Spring/fall	Fall
Sunflower	West North Central, New England, East South Central, East North Central, Mountain, Middle Atlantic, South Atlantic, Pacific, West South Central British Columbia; western Yukon Territory; southern Alberta, Saskatchewan, Manitoba, Ontario, and Quebec; New Brunswick, Nova Scotia, and Prince Edward Island	Summer/fall	Fall

A common sunflower in bloom is extremely attractive to birds.

Invading Plant Species

Some non-native plants have proven so hardy and lived on the continent so long, we have come to think of them as belonging here. In truth, many of these invasive species are spreading across North America, crowding out native plants. They don't feed the birds and other animals as well as native plants do, so when we can, it's a good idea to weed them out and replace them with species native to your area. Following is a list of plants to look for and remove:

Alphalpha
Bamboo
Black locust (in Canada)
Blue grass (both Canada and Kentucky
  varieties are from Eurasia)
Canadian thistle
Cedar
Common buckthorn
Dog strangling vine (Canada)
English ivy
Garlic mustard
Glossy buckthorn
Himalayan blackberry (Western North
  America)
Hoary Alyssum
Kudzu vine (United States)
Leafy spurge
Lilac
Nodding thistle
Norway maple
Scotch broom
Siberian peashrub

Smooth broom grass
Spotted knapweed
St. John's wort
Tatarian honeysuckle
Teasel
White mulberry
Wild marjoram
Yellow and white sweet clover

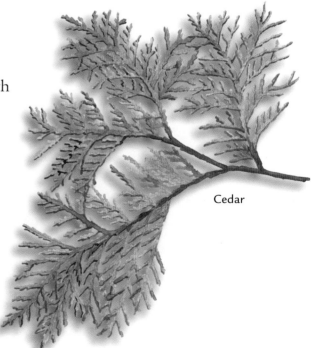

Cedar

8 Birdhouses and Nest Boxes

Once you've established the feeding stations in your yard, you may want to set up some birdhouses and nest boxes. Birdhouses and nest boxes provide an additional dimension to the wild bird habitat you're providing by giving birds not only a place to raise their young during spring and summer, but also a warm place to stay during the autumn and winter.

Some may think it redundant to provide birdhouses and nest boxes in your yard, believing that nature has already provided ample sites for birds to nest. Although this used to be true, it is no longer the case as our surroundings become more developed and less wild. Bird species that were once able to nest in cavities in wooden fence posts or in established trees near farmlands are now faced with a landscape of fences with metal posts and housing developments with few or no mature trees.

Wild birds will still find nesting sites in all sorts of interesting places. Bird-watchers in Atlanta can see peregrine falcons that nest atop one of the city's skyscrapers, and those in New York City can marvel at the variety of bird life found in Central Park. Students and alumni of Stanford University in California are so interested in the approximately 125 avian species found on campus that a part of the school's alumni Web site is devoted to the birds of Stanford. In Canada, bird watchers are so avid that each province and territory lists birds found there.

The Difference Between Houses and Boxes

As you start to research what's available to house wild birds in your yard, you discover that two basic choices—birdhouses and nest boxes—are available. Some books and Web sites use the terms interchangeably, and although they serve essentially the same purpose—providing a safe haven for nesting wild birds—birdhouses and nest boxes differ somewhat in their appearance and function. Birdhouses tend to be more decorative, whereas nest boxes are more utilitarian. Birdhouses typically offer more security for nesting birds because the nest itself cannot be accessed easily, whereas nest boxes have a lift-up roof or sliding side panel that provides fairly easy access to the nest and chicks. Base your choice on your personal tastes and the different types of birds that visit your yard.

You may find that a compromise nest site, called a nesting shelf, fills the needs of your visitors. The nesting shelf, which resembles a small wooden porch, provides protection from the elements with its roof, floor, and enclosed sides, but it also offers access to the great outdoors through the open side or sides. Some nesting shelves have one open side, whereas others have two. Robins and barn swallows are among the birds attracted to nesting shelves. Although nesting shelves are fairly easy to make, they can be purchased at a bird specialty store.

Nest Box Specifics and Shapes

Whether you choose to purchase or make birdhouses or nest boxes for your yard, you will find several designs are available. These include the standard box, the Peterson box, the log nest box, the PVC pipe house, the purple martin house, the wren house, and the gourd house.

Let's look at each in more detail: first, the standard box. As the name suggests, a standard box is a straightforward rectangular box with a sloped, slightly overhanging roof and an access hole drilled close to the roof's overhang. In some designs, the standard box has a hinged roof; in others, it's the hinged side panel that allows access to the nesting cavity. Roof access to the nest makes observation easier, whereas side-entry panels make cleaning out the boxes at the end of the nesting season quicker.

The Peterson box is a variation on the standard box design that was created by bird-watcher and nature photographer Dick Peterson. The Peterson box features an oval, rather than a round, entrance hole, and it redesigns the traditional rectangle into a more wedge-shape box. This

You can attract many different kinds of birds in the winter with suet.

design makes the nest box less likely to be attacked by predators, and it also requires that the birds use fewer nesting materials than a traditional box. The Peterson box also features a drop-down front panel that lets bird-watchers observe nesting activities with relative ease.

The log nest box offers a more natural-looking alternative to a squared-off conventional box. Log nest boxes start out as sections of real logs.

If your yard is small, don't despair. Use a trellis against a wall or a fence and then plant fast-climbing roses. You can also add some thick hedges made of holly, for instance, to offer birds a safe place to hide and nest.

They are modified slightly when an access panel (usually the roof) is added to enclose the nesting cavity.

PVC pipe houses offer durability and utility. When constructing a house out of PVC pipe, roughen the interior slightly with sandpaper or carefully etch ridges with a handheld router to give the nesting birds some traction inside their homes.

People who live in prairie regions usually think of purple martin houses when someone mentions the word "birdhouse." These split-level dwellings that feature porches in front of the multiple entrance holes perch on posts in many backyards in the region, and they can accommodate the nesting needs of several pairs of birds because purple martins are communal nesters. Don't open the doors on these houses or put them up until you begin to see purple martin scouts—or until the date you know they generally return. This will prevent house sparrows from taking them over. Purple martins don't like to nest near these aggressive little birds.

The diamond shape of a wren house works well for various smaller species, including sparrows, chickadees, titmice, and swallows. They feature slightly overhanging, peaked roofs with entrance holes drilled high at the top of the peak on the front of the house.

Gourd houses offer a natural alternative to wooden nest boxes. They are made from dried calabash or other hard-shelled gourds. Once the gourds have dried completely, a hole is drilled in the side and the gourd seeds are emptied out. The gourd is then ready to be decorated and used as a birdhouse. Purple martins are attracted to gourd homes.

Handmade or Manufactured?

As with the bird feeders we discussed in Chapter 5, the choice of whether you want to build or buy your birdhouses and nest boxes is up to you. A number of books and Web sites offer birdhouse plans for the do-it-yourselfer, or a wide variety of styles and designs are available at discount, pet supply, feed, or bird specialty stores.

Material Choices

Whether you decide to purchase or to handcraft birdhouses and nest boxes for your yard, you need to keep some basic information about the material choices and basic designs in mind as you make your selections.

First, birdhouses should not be made out of metal. Metal conducts heat very well, which means that birds inside a metal house could become overheated very quickly. Select a house made out of wood or PVC pipe instead of metal. Popular wood choices include water-resistant varieties, such as redwood, cedar, cypress, and pine.

If you provide a dovecote, you will attract these interesting birds. It's always fun to watch them waddle on the ground as they eat and then bathe in family groups.

Safe, Durable, Practical Houses and Boxes

When shopping for a birdhouse or nest box, keep the following concepts in mind:

Safety: Is the house or box safe for wild birds? Is it well constructed and free from nails or screws—inside and out—that could possibly poke or injure a bird?

Durability: Is the house or box securely put together and able to withstand exposure to elements? Is it made of materials (wood or PVC pipe, for example) that will hold up in rainy or snowy situations?

Practicality: Will the house or box be useful to a nesting pair of birds? Some styles of birdhouse are purely decorative. They are too small to comfortably hold a family of birds. Use decorative birdhouses as accents in your yard, but be sure to provide an ample supply of usable houses and boxes, too.

Is the house or box suitable for the birds you wish to attract? Remember that wild birds like to be snug and secure in their nests, but they can't be so snug that the chicks are crammed together constantly. Ask the staff at your local pet supply or bird specialty store for birdhouse and nest box size recommendations for the birds you hope to bring to your yard.

Will the house be easy for you to clean and maintain between nesting seasons? Try to select designs that are simple and straightforward, such as those that have built-in access panels to the nesting area, either through the roof or through the side of the house or box. If you can perform routine maintenance on the house or box quickly and easily, chances are you'll be more inclined to maintain it than a house or box that features an unworkable design as far as cleaning and maintenance go.

When choosing a wooden house or box, make sure the wood is untreated lumber. Untreated lumber means that the lumber doesn't contain preservatives (which treated lumber has). In the past, some preservatives used to treat lumber contained arsenic, which can be harmful. Some companies have come up with other, less-harmful preservatives, such as those containing copper, but to be safe, use only untreated lumber for your bird-related building.

The house or box should be held together with rustproof screws or nails, rather than staples or glue. It should fit together snugly, with minimal gaps between the joints of the wood, and it should be made of sturdy material. Flimsy houses are more likely to split or fall apart, which generally means the end of the nest inside.

The roof of the house or box should extend over the entrance hole, and it should slope to allow rain or snow to drain without standing. The birdhouse or nest box walls should be at least 3/4 of an inch (1.90 centimeters) thick to provide adequate warmth, security, and protection from predators. The insides of the walls should be roughly finished or grooved to give the birds inside ample opportunity to climb out of the box, and the floor should be recessed to provide a dry nesting site. Holes should be drilled in the floor for drainage and in the sides of the box (ideally, right near the roofline) to provide adequate ventilation. A well-designed birdhouse or nest box should allow easy access to the nest, usually through a hinged panel either in the roof or the side.

The size of the box is important, too, because you want the nesting birds to feel secure, but not too crowded. The smallest box that will realistically attract birds is one that measures 4 by 4 by 8 inches (10.16 by 10.16 by 20.32 centimeters), which is the size favored by wrens, titmice, and chickadees, whereas nuthatches and downy woodpeckers use boxes that measure 4 by 4 by 10 inches (10.16 by 10.16 by 25.3 centimeters). Swallows favor boxes that measure 5 by 5 by 6 inches (12.7 by 12.7 by 15.24 centimeters), and finches are attracted to boxes that measure 6 inches (15.24 centimeters) square. Hairy and redheaded woodpeckers, as well as flycatchers, use boxes that measure 6 by 6 by 15 inches (15.24 by 15.24 by 38.1 centimeters), and flickers are attracted to boxes that measure 7 by 7 by 18 inches (17.78 by 17.78 by 45.72 centimeters).

Make an Entrance: Hole Sizes and Perches

A well-designed birdhouse or nest box should have an appropriate-sized entrance hole. The size of the hole will be determined by the overall size of the box itself and the kind of bird you're trying to attract.

Here's a look at the entrance hole size that will attract different wild birds:

Measurement	Likely tenants
1–1 1/2 inches (2.54–3.81 centimeters)	wrens
1 1/8–1 1/2 inches (2.86–3.81 centimeters)	chickadees, nuthatches
1 1/8–1 1/2 inches (2.86–3.81 centimeters)	titmice, prothonotary warblers, downy woodpeckers
1 3/8–2 inches (3.49–5.08 centimeters)	finches
1 3/8–1 9/16 inches (3.49–3.97 centimeters)	bluebirds
1 1/2–2 1/2 inches (3.81–6.35 centimeters)	flycatchers, purple martins, tree swallows, violet-green swallows
1 1/2–2 3/4 inches (3.81–6.98 centimeters)	hairy woodpeckers
1 3/4–2 3/4 inches (4.44–6.98 centimeters)	red-bellied or red-headed woodpeckers
2–3 inches (5.08–7.62 centimeters)	northern flickers
2 1/2–4 inches (6.35–10.16 centimeters)	screech or saw-whet owls
6–8 inches (15.24–20.32 centimeters)	barn or barred owls

The goal of entrance hole selection is to attract the birds you want to nest in your yard, while discouraging those you don't want. Many people place pigeons, starlings, and sparrows in this latter category, whereas other bird-watchers welcome all feathered visitors with full feeders and empty houses.

Although the house or box needs the right-sized entrance, it doesn't need a perch. Perches allow predators to gain access to the adult birds on the nest or the chicks inside the house. A bird doesn't require a perch to get in and out of the house, so leave it off if you are constructing a house or box, and don't purchase a house or box with this feature.

Enter the Birds

To give your birdhouses and nest boxes the best chance of attracting avian tenants, set them up in late winter or very early spring. By doing this, you will give the birds that come to your yard the greatest amount of time to inspect the boxes and get them ready for nesting season.

Although you might expect your yard to be overflowing with nesting birds in your houses and boxes, please keep in mind that only 86 of the 650 North American wild-bird species are likely to nest in your houses and boxes. These 86 are called cavity nesters, and they would nest in natural cavities in trees or fence posts if you didn't set up the houses and boxes for their use.

Woodpeckers are one of the most commonly known cavity

Some ducks prefer to live near the ground, but these two prefer this raised duck house.

Birds That May Use Nest Boxes or Birdhouses	
Bluebirds	Owls
Chickadees	Purple martins
Ducks	Swallows
Finches	Titmice
Flycatchers	Woodpeckers
Nuthatches	Wrens

nesters and deserve special attention because they not only nest in cavities but also help create them. Woodpeckers create new nesting holes every spring and are considered primary cavity nesters because they both build and nest in the cavities. After the woodpeckers use and abandon a nest, other species, such as wrens, swallows, and bluebirds, move in the following year. These birds are called secondary cavity nesters because they only nest in the cavities; they don't actually build them.

Studies have shown that birds that nest in cavities have a 60 to 80 percent success rate in raising their young, as compared with a 20 to 40 percent success rate for birds that nest in traditional open nests. Birds that nest in cavities can raise their chicks in the nest for 16 to 22 days before the young birds fledge, as compared with a 9-to-11-day window between hatching and fledging that chicks in open nests have.

You don't need to provide a home for swallows, but they do need water and a mud source to build the nests they attach to sides and corners of various structures. Give these birds the supplies, peace and quiet, and space, and they'll build their own nests.

Although it would seem that cavity nesting would be the preferred way to raise chicks, not all birds have the characteristics required to succeed in a cavity nest. Successful cavity nesters must have strong feet to climb in and out of a cavity nest, and they must be curious and inquisitive enough to explore potential cavities without fear.

As the human population increases, more wild lands are being developed, which means there are fewer suitable nesting sites for wild birds. As a result, there is strong competition for the wild sites that remain. By putting up birdhouses and nest boxes, you can help do your part to improve the environment and also provide for future generations of wild birds.

Placing the Houses

To ensure that your birdhouses and nest boxes have the greatest chance of being used, you'll need to put a little thought into where you'll place them in your yard. The old real estate adage of "location, location, location" applies to birdhouses as well as human houses, so take a little time to consider house and box placement.

For birds to survive in their habitat, they must have access to a steady supply of food and water, as well as adequate cover in which to hide from potential predators. Review Chapters 5 and 7 to ensure that you've set up a suitable avian habitat in your yard, and take steps to improve any areas that need it. Resist the temptation to prune and shape your trees perfectly; this will afford birds that nest in the trees plenty of nesting sites. Leave a few brush piles around your yard so that ground-nesting birds will have suitable locations, too.

Next, check the potential height. Houses and boxes must be placed high enough so nesting birds feel secure; this will help protect them from cats, snakes, and other predators.

Here are some suggested heights at which to place your birdhouses:

Distance from ground	Birds that prefer this height
5–10 feet (1.52–3.04 meters)	bluebirds
5–12 feet (1.52–3.66 meters)	prothonotary warblers
5–15 feet (1.52–4.57 meters)	swallows
5–20 feet (1.52–6.09 meters)	nuthatches
6–10 feet (1.83–3.04 meters)	wrens
6–15 feet (1.83–4.57 meters)	titmice and chickadees
6–20 feet (1.83–6.09 meters)	downy woodpeckers and northern flickers
8–20 feet (2.44–6.09 meters)	flycatchers
10–30 feet (3.04–9.14 meters)	screech owls
12–18 feet (3.66–5.49 meters)	barn owls
12–20 feet (3.66–6.09 meters)	golden-fronted, hairy, red-bellied and redheaded woodpeckers
15–20 feet (4.57–6.09 meters)	purple martins

As you mount your houses on poles, make sure the poles are firmly anchored in the ground. Install predator guards, too, to prevent cats, raccoons, snakes, and other predators from gaining access to the houses and the chicks inside. As an added precaution against predators, install the post-mounted houses in your yard far enough away from trees to prevent predators from getting to the houses, but close enough to shrubs and other foliage so the nesting birds feel comfortable in their surroundings. Use the trees to hold your decorative birdhouses only.

Next, consider the wind and weather conditions unique to your yard and your area. Hang your houses and boxes so they receive the benefits of good things, such as morning sun and afternoon shade, while minimizing bad things, such as prevailing winds that could blow rain into the house or box.

Cleaning Considerations

Bird-watchers are divided on the question of whether or not birdhouses and nest boxes should be cleaned after nesting season. On one hand, birds in the wild don't have the benefit of a clean-up crew following behind them after they've left the nest. Nest sites are occupied year after year without cleaning by humans.

On the other hand, bird-houses and nest boxes can benefit from an annual cleaning after nesting season to ensure that other tenants, such as mice or

Cleaning nest boxes is optional, but if you plan to do so, design or buy nest boxes that have removable parts.

rats, haven't moved in. In other cases, annual cleanings can help alleviate problems with blowflies and other parasites that can take advantage of nestlings.

If you choose to clean out the houses and boxes in your yard, wear gloves and a dust mask during the cleaning process. This gear will help keep your allergies in check, and it will also protect you from exposure to

> ### Adding to the Nesting Mix
>
> Besides providing birdhouses and nest boxes, you can also offer nesting materials to the birds in your yard. These can include dryer lint, pet or human hair removed from brushes, moss, short pieces of string or yarn, and paper scraps from your home shredder. Also, provide a small mud puddle in your yard for swallows and other birds that build their nests from earth.

Hantavirus or other potentially harmful germs. In addition, the droppings, or waste products, of wild birds can carry the spores of *Histoplasma capsulatum*, a fungus that causes an infection called histoplasmosis. The fungus acts as a parasite on the cells of the body's defense system. (Bill Garcia, MICP, ed. *Mosby's Emergency Dictionary*, 2nd Ed. Mosby, St. Louis, 1989.) Always wet down any bird droppings before you clean them. This will help reduce your chance of contracting histoplasmosis.

Exotic Newcastle disease can affect any bird, whether wild or a pet or poultry. If you have a pet bird, you must take great care to prevent it from contracting this deadly and highly infectious disease. After any direct contact with wild birds, such as cleaning a birdhouse or bird nest, take care to protect your pet bird. Don't go anywhere near your bird or the rooms which it might visit or reside in until you and your clothing are clean. Remove your clothing in the garage, if possible, and wash it there if your machine is located there. If you have a machine in another part of the house or a room located elsewhere in your apartment complex, remove your clothing in your bathroom, but put the clothing in a plastic bag to wash later. Use a fastener to close the bag. When you can, wash your clothing in hot water and dry it. Bathe or shower immediately, taking care to wash all body hair, including that on your head, arms, and legs. Although this may sound excessive, consider that in summer 2003 more than 3.5 million birds died in an outbreak in the West. Of those, about 100,000 were exotics and backyard pets. Many had to be euthanized to prevent the spread of the disease.

9 What to Do if You Find an Injured Bird

You walk out into your backyard one late spring morning and notice a baby bird flapping and fluttering on the ground near your bird feeder. It has most of its feathers and appears to be uninjured. You know that a pair of that species has nested in a tree nearby, and you presume this is one of their offspring on the ground in front of you. You don't see the parent birds, and you wonder if the bird has been abandoned.

The Law

Although you may be strongly tempted to rush in and assist Mother Nature at this point, it's best to leave the little sparrow where it is and observe carefully. Go back into the house if you can see the bird from there and watch; the parent birds will probably fly by to check on their fledgling in due time. Fledgling birds are those that have attained some limited flying skills, and they improve their abilities under the watchful eyes of their parents. Although you may not see the adult birds right away, they are likely keeping an eye on their chick.

Here is a list of situations when you can intervene on behalf of a baby bird:

- You see dead parent birds.
- You see a naked hatchling on the ground.
- You see the chick is obviously injured.
- A child or a pet dog or cat brings the chick to you.

If the bird has no feathers and cannot stand but appears uninjured, it probably fell out of its nest. Create a substitute nest by lining a plastic berry basket or margarine tub with toilet tissue or other soft material. Place the bird in the makeshift nest and duct tape the nest to the shady side of the tree where you found the chick. Make sure the parent birds have found their chick and are feeding it. If not, you may have to turn the bird over to a wildlife rehabilitator.

Who to Call

If you find an injured or abandoned baby bird, contact one of the following animal care professionals as soon as possible:

- Wildlife rehabilitator
- Animal shelter or animal control agency
- Wildlife veterinarian (Your veterinarian is a good contact for information.)
- State, provincial or territorial wildlife agency

Look for listings for these professionals in your telephone book or online. Remember that it's illegal in most states, territories, and provinces to keep a wild bird unless you are a licensed wildlife rehabilitator, so you need to get the bird to the appropriate people as soon as you can.

What to Do Until Help Arrives

If the bird you've found is injured and you will need to transport it to a veterinary clinic or wildlife rehabilitation facility, it's important to keep the chick warm and quiet until you can get it some help. To do this, put the bird in a small cardboard box or paper bag with air holes punched in it. Keep the container away from children and pets, and transport it to a qualified wildlife care professional as soon as possible.

When you have the baby bird in your car, make sure to place its container out of direct sun and away from direct exposure to heat or air conditioning. Keep the car as quiet as you can to minimize stress on the bird.

If you find an injured wild bird, take it to a wildlife rehabilitator. Most birds are protected by law in the United States and Canada: It's illegal to keep them.

Helping Escaped Exotic Cage Birds

Some backyard bird feeders may feed former pet parakeets, cockatiels, and other parrot species that show up. Known colonies of parrots can be found in Chicago; Bridgeport, Connecticut; San Francisco; Seattle; Houston and San Antonio, Texas; and New York City, as well as other locations around the United States.

It's safe to assume these parrots escaped from homes, found enough food in the wild to survive, and banded together with other escapees to form somewhat mixed flocks.

If you see an escaped pet bird at your feeder, here are some steps you can take to try to reunite the bird with its owner.

Check your local newspaper to see if any parrots are listed in the "lost pets" section of the classifieds. Determine if the bird at your feeder matches the description of any birds listed in the ads and contact the owners if you have a match.

Call bird specialty stores and avian veterinary offices in your area to see if any lost birds have been reported. Let the receptionist know what type of parrot is visiting your feeder, and leave your phone number in case someone calls in a report that matches your visiting bird.

Notify your local animal shelter or humane society about the parrot at your feeder. Again, leave your phone number in case someone calls to report a lost parrot.

Keep an injured chick warm and quiet until you can get it to a wildlife rehabilitator.

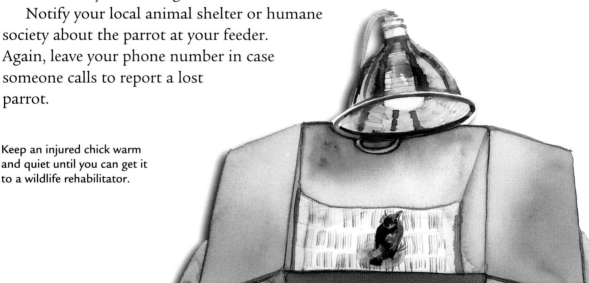

Finding Help

There are many laws in place to protect native and migratory birds. If you find a featherless chick and cannot return it to its nest, call the following offices for regulations and phone numbers for people who can help.

U.S. Fish and Wildlife Service Offices by Region

Office of the Regional Director
Great Lakes-Big Rivers Region
Federal Building
1 Federal Drive
Fort Snelling, MN 55111-4056
Telephone: (612) 713-5301
Fax: (612) 713-5284

Office of the Regional Director
Northeast Region
300 Westgate Center Drive
Hadley, MA 01035-9589
Telephone: (413) 253-8300
Fax: (413) 253-8308

Office of the Regional Director
Southeast Region
1875 Century Boulevard, Suite 400
Atlanta, GA 30345-3319
Telephone: (404) 679-4000
Fax: (404) 679-4006

Office of the Regional Director
Mountain-Prairie Region
Denver Federal Center
P.O. Box 25486
Denver, CO 80225-0286
Telephone: (303) 236-7920
Fax: (303) 236-8295

Office of the Regional Director
Pacific Region
Eastside Federal Complex
911 NE 11th Ave.
Portland, OR 97232-4181
Telephone: (503) 231-6118
Fax: (503) 872-2716

Office of the Regional Director
Alaska Region
1011 E. Tudor Rd.
Anchorage, AK 99503-6199
Telephone: (907) 786-3542
Fax: (907) 786-3306

Office of the Regional Director
Southwest Region
P.O. Box 1306
Albuquerque, NM 87103-1306
Telephone: (505) 248-6282
Fax: (505) 248-6845

Director, U.S. Fish and Wildlife Service
Main Interior, 3256 MIB
1849 C Street NW, Room 3238
Washington, DC 20240-0001
Telephone: (202) 208-4717
Fax: (202) 208-6965

Canadian Wildlife Offices

Environment Canada operates one national and several regional offices across Canada. Contact the office nearest you for information on wild bird conservation programs.

National Office
Ottawa ON, K1A 0H3
Telephone: (800) 668-6767
[in Canada only] or (819) 997-2800
TTY: (819) 994-0736
Fax: (819) 953-2225

Atlantic
(New Brunswick, Nova Scotia, Prince Edward Island, Newfoundland and Labrador)
45 Alderney Drive, Dartmouth NS, B2Y 2N6
Telephone: (902) 426-7231
Fax: (902) 426-6348

Québec
Information Centre, Environment Canada - Québec Region
1141 route de l'Église, C.P. 10100, Sainte-Foy QC, G1V 4H5
Telephone: (800) 463-4311
[in Canada only]
Fax: (418) 648-4613

Ontario
4905 Dufferin Street, Downsview ON, M3H 5T4
Telephone: (416) 739-4809
Fax: (416) 739-4776

Prairies, NWT, and Nunavut
(Prairie and Northern Region)

Alberta Office
Rm 200, 4999-98 Avenue, Edmonton AB, T6B 2X3
Telephone: (780) 951-8600
Fax: (780) 495-2615

Manitoba Office
150 - 123 Main Street, Winnipeg MB, R3C 4W2
Telephone: (800) 263-0595
Fax: (204) 983-0964

B.C. and Yukon
(Pacific and Yukon Region)

British Columbia Office
Suite 201 - 401 Burrard Street, Vancouver BC, V6C 3S5
Telephone: (604) 664-9100
Fax: (604) 664-9195

Yukon Office
Canadian Wildlife Service, 91782 Alaska Highway, Yukon Y1A 5B7
Telephone: (867) 393-6700
Fax: (867) 667-7962

10 Organizations that Help and Study Wild Birds

The bulk of this chapter is devoted to lists that will help you with different aspects of watching birds. If you need more information about local birding opportunities, contact a local bird club or an Audubon Society center or chapter in your area. If you've seen a rare bird, you can call the sighting in to a Rare Bird Hotline in your area, and if you want to search for birds in cyberspace, we've provided a listing of online birding sites.

The Audubon Society

The Audubon Society was first organized by George Bird Grinnell, editor of *Forest and Stream* magazine, in 1886. Grinnell named his conservation organization after noted painter and naturalist John James Audubon. This Audubon Society disbanded in 1888 after Grinnell was overwhelmed by the initial response to this first U.S. conservation organization.

The Audubon Society next surfaced in Massachusetts in 1896, when a group of women against the senseless shooting of birds for fashion gathered together to protest these acts. Within 3 years, 16 states had formed Audubon Society chapters. The groups began forging a national alliance in 1901, and by 1905, the

Once you've decided to watch birds in locations beyond your backyard, a national park might be a good place to start.

National Association of Audubon Societies for the Protection of Wild Birds and Animals was formed. The group's name was changed in 1940 to the National Audubon Society.

Since its formation in the late 1800s, the Audubon Society has worked to pass laws to protect wild birds and animals. It has also lobbied to have wild areas set aside as nature preserves, and it has sponsored research projects to study and preserve various species.

Today, the Audubon Society has more than 500 chapters and 27 state offices around the country. It continues to act as an advocate for wildlife conservation and education, and it provides information and resources to nature lovers throughout the United States.

Birding Hotlines

Bird clubs, Audubon Society chapters, and other organizations provide special birding hotlines for bird-watchers to report sightings of rare or unusual species. A list of numbers for U.S. states and Canadian provinces and territories is provided. If your region is not listed, contact your local bird club or Audubon Society chapter for more information on rare bird alerts in your area.

Bird Studies Canada

Bird Studies Canada (BSC) is one of the country's leading conservation organizations. It offers training, conservation, and scientific work that involves volunteers and scientists from across Canada.

BSC is an outgrowth of the Long Point Bird Observatory in Ontario. Members of the Ontario Bird Banding Association built field bird banding stations on Long Point, a sandspit in Lake Erie, beginning in 1959. The observatory followed in 1960, and field research was soon underway. Volunteers and staff monitored migratory routes and studied the behavior of resident species such as kingbirds and tree swallows.

By the mid-1970s, the observatory was involved in a variety of projects, including bird study workshops for teens and provincial studies of feeder birds. By the late 1980s, the observatory had become the official home of the Long Point Waterfowl and Wetlands Research Fund, and it had partnered with the Canadian Nature Federation as national representatives for BirdLife International.

In 1994, a committee of Canadian ornithologists and conservationists recommended that the observatory create BSC as a sister organization in order to continue the observatory's work regionally, nationally, and internationally. The BSC was officially created in 1998 by a vote of observatory members.

Rare-Bird Hotline Numbers by State

United States

Alabama (256) 751-4788

Alaska (907) 451-9213

Arizona

Phoenix (602) 832-8745

Tucson (520) 798-1005

Arkansas (501) 753-5853

California

Northwest (707) 822-5666

Los Angeles (323) 874-1318

Monterey (831) 626-6605

Morro Bay (805) 528-7182

Northern (415) 681-7422

Orange County (949) 487-6869

Sacramento (916) 783-2331

Southeast (909) 793-5599

San Diego (619) 688-2473

Santa Barbara (805) 964-8240

Southern (818) 952-5502

Colorado (303) 424-2144

Connecticut (203) 254-3665

Delaware (302) 658-2747

District of Columbia (301) 652-1088

Florida (561) 340-0079

Georgia (770) 493-8862

Idaho

Northern (208) 882-6195

Southwest (208) 368-6096

Southern (208) 236-3337

Illinois

Central (217) 785-1083

Chicago (847) 265-2118

Dupage (630) 406-8111

Northwest (815) 965-3095

Indiana (317) 767-4727

Iowa (712) 364-2863

Kansas (316) 229-2777

Kentucky (502) 326-0878

Louisiana (877) 834-2473

Maine (207) 781-2332

Maryland (301) 652-1088

Massachusetts (888) 224-6444

Michigan (616) 471-4919

Minnesota (800) 657-3700 or
(763) 780-8890

Mississippi (228) 435-7227

Missouri (573) 445-9115

Montana (406) 721-9799

Nebraska (402) 292-5325

Nevada

Northern (775) 324-2473

Southern (702) 390-8463

New Hampshire (603) 224-9900

New Jersey (732) 872-2595

New Mexico (505) 323-9323

New York

Buffalo (716) 896-1271

Chautauqua County (716) 595-8250

Finger Lakes (607) 254-2429

Hudson/Mohawk (518) 439-8080

New York (212) 979-3070

Rochester (585) 425-4630

Syracuse (315) 637-0318

North Carolina (704) 332-2473

North Dakota (701) 355-8544

Ohio
Cincinnati (513) 521-2847
Cleveland (330) 467-1930
Columbus (614) 221-9736
Blendon Woods Park (614) 895-6222
Southwest (937) 640-2473
Northwest Ohio (419) 877-9640
Oklahoma (918) 669-6646
Oregon (503) 292-6855
Pennsylvania
Eastern (610) 252-3455
Central (717) 255-1212, ext. 5761
Philadelphia (215) 567-2473
Berks County (610) 376-6000,
   ext. 2473

Schuylkill County (570) 622-6013
Western (412) 963-0560
Wilkes-Barre (570) 825-2473
Rhode Island (401) 949-3870
South Carolina (704) 332-2473
South Dakota (605) 773-6460
Tennessee (615) 356-7636
Texas (713) 369-9673
Utah (801) 538-4730
Vermont (802) 457-2779
Virginia (301) 652-1088
Washington (206) 281-9172
Wisconsin (414) 352-3857
Wyoming (307) 265-2473

Canada

Alberta
Calgary (403) 221-4519
Edmonton (780) 433-2473
British Columbia
Okanagan Valley (250) 491-7738
Vancouver (604) 737-3074
Victoria (250) 592-3381
New Brunswick
Shediac/Moncton (506) 384-6397
   (French)
Ontario
Hamilton (905) 381-0329
Oshawa (905) 576-2738
Ottawa/Hull (613) 860-9000
Sault Ste. Marie (705) 256-2790
Toronto (416) 350-3000, x 2293
Windsor/Detroit (248) 477-1360
Windsor/Pt. Pelee (519) 252-2473

Québec
Eastern Québec (French)
   (418) 660-9089
Sagueny/Lac St. Jean (French)
   (418) 696-1868
Bas St. Laurent (French)
   (418) 725-5118
Coeur-du-Québec (French)
   (819) 370-6720
Western Québec (French)
   (819) 778-0737
Montreal (English)
   (514) 989-5076
Saskatchewan
Regina (306) 949-2505

Birding on the Web

Many sites relating to wild birds can be found on the Internet. Some report on the activities of local bird clubs, whereas others provide checklists and other information about birds commonly seen in a particular region. Still others offer birders a chance to shop for specific products or to locate bird-watching travel opportunities.

Use the list provided below as a jumping-off point. Search for sites closer to your home by entering the name of your state or province into your favorite search engine, then get ready to surf!

Online Resources

Listed below are some of the Web sites that relate to wild birds. You can find more by pointing your Web browser to "wild birds" or "backyard bird feeding."

American Birding Association: *www.americanbirding.org*
Audubon Cooperative Sanctuary System of Canada: *www.acssc.ca*
Audubon International: *www.audubonintl.org*
Avibase Bird Checklists of the World: *www.bsc-eoc.org/avibase/avibase.jsp*
Birder.com: *www.birder.com*
Birding in Canada: *www.web-nat.com/bic*
Birding.com: *www.birding.com*
BirdLife International: *www.birdlife.net*
Bird Studies Canada: *www.bsc-eoc.org*
Birdwatching Dot Com: *www.birdwatching.com*
Canadian Nature Federation: *www.cnf.ca*
Canadian Wildlife Service: *www.cws-scf.ec.gc.ca/index_e.cfm*
Cornell University Lab of Ornithology: *birds.cornell.edu*
eNature/*National Geographic* online birding guide:
   enature.nationalgeographic.com (select "Field Guides")
Important Bird Areas of Canada: *www.ibacanada.com*
Important Bird Areas of the United States: *www.abcbirds.org/iba*
International Migratory Bird Day: *www.birdday.org*
National Audubon Society/Cornell University joint venture site: *www.birdsource.org*
National Audubon Society: *www.audubon.org*
National Bird Feeding Society: *www.birdfeeding.org*
National Wildlife Refuges site: *refuges.fws.gov*
Peterson Field Guides: *www.houghtonmifflinbooks.com/peterson*
US Fish and Wildlife Service's wild bird pages: *birds.fws.gov*
Wildbirds.com: *www.wildbirds.com*

11 Conservation

Although conservation may seem like a topic from World War II history or an idea some of us studied in junior high school science class, it's a concept that has relevance today. Backyard bird-watchers do their part to conserve resources and to improve the environment by setting up wildlife-friendly yards and by limiting the types of weed killers, insecticides and other harmful chemicals they use to maintain their yards.

In this chapter, we'll take a look back at where backyard bird feeding began, as well as offer some bird history and some additional suggestions for conservation you can implement around your home.

A Bit of Bird History

Birds have been part of the North American landscape for millions of years. The fossil record shows that large birds of prey, such as condors, have been on the continent for 13 to 15 million years, whereas smaller birds, such as conures, have been around for about 20 million years. Shorebirds, such as pelicans, have been around for about 30 million years.

Native Americans worshiped some birds, such as eagles and condors, as deities; used others, such as grouse and turkey, as food sources; and tamed others, mostly parrot species, as companions.

When European settlers came to America, they used some of the native bird species, such as pigeons, as food. At the time the first settlers arrived, it's estimated that about 4 billion passenger pigeons lived on the North American continent, which likely made the settlers think the pigeons would be around forever.

Later, people hunted other species, such as egrets, to satisfy the whims of fashion. Still other species, such as the Carolina parakeet, were considered pest species because they damaged farmers' crops. These birds were killed by the thousands. Birds of prey suffered, too, because their scavenging efforts on carcasses of already dead livestock were perceived as predatory.

The Beginnings of the Conservation Movement

The American conservation movement can trace its beginnings to an 1847 speech in Vermont by George Perkins Marsh, who drew attention to the destructive force human activities had on the land, especially the nation's forests. In the speech, Marsh also called for management of forested land to conserve natural resources.

The U.S. federal government began to do its part for the conservation movement in the 1840s, too. In 1849, it established the Department of the Interior. This act was followed up in the 1850s by reports from the Commissioner of Patents, who apparently did more than just oversee the Patent Office at this time, warning of the consequences of unmanaged deforestation. During the 1850s and 1860s, the War Department's reports of surveys in the West included information about the native plants and wildlife. In 1864, the U.S. government set aside Yosemite as a public park for the people of California and in 1872, it established the first national park anywhere in the world: Yellowstone.

During this same time, conservation movements were also forming in cities and

Although North America has no native wild parrots today, Carolina parakeets were once common in the United States.

states. In 1858, park commissioners in New York City selected a landscape design for the new Central Park, which was the first major rural park in a U.S. city. Although altered somewhat over time, the original design by Frederick Law Olmsted and Calvert Vaux established Central Park's identity and set the standard for landscape design at the time. And it holds up well today.

On April 10, 1872, the first trees were planted in Nebraska for what would become Arbor Day. By 1907, all states celebrated Arbor Day, which gave schoolchildren across the country the opportunity to learn about the importance of planting trees for the future.

Conservation efforts were taking shape in Canada, too. North America's first waterfowl refuge was

---

The Beginning of Backyard Bird Feeding

Backyard bird feeding in the United States can trace its beginnings to the efforts of Mrs. E.B. Davenport of Brattleboro, Vermont, who was one of the first recorded American backyard bird feeders. Mrs. Davenport's bird-feeding efforts were documented in *Birds of Village and Field*, written by Florence A. Merriam in 1898. Among the birds that Mrs. Davenport's feeders attracted were ruffed grouse, chickadees, and blue jays. Her feeders offered a wide variety of foods, including buckwheat, suet, sunflower seeds, nutmeats, cracked corn, and cornbread.

The first commercial hummingbird feeder made its appearance around 1900. A Massachusetts woman named Caroline G. Soule was among the first to feed hummingbirds. Her feeder consisted of a bottle of sugar water with an artificial trumpet flower attached to act as an attractant.

---

established in 1887 at Last Mountain Lake in Saskatchewan, which is still a popular destination for bird lovers today. The site became Canada's first cooperative wildlife area in 1966, and it has been designated as a "Wetland of International Importance" due to the number of migratory birds that stop at the lake each year.

People began to realize the importance of the protection of wild-bird species in the mid-1880s and founded the American Ornithologists' Union in 1884 and the Audubon Society in 1886. In 1894, the first Bird Day was observed in Pennsylvania. This event, which was often piggybacked onto Arbor Day celebrations, stressed the importance of protecting native wild-bird species. By 1897, a book called *Citizen Bird* was in wide circulation, and it reportedly helped foster interest in and enthusiasm for bird-watching among young people.

In 1892, the Sierra Club was formed, and in 1894, Congress passed an act that made it illegal to hunt birds and animals in national parks.

The End of the Line for Some Pigeons and Parakeets

Unfortunately, these conservation efforts came too late to save the Carolina parakeet and the passenger pigeon, two Native American species of birds that were hunted into extinction in about 100 years. The Carolina parakeet, whose range included the southern and eastern United States and as far west as the plains of Nebraska and Colorado, was a pest species because it began to favor farm crops over its traditional diet of cockleburs. The passenger pigeon, which once comprised 25 to 40 percent of all the land birds that lived in the United States, lived in the northeastern and midwestern United States, was considered a game bird, and was shot for sport and for food.

Habitat destruction by humans also helped make the Carolina parakeet and the passenger pigeon extinct. Both species lived in forests, which were cleared by settlers in need of flat land to grow crops. Fewer forests meant fewer suitable trees in which the birds could nest, which meant fewer nests in which to raise young. The passenger pigeon was particularly affected by deforestation because it required large nesting colonies to reproduce successfully.

According to Christopher Cokinos, author of *Hope Is the Thing with Feathers*, the Carolina parakeet faced the additional challenge from an unlikely source: European honeybees. The bees competed for the same types of tree hollows that the parakeets did, and the birds were unable to adapt to other nesting locales.

In the early 1800s, large flocks of both birds were still common sights in the eastern and midwestern United States. By 1844, though, things were changing for the Carolina parakeet. Naturalist John James Audubon wrote in *The Birds of America, 1840–1844* that "our parakeets are very rapidly diminishing in number; and

The thick-billed parrot is one of two parrots native to the United States. It can now be found only in zoos and in Mexico. To date, reintroduction programs have been largely unsuccessful.

in some districts, where twenty-five years ago they were plentiful, scarcely any are now to be seen." By 1874, ornithologists were predicting extinction for the Carolina parakeet and steps were taken to capture both Carolina parakeets and passenger pigeons to set up captive-breeding programs in zoos.

Neither the passenger pigeon nor the Carolina parakeet reproduced well in captivity, and by 1900, there were only a few birds kept in zoos. The last Carolina parakeet died in 1918 in captivity in the Cincinnati (Ohio) Zoo, a few years after the last passenger pigeon, which died in 1914 in the same aviary at the zoo. The zoo has turned their aviary into the Passenger Pigeon Memorial and uses it to educate zoo visitors about endangered species, extinction, and conservation.

> ## Percy Taverner: Canadian Ornithologist
>
> Percy Algernon Taverner (1875–1947) was the first ornithologist at the Canadian National Museum of Natural Science. He joined the museum staff in 1911 and served until his retirement in 1942.
>
> As part of his work at the Museum, Taverner developed an innovative series of maps and indices that provided up-to-date information for bird-watchers on species seen in Canada. He was instrumental in having Ontario's Point Pelee designated as a national park and having Bonaventure I and Perce Rock in the Gulf of St. Lawrence designated as bird sanctuaries. Taverner also wrote about 300 articles and books on the birds of Canada, including *Birds of Eastern Canada*, which was published in 1919 and was considered a major work for its time.

DDT and Other Chemicals

After the Carolina parakeet and the passenger pigeon became extinct, efforts were made to start preserving native bird species in earnest. International cooperation between Great Britain (acting on behalf of Canada) and the United States resulted in the Migratory Bird Convention Act, which protects wild bird populations from harm. By the 1940s, laws had been passed to stop overhunting of birds of prey and other native bird species in the United States, and Canada had created the Dominion Wildlife Service, which had bird conservation as one of its responsibilities.

But a new threat soon appeared on the scene: chemical poisoning. The pesticide dichlorodiphenyltrichloroethane, or DDT, which had proven so effective in controlling mosquitoes and other insects around the world during World War II, was in widespread use. Over time, breeding populations of many bird species decreased, and scientists soon discovered that increased levels of DDT found in the bodies of parent birds led to poor fertility, deformed chicks, and weak eggshells that could not withstand the pressure of a parent bird's weight.

Because DDT is a "persistent pesticide," which means it remains in the environment for years after it was first introduced, its effects on wild birds were seen for many years. It was first used in large quantities in the United States in the late 1940s, and its use continued until 1973. According to the Environmental Protection Agency, the peak year for usage was 1959, when nearly 80 million pounds of the insecticide were applied. Overall, about 675,000 tons of DDT was applied across the United States during its useful life span.

Sadly, insects adapted to DDT, but fish, birds, and mammals took longer to recover. Author Rachel Carson was one of the first people to bring attention to the environmental problems caused by DDT. In 1958, a friend of hers told Carson

Martha, the Last Passenger Pigeon

The last passenger pigeon kept in captivity was Martha, who lived at the Cincinnati Zoo from 1902 to 1914. She lived an undistinguished life in her enclosure until July 10, 1910, when her mate, George, died and she became the last captive passenger pigeon. At first, people refused to believe she was the last of her kind left alive, but they began to believe the story after ornithologists and scientists from around the country came to see her.

Martha died on September 1, 1914. Her body was preserved in ice and shipped to the Smithsonian Institution, where it was examined and stuffed. Martha has left the Smithsonian twice since 1914: She was the featured attraction at the San Diego Zoo's 50th anniversary and at the dedication of the Passenger Pigeon Memorial at the Cincinnati Zoo. Today, Martha's remains are part of the Smithsonian's permanent collection.

Project Feeder Watch

Project FeederWatch, which involves some 15,000 backyard bird-watchers in the United States and Canada, began in 1976 when Dr. Erica Dunn started the Ontario Feeder Bird Survey. After the project grew to include some 500 feeders in Canada, Dr. Dunn and the staff of the Long Point Bird Observatory determined that a continent-wide study was required to adequately monitor large-scale bird movement. In 1986, the project was expanded and became a partnership between Cornell University's ornithology lab and the Observatory (now Bird Studies Canada). In subsequent years, the National Audubon Society and the Canadian Nature Federation joined the partnership, which annually monitors the movements of birds during their winter visits to backyard feeders.

---

about the die-off of many birds on Cape Cod after the area had been treated with DDT. Carson began researching the problem and presented the story 4 years later in her classic book, *Silent Spring*.

Endangered Species

Besides outlawing the use of DDT in 1973, the U.S. government passed the Endangered Species Act that same year. This act offered federal protection to bald eagles, California condors, Aleutian geese, and other species in danger of becoming extinct. This protection included the establishment of nesting areas that will remain free from development, the cleanup of waterways, field studies on established populations, and public education.

At the same time, Canada passed the Wildlife Act, which authorized the establishment of National Wildlife Areas, as well as federal research, conservation, and education efforts.

Making a Comeback: The Brown Pelican, Bald Eagle, and California Condor

Although we didn't move fast enough to save the Carolina parakeet or the passenger pigeon, great strides were made at the end of the twentieth century to preserve some endangered avian species for future generations. Three good examples of these efforts are the brown pelican, the bald eagle and the California condor.

Back to the Beach

The brown pelican, a common sea-side sight on the East and West Coasts and the Gulf of Mexico, suffered greatly after DDT washed into American rivers and streams between the late 1940s and the 1960s; large numbers of fish died off. Pelicans that ate the fish also ingested DDT, which caused reproductive problems for the birds. In some California nesting colonies in the 1970s, the brown pelican was almost wiped out because the parent birds in the colony could not successfully incubate their eggs because the eggs had thinner-than-normal shells that could not hold up during incubation.

DDT, a potent pesticide, almost caused the extinction of the brown pelican. The species began making a comeback in the early 1970s after the use of DDT was banned.

The brown pelican also suffered from habitat loss, decline of feeder fish populations, and encounters with monofilament fishing line, which can cripple or kill a pelican. Education of fishing enthusiasts has resolved the last issue, whereas the first two remain as factors in controlling the current brown pelican population.

After DDT was banned in 1973, the brown pelican began making a slow, steady comeback. Today, it is a bird normally seen in flight or perching at a beach or pier along the coastline.

The Eagle Flies Again

The bald eagle was once a fairly common sight in North America, with its range reported to include all the states in the continental U.S. and Alaska, and across Canada, especially near waterways. Biologists estimate that between a quarter- and a half-million eagles could be found on the North American continent in the early 1600s.

Eagles suffered the loss of their habitat when settlements caused the prime nesting trees to be felled for lumber. Settlers who wanted to establish ranches considered eagles a threat to their livestock, even though the eagle's traditional role as a scavenger would protect healthy livestock from predation. Eagles also fell victim to poisons set out in animal carcasses to harm coyotes or foxes, and lead pellets in animals killed (but not recovered by) hunters.

By the beginning of the twentieth century, it was becoming clear that bald eagles were becoming endangered. Fortunately, people became concerned and took action to protect our national symbol from extinction.

The Bald Eagle Protection Act helped bring this beautiful raptor back from the verge of extinction. Imagine if we had let our national symbol become extinct.

The Bald Eagle Protection Act, passed in 1940 in the United States, made it illegal to kill eagles or to possess their talons, feathers, or eggs. Additional efforts by the federal government included protecting the eagles' nesting sites in Alaska, as well as cleaning up the nation's waterways and reducing the amount of pollutants released into the environment.

Thanks to these efforts, the bald eagle today has made a strong comeback. Today, these birds are most commonly seen in Alaska and along the Canadian west coast.

Soaring High Over the West

For thousands of years, California condors flew high over California and other parts of the West. These large vultures performed an important role in the local ecosystems, scavenging carcasses of dead animals.

As settlement grew in the West, some people misunderstood the condor's role in the wild and perceived these birds as predators that stole livestock from ranchers' herds, which led to the birds being hunted. The development of the West also took its toll on the condor as civilization began to fill in the wide-open spaces these birds called home. With civilization eventually came pesticides and other chemical controls on the environment. These also contributed to the decline of wild condors.

By 1985, the outlook for the condor was bleak. Only nine birds remained in the wild, and the decision was made to capture all remaining birds in an attempt to protect them in a captive setting until the population could be stabilized. The San Diego and Los Angeles zoos joined forces to bring the condor back from the edge of extinction.

In just a few short years, the population of condors in captivity rose from the original 9 to 32. Within 7 years of the program's start, birds were released back into the wild, and by 1996, the program contained 121 birds. By 2003, the program had more than 200 condors under its care. Some were still being raised in zoos, whereas others had been released in the wilds of California, Arizona, and Baja California, Mexico.

With planning, hard work, and the dedication of many conservationists and zoos, the California condor has been successfully reintroduced to the wild. Once, there were so few remaining that it appeared as if the California condor would become extinct.

Things You Can Do to Be a Conservationist

Join your local zoological society. Many zoos across the country contribute money toward preserving endangered species both in their facilities and in the wild.

- Join a conservation organization such as the Audubon Society. Audubon Society chapters can be found in most states and in other countries. Check your phone book or search online for a chapter near you.
- Reduce, reuse, and recycle. It's simple enough and seen often enough, yet we fail to follow through on these simple steps to reduce the amount of refuse that goes to landfills each year.
- Create a wildlife-friendly yard. See Chapter 7, "Creating a Backyard Habitat," for more information.
- Support companies that support conservation. Manufacturers of products as diverse as home appliances, office furniture, automobiles, and household cleaners are taking steps to be more environmentally friendly, or "green." You can research them online by using your Web browser to search for "green" companies.
- Use water wisely. Design your landscaping with water savings in mind, and use water in your home intelligently. Don't use the dishwasher or washing machine when it's only half full, and try not to let the faucet run when you brush your teeth or shave. Do the same with your electricity and natural gas usage. Conservation today means more resources for tomorrow.
- Support recycling efforts in your community. You not only have the chance to recover your deposit fee on soda bottles and other recyclable materials, but also help the environment by putting less trash in landfills.
- Volunteer to serve on committees that deal with conservation and land use in your community. Your knowledge of the local bird species can come in handy if questions arise about migratory flight paths, nesting habits, or other concerns relating to development and conservation.
- Take part in community cleanup days. You can help make your city or town nicer to live in, and you'll meet some people who may share your interest in and enthusiasm for wild birds.
- Offer your expertise as a guest speaker to local civic groups. You can help spread the word about birds or other nature-related topics to scout groups, civic organizations, preschools, or senior centers.

U.S. Audubon Centers by Region

Pacific

Bobelaine Audubon Sanctuary, c/o 215 Ardmore Ave., Roseville, CA 95678-5101; (916) 783-8305.

Dungeness River Audubon Center, Railroad Bridge Park, 2151 Hendrickson Rd., Sequim, WA 98382; (360) 681-4076.

Kern River Preserve, P.O. Box 1662, Weldon, CA 93283; (760) 378-2531.

Mayacamas Mountains Audubon Sanctuary, 108 Philip Dr., Healdsburg, CA 95448; (707) 473-0601.

Paul L. Wattis Sanctuary, 1318 Ramirez Rd., Marysville, CA 95901; (530) 743-7202.

Starr Ranch Sanctuary, 100 Bell Canyon Rd., Trabuco Canyon, CA 92679; (949) 858-0309.

Tahoma Audubon Center, 2917 Morrison Rd. West, University Place, WA 98466; (253) 565-9278.

Ten Mile Creek Sanctuary, P.O. Box 496, Yachats, OR 97498; (541) 547-4227.

The Audubon Center, Los Angeles, 6042 Monte Vista St., Los Angeles, CA 90042; (323) 254-0252.

Tiburon Audubon Center and Sanctuary, 376 Greenwood Beach Rd., Tiburon, CA 94920; (415) 388-2524.

Williams Sisters Ranch Sanctuary, c/o 100 Bell Canyon Rd., Trabuco Canyon, CA 92679; (949) 858-0309.

Mountain

Appleton-Whittell Research Ranch, 366 Research Ranch Rd., HC 1 Box 44, Elgin, AZ 85611; (520) 455-5522.

Audubon Center at Beartooth Ranch, c/o Audubon Wyoming, 101 Garden Creek Rd., Casper, WY 82604; (307) 235-3485.

Audubon Center at Garden Creek, c/o Audubon Wyoming, 101 Garden Creek Rd., Casper, WY 82604; (307) 235-3485.

Edward L. & Charles E. Gillmor Sanctuary, 3868 Marsha Dr., West Valley, UT 84120; (801) 966-0464.

Grand Valley Audubon Center, P.O. Box 1211, Grand Junction, CO 81502; (970) 241-4670.

Randall Davey Audubon Center, 1800 Upper Canyon Rd., Santa Fe, NM 87501; (505) 983-4609.

West North Central

Audubon Center of the North Woods, P.O. Box 530, Sandstone, MN 55072; (320) 245-2648.

Edward M. Brigham III Sanctuary, 2646 90 R Ave. SE, Spiritwood, ND 58481; (701) 298-3373.

Lillian Annette Rowe Sanctuary and Audubon Center, 44450 Elm Island Rd., Gibbon, NE 68840; (308) 468-5282.

Ozark Gateway Audubon Center, c/o Audubon Missouri, 212 W 8th St., Joplin, MO 64801; (417) 623-3254.

Spring Creek Prairie Audubon Center, P.O. Box 117, 11700 SW 100th St., Denton, NE 68339; (402) 797-2301.

Sugar Creek Audubon Sanctuary, 224 420th Ave., Grinnell, IA 50112; (614) 236-6600.

West South Central

Paul J. Rainey Wildlife Sanctuary, P.O. Box 187, Perry, LA 70575; (337) 652-2496.

Sabal Palm Grove Audubon Center and Sanctuary, P.O Box 5169, Brownsville, TX 78523; (956) 541-8034.

Texas Coastal Islands Sanctuary, 2525 Wallingwood, Suite 301, Austin, TX 78746; (512) 306-0225.

East North Central

Aullwood Audubon Center and Farm, 1000 Aullwood Rd., Dayton, OH 45414; (937) 890-7360.

Hunt Hill Audubon Sanctuary and Camp, N. 2384 Hunt Hill Rd., Sarona, WI 54870; (715) 635-6543.

Schlitz Audubon Center, 1111 East Brown Deer Rd., Bayside, WI 53217; (414) 352-2880.

East South Central

Clyde E. Buckley Wildlife Sanctuary and Audubon Center, 1305 Germany Rd., Frankfort, KY 40601; (859) 873-5711.

Strawberry Plains Audubon Center, 285 Plains Rd., Holly Springs, MS 38635; (662) 252-1155.

Middle Atlantic

Audubon Center at Knox Farm State Park, c/o Audubon New York, 200 Trillium Lane, Albany, NY 12203; (518) 869-9731.

Beaver Meadow Audubon Center, 1610 Welch Rd., North Java, NY 14113; (716) 457-3228.

Benjamin Olewine III Nature Center at the Wildwood Lake Sanctuary, 100 Wildwood Way, Harrisburg, PA 17110; (717) 221-0292.

Buttercup Farm Audubon Center and Sanctuary, P.O. Box 1, Craryville, NY 12521; (518) 325-5203.

Constitution Marsh Audubon Center and Sanctuary, P.O. Box 174, Cold Spring, NY 10516; (845) 265-2601.

Jamestown Audubon Center, 1600 Riverside Rd., Jamestown, NY 14701; (716) 569-2345.

Kaler's Pond Audubon Center, P.O. Box 802, Center Moriches, NY 11934; (631) 878-5576.

Mill Grove Audubon Wildlife Sanctuary, 1201 Pawlings Rd., P.O. Box 7125, Audubon, PA 19407; (610) 665-5593.

Prospect Park Audubon Center, 95 Prospect Park West, Brooklyn, NY 11215; (718) 965-8945.

Ramshorn-Livingston Audubon Center and Sanctuary, P.O. Box 1, Craryville, NY 12521; (518) 325-5203.

Rheinstrom Hill Audubon Center and Sanctuary, P.O. Box 1, Craryville, NY 12521; (518) 325-5203.

Theodore Roosevelt Audubon Center and Sanctuary, 134 Cove Rd., Oyster Bay, NY 11771; (516) 922-3200.

South Atlantic

Audubon Center for Birds of Prey, 1101 Audubon Way, Maitland, FL 32751; (407) 644-0190.

Audubon Resource Center at Lettuce Lake, P.O. Box 320025, Tampa, FL 33679; (813) 983-0258.

Bird Island, Colclough Pond, Egret Island, Sabal Point, Saddle Creek, St. John's Marsh, Sister Vesta Newcomb, Turkey Creek, c/o Audubon of Florida, 1331 Palmetto Ave., Suite 110, Winter Park, FL 32789; (407) 539-5700.

Blair Audubon Center at Corkscrew Swamp Sanctuary, 375 Sanctuary Rd. West, Naples, FL 34120; (239) 348-9151.

Everglades Education Center, 444 Brickell Ave., Suite 850, Miami, FL 33131; (305) 371-6399.

Florida Coastal Islands Sanctuary, 410 Ware Blvd., Suite 702, Tampa, FL 33619; (813) 623-6826.

Francis Beidler Forest Audubon Center and Sanctuary, 336 Sanctuary Rd., Harleyville, SC 29448; (843) 462-2150.

Jean Ellen du Pont Shehan Audubon Sanctuary, 23000 Wells Point Rd., Bozman, MD 21612; (410) 745-9283.

Kissimmee Prairie Sanctuary, 100 Riverwoods Circle, Lorida, FL 33857; (941) 467-8497.

Lake Okeechobee Sanctuaries, 100 Riverwoods Circle, Lorida, FL 33857; (941) 467-8497.

North Carolina Coastal Office and Sanctuaries, 3806-B Park Ave., Wilmington, NC 28403; (910) 798-8376.

Pickering Creek Audubon Center, 11450 Audubon Lane, Easton, MD 21601; (410) 822-4903.

Pine Island Sanctuary, c/o Audubon North Carolina, 410 Airport Rd., Chapel Hill, NC 27514; (919) 929-3899.

Ridge Audubon Center, P.O. Box 148, Babson Park, FL 33827; (863) 638-1355.

Rookery Bay Sanctuary, c/o Corkscrew Swamp Sanctuary, 375 Sanctuary Rd. West, Naples, FL 34120; (239) 348-9151.

Silver Bluff Audubon Center and Sanctuary, 4542 Silver Bluff Rd., Jackson, SC 29831; (803) 827-0781.

Street Audubon Center, 115 Lameraux Rd., Winter Haven, FL 33884; (941) 324-7304.

New England

Audubon Center at Bent of the River, 185 East Flat Hill Rd., Southbury, CT 06488; (203) 264-5098.

Audubon Center in Greenwich, 613 Riversville Rd., Greenwich, CT 06831; (203) 869-5272.

Audubon Guilford Salt Meadows Sanctuary, 330 Mulberry Point Rd., Guilford, CT 06437; (203) 458-9981.

Audubon Miles Wildlife Sanctuary, 99 West Cornwall Rd., Sharon, CT 06069; (860) 364-0048.

Borestone Mountain Wildlife Sanctuary, June through October, RR2 Box 1582, Guilford, ME 04443; (207) 631-4050.

East Point Sanctuary, Fore River Sanctuary, Hamilton Sanctuary, Hunter Cove Sanctuary, Josephine Newman Sanctuary, Mast Landing Sanctuary, c/o Maine Audubon, 20 Gilsland Farm Rd., Falmouth, ME 04105; (207) 781-2330.

Fields Pond Audubon Center, 216 Fields Pond Rd., Holden, ME 04429; (207) 989-2591.

Gilsland Farm Audubon Center and Sanctuary, c/o Maine Audubon, 20 Gilsland Farm Rd., Falmouth, ME 04105; (207) 781-2330.

Green Mountain Audubon Center, 255 Sherman Hollow Rd., Huntington, VT 05462; (802) 434-3068.

High Pond Audubon Camp, June through August, High Pond Rd., Brandon, VT; (802) 273-2170.

Hog Island, Audubon Camp in Maine, 11 Audubon Rd., Bremen, ME 04551; (207) 529-5148.

Scarborough Marsh Audubon Center, c/o Maine Audubon, 20 Gilsland Farm Rd., Falmouth, ME 04105; (207) 781-2330.

Sharon Audubon Center, 325 Cornwall Bridge Rd., Sharon, CT 06069; (860) 364-0520.

Todd Wildlife Sanctuary, 11 Audubon Rd., Bremen, ME 04551; (207) 529-5148.

Canadian Birding and Conservation Organizations

Alberta Environmental Network Society, 1 - 6328A 104 St., Edmonton, AB T6H 2K9; (780) 439-1916.

Bird Studies Canada/Études d'Oiseaux Canada, P.O. Box 160, Port Rowan, ON N0E 1M0; (888) 448-BIRD.

Canadian Environmental Network, 300-945 Wellington St., Ottawa, ON 1Y 2X5; (613) 728-9810.

Canadian Nature Federation, 1 Nicholas St., Suite 606, Ottawa, ON K1N 7B7; (613) 562-3447.

Canadian Wildlife Federation, 350 Michael Cowpland Dr., Kanata, ON K2M 2W1; (800) 563-WILD or (613) 599-9594 (Ottawa area).

Manitoba Naturalists Society, 401-63 Albert St., Winnipeg, MB R3B 1G4; (204) 943-9029.

The Natural History Society of Newfoundland and Labrador, P.O. Box 1013, St. John's, NF A1C 5M3.

The Natural History Society of Prince Edward Island, P.O. Box 2346, Charlottetown, PE C1A 8C1; (902) 629-1350.

Nature Conservancy of Canada, 110 Eglinton Ave. W., Suite 400, Toronto, ON M4R 1A3; (800) 465-0029.

Nature Saskatchewan, 206 - 1860 Lorne St., Regina, SK S4P 2L7; (306) 780-9273, or (800) 667-4668 (Saskatchewan only).

New Brunswick Federation of Naturalists, 277 Douglas Ave., Saint John, NB E2K 1E5.

Nova Scotia Bird Society, Nova Scotia Museum of Natural History, 1747 Summer St., Halifax, NS B3H 3A6.

The Ontario Field Ornithologists, Box 455, Station R, Toronto, ON M4G 4E1.

Province of Quebec Society for the Protection of Birds, P.O.Box 43, Station B, Montreal, QC H3B 3J5.

Wild Bird Trust of British Columbia, 124-1489 Marine Dr., West Vancouver, BC V7T 1B8; (604) 922-1550.

Wildlife Habitat Canada, 1750 Courtwood Crescent, Suite 310, Ottawa, ON K2C 2B5; (800) 669-7919 or (613) 722-2090.

Yukon Bird Club, Box 31054, Whitehorse, YT Y1A 5P7.

The Audubon Cooperative Sanctuary System

The Audubon Cooperative Sanctuary System program was developed by the Audubon Society of New York in 1991. As the program grew, it became part of Audubon International and is now active in the United States, Australia, Costa Rica, Germany, Guam, Ireland, the Philippines, Scotland, Singapore, Spain, and Sweden.

The Audubon Cooperative Sanctuary System of Canada began to develop in the early 1990s, and soon it was evident that interest in Canada was great enough to develop a Canadian-based and operated organization. The Audubon Cooperative Sanctuary System of Canada was incorporated in 1995. It offers programs for golf courses, homeowners, companies, and schools to develop wildlife-friendly habitats. For more information, contact the Audubon Cooperative Sanctuary System of Canada, 115 First St., Suite 116, Collingwood, ON L9Y 1A5; (705) 446-1532.

Bibliography

Attracting Birds to Your Backyard: 536 Ways to Turn Your Yard and Garden into a Haven for Your Favorite Birds. Sally Roth. Rodale Inc., Emmaus, Pennsylvania. 1998.

The Backyard Bird Feeder's Bible: The A-to-Z Guide to Feeders, Seed Mixes, Projects and Treats. Sally Roth. Rodale Inc., Emmaus, Pennsylvania. 2000.

The Backyard Birdhouse Book: Building Nestboxes and Creating Natural Habitats. Rene and Christyna M. Laubach. Storey Books, Pownal, Vermont. 1998.

The Backyard Bird Watcher. George H. Harrison. Fireside Books, New York. 1979.

The Bird Feeder Book: An Easy Guide to Attracting, Identifying and Understanding Your Feeder Birds. Donald and Lillian Stokes. Little, Brown and Company, Boston. 1987.

The Birdfeeder's Handbook. Sheila Buff. Lyons & Burford, New York. 1991.

The Bird-Friendly Backyard: Natural Gardening for Birds. Julie Zickefoose. Rodale Inc., Emmaus, Pennsylvania. 2001.

Birdhouses & Feeders You Can Make. Paul Gerhards. Stackpole Books, Mechanicsburg, Pennsylvania. 1999.

Bird Watching for Dummies. Bill Thompson. IDG Books Worldwide, Foster City, California. 1997.

Birding for Beginners. Sheila Buff. Lyons & Burford, New York. 1993.

Birds: Their Life, Their Ways, Their World. Reader's Digest Association, Pleasantville, NY. 1979.

The Birdwatcher's Companion: An Encyclopedic Handbook of North American Birdlife. Christopher Leahy. Hill and Wang, New York. 1982.

The California Condor: A Saga of Natural History and Conservation. Noel and Helen Snyder. Academic Press, San Diego, California. 2000.

A Complete Guide to Bird Feeding. John V. Dennis. Alfred A. Knopf, New York. 1978.

Getting Started in Birdwatching. Edward W. Cronin Jr. Houghton Mifflin Co., Boston. 1986.

Grzimek's Animal Life Encyclopedia. Van Nostrand Reinhold Company, Inc., New York. 1975.

Hope Is the Thing With Feathers. Christopher Cokinos. Jeremy P. Tarcher/Putnam, New York. 2000.

How to Know the Birds. Roger Tory Peterson. Gramercy Publishing Co., New York. 1977.

Impeccable Birdfeeding. Bill Adler Jr. Chicago Review Press Inc., Chicago. 1992.

National Audubon Society Birder's Handbook. Stephen W. Kress, PhD. Dorling Kindersley, New York. 2000.

National Audubon Society North American Birdfeeder Handbook. Robert Burton. Dorling Kindersley, New York. 1992.

North American Birds with Roger Tory Peterson. Simon and Schuster Interactive, New York. 2000.

Peterson First Guide to Birds. Houghton Mifflin Co., Boston. 1980.

Random House Atlas of Bird Migration. Random House, New York. 1995.

Reader's Digest Field Guide to North American Wildlife: Birds. Reader's Digest Association, Pleasantville, New York. 1998.

The Return of the Bald Eagle. Priscilla Tucker. Stackpole Books, Mechanicsburg, Pennsylvania. 1994.

The Return of the Brown Pelican. Joseph E. Brown. Louisiana State University Press, Baton Rouge, Louisiana. 1983.

Stokes Beginner's Guide to Birds, Western Region. Donald and Lillian Stokes. Little, Brown and Company, New York. 1996.

Where the Birds Are: A Guide to All 50 States and Canada. John Oliver Jones. William Morrow and Co., New York. 1990.

Would You Lend Your Toothbrush? Heather Brazier. Harper Perennial, Toronto. 1995.

Index

NOTES

NOTES